The Musicals of Cole Porter

The Musicals of
Cole Porter

Broadway, Hollywood, Television

BERNARD F. DICK

University Press of Mississippi / Jackson

The University Press of Mississippi is the scholarly publishing agency of the
Mississippi Institutions of Higher Learning: Alcorn State University,
Delta State University, Jackson State University, Mississippi State University,
Mississippi University for Women, Mississippi Valley State University,
University of Mississippi, and University of Southern Mississippi.

www.upress.state.ms.us

The University Press of Mississippi is a member of
the Association of University Presses.

Copyright © 2025 by University Press of Mississippi
All rights reserved
Manufactured in the United States of America

∞

Publisher: University Press of Mississippi, Jackson, USA
Authorised GPSR Safety Representative: Easy Access System Europe -
Mustamäe tee 50, 10621 Tallinn, Estonia, gpsr.requests@easproject.com

Library of Congress Control Number 2024059214
Hardback ISBN 978-1-4968-5612-8
Epub single ISBN 978-1-4968-5613-5
Epub institutional ISBN 978-1-4968-5614-2
PDF single ISBN 978-1-4968-5615-9
PDF institutional ISBN 978-1-4968-5616-6

British Library Cataloging-in-Publication Data available

For Kristine Krueger (1954–2023)

Contents

INTRODUCTION IX

CHAPTER 1: Following His Fancy: *See America First, Hitchy-Koo of 1919, Greenwich Village Follies,* and *Paris* 3

CHAPTER 2: The List Song: *Wake Up and Dream, Fifty Million Frenchmen,* and *The New Yorkers* 12

CHAPTER 3: Ça, c'est l'amour: The Cole Porter Love Song 20

CHAPTER 4: La vie est gai: *Gay Divorce* 33

CHAPTER 5: An Errant Nymph and an Ex-Evangelist: *Nymph Errant* and *Anything Goes* 42

CHAPTER 6: A Cole Porter Primer: Prosody and Figurative Language . . . 56

CHAPTER 7: Strange Bedfellows: Cole Porter and Moss Hart's *Jubilee* . . . 66

CHAPTER 8: Triple Threat: Ethel Merman, Jimmy Durante, and Bob Hope in *Red, Hot and Blue* 72

CHAPTER 9: 1938, A Year to Remember: *You Never Know* and *Leave It to Me* 76

CHAPTER 10: Porter's Bawdy: *Du Barry Was a Lady* 84

CHAPTER 11: The War Years: *Panama Hattie, Let's Face It!, Something for the Boys,* and *Mexican Hayride* 90

CHAPTER 12: Strange Interludes: *Seven Lively Arts* and
Around the World. 109

CHAPTER 13: Journey's End: *Kiss Me, Kate*. 121

CHAPTER 14: Regards to Broadway: *Out of This World, Can-Can*,
and *Silk Stockings* 143

CHAPTER 15: Porter in Hollywood 172

CHAPTER 16: A Less-Than-Grand Finale: *Aladdin* 185

EPILOGUE. 191

THE MUSICALS OF COLE PORTER (1891–1964) 195

NOTES 199

INDEX. 205

Introduction

In 2006, the Library of America's American Poets Project published *Cole Porter: Selected Lyrics*, edited and with an introduction by Robert Kimball. To see Porter's lyrics printed as poetry, not as sheet music or as musical numbers in a conductor's score, is to experience them as poems before they took on musical flesh. In "Burnt Norton," the first of the *Four Quartets*, T. S. Eliot observed that "words move, music moves / Only in time." The words do not necessarily have to inhere within a piece of music to becomes musical; they can generate a music of their own through a harmonious blend of stressed and unstressed which produces a melodious effect that can be both heard and felt. In Porter's "Night and Day," you can both feel and hear the "beat beat beat" of a tom-tom, the "tick tick tock" of a clock, and the "drip drip drip" of raindrops. The sounds exist within the words; the musical setting adds another dimension.

In *A Cole Porter Companion*, a group of eminent musicologists have analyzed the music that Porter wrote for his Broadway and Hollywood musicals. I have chosen to do the opposite and treat Porter's lyrics as poetry, prior to their musical incarnation. Porter was more than a songwriter; he was a poet who told stories in song.

The Musicals of Cole Porter: Broadway, Hollywood, Television is critical study of Cole Porter's Broadway and movie musicals, and his one foray into live television, *Aladdin*; it covers the period from his first failure, *See America First* (1916), to the moderately successful *Silk Stockings* (1955), which ended his Broadway career. The approach is roughly chronological, interspersed with a chapter on Porter's "list songs" that owe much to operas such as Mozart's *Don Giovanni* and Rossini's *The Barber of Seville* (chapter 2); another on his love songs, often bittersweet and bleakly poignant (chapter 3); and, above all, one on his creative use of rhythm, rhyme, and figurative language (chapter 6).

In *Rhetoric in Shakespeare's Time*, Sister Miriam Joseph noted that Shakespeare knew two hundred figures of speech, not necessarily by name but by being able to use them creatively, which is far more important. Porter could not claim to know two hundred, but an analysis of his lyrics, beginning with the songs that he wrote for Yale varsity shows, reveal a young composer working diligently at his craft, paying close attention to ways of alternating the flow of stressed and unstressed syllables into melodic patterns. One should remember that at Worcester Academy in Worcester, Massachusetts, Porter had a traditional classical education, heavy on Latin, Greek, French, and English. From his readings in classical poetry, he learned that accents can shift, so that a verb like "*Cano*" (Latin for "I sing") with an accent on the first syllable can undergo displacement as in the opening of Virgil's *Aeneid* ("*Arma virumque cano*," "*I sing of arms and the man*") in which the accent is transferred from the first syllable, **ca**-no, to the last (can-**o**). In "Can-Can," the final number in Porter's 1953 musical of the same title, he resorted to accent displacement to get "Can-**can**" to rhyme with "Lesbi-**an**" and "Angli-**can**."

Porter was enamored of rhyme: end rhyme, internal rhyme, and even off rhyme (imperfect rhyme). In the title song in *Anything Goes*, to get "intrude" to rhyme with "nud," he hyphenated the line, "When ev'ry night, the set that's **smart is** in- / **Trud**ing in **nud**ist **parties** in **stud**ios."

If *Kiss Me, Kate* receives more space here than any other musical, it is because it is Porter's crowning achievement, a model of adaptation, thanks to Bella Spewack (less so to her husband, Sam), who made Shakespeare's problematic *The Taming of the Shrew* palatable to audiences by turning it into a romantic comedy of remarriage on the order of films like *The Awful Truth* (1937) and *His Girl Friday* (1940), which Porter dressed up in Elizabethan finery, with three songs taken straight from the text: "I've Come to Wive It Wealthily in Padua," "Were Thine That Special Face," and "Where Is the Life That Late I Led?"

I have followed the discussions of the stage musicals with their Hollywood transfers so that a separate chapter on the movie versions will be unnecessary. The (mostly) original musicals that Porter wrote for MGM and Columbia Pictures are given a separate chapter.

I have not written a biography, although biographical details have been woven in where appropriate. Porter has been well served by his biographers, notably William McBrien in *Cole Porter*. What is needed is a study of Porter's body of work, to which I have tried to do justice—hence, the subtitle: *Broadway, Hollywood, Television*.

I wish to acknowledge the help of the late Kristine Krueger of the National Film Information Service at the Margaret Herrick Library in Beverly Hills for introducing me to its holdings, which still continue to amaze; the Special Collections staff of the New York Public Library of the Performing Arts, where I was able to analyze the books of Porter's musicals; and my musician friends, Dr. James Pegolotti and Leonard Moskowitz, for their help in understanding the music behind Porter's lyrics.

I must also acknowledge the valuable suggestions of the first reader whose thoroughness went far beyond an honorarium. This book is all the better for them. I also owe much to two teachers, Mr. James Driscoll, who taught American and British literature at the Scranton Preparatory School and showed me that by scanning poetry one can to hear the music imbedded in the verse; and Father William Kelly, SJ, who gave a radical course in Freshman English at the University of Scranton, in which the only text was Palgrave's *Golden Treasury*. I now understand why Cole Porter has his own volume in the Library of America's American Poets Project.

The Musicals of Cole Porter

CHAPTER 1

Following His Fancy

See America First, Hitchy-Koo of 1919, Greenwich Village Follies, and Paris

On October 8, 1928, *Paris*, a three-act musical with five songs by Cole Porter and a book by Martin Brown, opened at the Music Box Theatre in New York for a run of 195 performances. It was a hit, quite the opposite of Porter's Broadway debut, *See America First* (1916), "an opera [*sic*] in two acts," which lasted a mere fifteen performances. He had learned much about musical theater in the intervening year.

See America First was an attempt to capitalize on the See America First Movement, begun in 1906 as an attempt to promote Western tourism. President William Howard Taft popularized the movement in 1912, hoping to persuade Americans to visit US national parks, claiming they had more to offer than anything in the Old World. That the movement was a benign form of nationalism was apparent to Porter, who planned his own *See America First* as a three-pronged satire: of the "westward, ho!" craze; the patriotic musical popularized by George M. Cohan in *Little Tommy Jones* (1904), with songs like "Give My Regards to Broadway" and "The Yankee Doodle Boy"; and European operetta, in which the hero or heroine, or both, pretend to be something other than they are until the grand unmasking. Johann Strauss's *Die Fledermaus* (1874) is the paradigm of this form: a woman's lover pretends to be her husband; the woman, a countess; her Viennese husband, French; and her maid, an actress. In other operettas, deception is simpler. In Victor Herbert's *The Red Mill* (1906), two vaudevillians disguise themselves as Sherlock Holmes and Dr. Watson, and two women exchange identities so they can marry their true loves. The mysterious Red Shadow in Sigmund Romberg's *The Desert Song* (1926) is a French captain (also the romantic lead), the head of a band of Moroccan rebels seeking independence from France. In operetta, a commoner does not marry into royalty—unless the commoner is somehow raised to that level, as is the case in Strauss's *The Gypsy Baron* (1886), in which a young man displays such heroism in battle that he is elevated to the nobility and can now marry his beloved, who in the second act was revealed to be a Hungarian princess.

In *See America First*, a pre-Trumpian ("America First") senator packs his daughter Polly off to a school in the California wilderness to live and study in nature's realm, hoping that there she will forget a British duke and find herself a red-blooded American. In "Pity Me, Please," Polly admits to being such an Anglophile that she pronounces "clerk" as "clark" and assumes "the park" means Hyde, not Central. Meanwhile, in "To Follow Every Fancy," Cecil, the duke, expresses his desire to give up a life of privilege, travel west, and live in a "peerless place," accompanied by equally adventuresome young men. Cecil's prototype is the Duke in Shakespeare's *As You Like It*, who has accepted voluntary exile in the Forest of Arden where, with his followers, he can enjoy a "life more sweet / Than that of painted pomp" (Act 2, 1). In the guise of a cowhand, Cecil finds himself in the vicinity of the Arcadian school where he encounters Polly, who finds him attractive but uncouth. Eventually Cecil reveals his identity, and Polly has found a British peer for herself and a bogus American for her father, who is willing to accept his future son-in-law after becoming smitten with Polly's chaperone, Sarah, which suggests a double pairing off like Olivia and Sebastian and Viola and Orsino in Shakespeare's *Twelfth Night*.

The characters in *See America First* are the stock figures of operetta: Cecil recalls Prince Karl in Sigmund Romberg's *The Student Prince*, who is posing as a typical Heidelberg University student; Polly is the "love-at-first-sight" ingénue like Mabel in Gilbert and Sullivan's *The Pirates of Penzance*; the villains, known as the Bad Men, sing in rhyme and are no more dangerous than Penzance's pirates; the senator and the sheriff, Blood, are throwbacks to the Major-General and the Sergeant of Police in *The Pirates of Penzance*; Native American women, who describe themselves as "nature's children undisturbed by brains" ("Entrance of Indian Maidens"), have nothing in common with the schoolgirls in Gilbert and Sullivan's *The Mikado* but are merely a touch of (politically incorrect) local color; and the young men who have accompanied Cecil and refer to themselves as "disguised aristocracy" are kin to Gilbert and Sullivan's pirates, who are "noblemen gone wrong."

See America First was not that different from the fraternity shows that Porter wrote at Yale: a blend of broad satire and collegiate humor that might have regaled the Yalies but left New Yorkers unimpressed. If Cecil had become so enamored of America that he gave up his title and applied for citizenship, Porter might have been hailed as an iconoclast for overturning the conventions of operetta. Despite its portrayal of Native Americans as benign savages, *See America First* achieved a modicum of authenticity in the casting of Chief Henry Red Eagle (né Henry Perley), an Algonquin actor and writer, as Lo, the Poor Indian.

Porter had great hopes for his first Broadway musical. "SHOW MOST ENTHUSIASTICALLY RECEIVED HAVE HIGH HOPES FOR BRILLIANT OPENING IN NEW YORK," Porter wired his mother on February 22, 1916, after the first matinee of the Schenectady, New York, tryout. The March 28 opening night was far from brilliant, and the show closed on April 8. One should remember that Porter composed the score when he was two years out of Yale and a mere twenty-three years old. Taken on its own terms, *See America First* is a clever pastiche of musical forms (solos, duets, men's and women's choruses, ensembles) and operetta conventions (disguise, imperiled love, revelations). The college-in-the-woods is really a finishing school, whose graduates turn out to be either intellectually or domestically inclined ("Something's Got to Be Done"). After Blood describes the first type—those who have cultivated a love of Byzantine art, classical philology, Browning and Shelley—the Indian maidens respond, "Something's got to be done." Actually, nothing can be done for those who have embraced the intellectual life. But for the second type, those who prefer domesticity, there is a remedy: they should be taught to choose caviar over cheese and crackers and marry for money. The Indian maidens agree: "That's what's got to be done!" The number is both satiric and cynical, reflecting Porter's awareness that in 1916, higher education for women consisted of colleges that graduated debutantes and those that graduated liberally educated women.

"When I Used to Lead the Ballet," which Porter had written for *The Pot of Gold* (1912), a Yale fraternity show, was added to the score of *See America First*. It is the reminiscence of a former "Premier Danseur" who partnered with Pavlova, wearing a costume that resembled a negligee and looking like the ad for a White Rock beverage. In *See America First*, it was sung by Felix Adler as Chief Blood-In-His-Eye and chorus. It might have been performed in drag at the fraternity house, but one doubts that it was on Broadway, where the sight of a Native American chief singing about his dancing days might generate some laughs and perhaps a few groans. Yet the song clearly has gay overtones; the White Rock ad in question featured a scantily clad young woman kneeling on a rock. The number was performed at the Yale-Brown 1912 football game at which Porter appeared, costumed as Pavlova. Gay-coded lyrics or playful gender bending?

The only *See America First* cast member who went on to a major career on both stage and screen was Clifton Webb (1889–1966) as Percy, one of the disguised aristocrats. He had a duet with Jeanne Cartier, "The Language of Flowers," in which the couple address each other not by first name but by the name of a flower. It's rather romantic until he calls her "Daffodilly" and she calls him "Pansy," which is also slang for an effeminate or gay male. Since the duet was interpolated from *Paranoia* (1914), which Porter had written for the Yale University Dramatic Association, it is evident that, at twenty, he had mastered the art of double entendre. To anyone who knew that Webb, who specialized in playing effete males (*Laura*, *The Razor's Edge*, the Mr. Belvedere series), was gay, "pansy" was an inside reference as well as a double entendre. Whether Porter knew Webb was gay in 1916 is uncertain, but they eventually became quite friendly, with Porter singing one letter "Devotedly, Cole." By 1935, Porter seems to have known about Webb's discreetly veiled sexuality, addressing him as "Cute Clifton" in a letter dated January 1935 and sending "love to the great Mabel." Although some have conjectured that "Mabel" was the famous cabaret artist Mabel Mercer, she was actually Webb's mother to whom he was devoted and whose death at ninety-one in 1960 left a permanent void in his life. Webb himself died six years later and is buried alongside his mother at Hollywood Forever Cemetery on Santa Monica Boulevard. Porter, who could be unsparingly satirical, included a reference to Webb and Mabel in "Farming," which Danny Kaye introduced in *Let's Face It!* (1941). The song envisioned a nationwide return to nature, with celebrities feeding hogs, shelling peas, and raising cattle. Even Webb joins the movement *sans* mother: "So Clifton Webb has parked his ma, Mabel . . . in a broken-down stable." Cruel? Historically speaking, anything is grist for the satirist's mill. Porter also has John Steinbeck "growing Grapes of Wrath." Some 1941 theatergoers might have gotten the reference to Clifton and Mabel, but one would have had to be an insider—and Porter was one—to know that in social circles they seemed more like a couple than son and mother.

See America First was two-edged satire as well as a two-edged sword that left the show in shreds and Porter in need of a comeback. He returned three years later with the revue, *Hitchy-Koo of 1919*, which did somewhat better: fifty-seven performances with twelve Porter songs, including one that became popular, "Old-Fashioned Garden," a floral effusion of phlox, hollyhocks, violets, eglantines, columbines, and marigolds that could have only thrived in a hot house. Then it was another flop, *Hitchy-Koo of 1922*, which barely lasted two weeks in Philadelphia and never reached New York. Porter seemed to be back on track with *The Greenwich Village Follies of 1924*, which racked up 127 performances—except that all seven of his songs were eventually replaced. To paraphrase Willy Loman, who made a distinction between being "liked" and "well liked" in Arthur Miller's *Death of a Salesman*, Cole Porter was known but not well-known. Rather than remain in the United States and establish himself as a Broadway composer like Jerome Kern, he preferred the high life with a mansion instead of a garret and a palazzo in lieu of a pensione. Paris was his true home. He knew both Paris and Paree—the former with the ever present laughter; the latter with the "laughter that hides the tears," as Porter wrote so poignantly in "You Don't Know Paree," introduced by William Gaxton in *Fifty Million Frenchmen* (1929).

It was in Paris/Paree that Porter (1891–1964) met his wife, Linda Lee Thomas (1883–1954), seven years his senior, whom he married in 1919. From 1920 to 1937, the Porters lived in a luxurious seventeenth-century Paris townhouse at 13 rue Monsieur in the fashionable seventh arrondissement when they were not traveling or renting a Venetian palazzo where Porter had his own gondola. The townhouse was marked by a circular entrance, a grand salon, rooms with exotic furnishings, and a garden enclosure with a piano and composing table that Linda had custom made for her husband.

Such a lifestyle comes with a price. Small wonder that his output was so paltry, compared to that of Jerome Kern, then Broadway's leading songwriter, who composed the complete scores to (or considerable portions of) twenty-eight Broadway musicals between 1915 and 1927, including *Sally* (1920) and *Sunny* (1925), with Marilyn Miller, and the classic *Show Boat* (1927). By the time *Paris* opened in 1928, Cole Porter had composed songs for three Broadway shows, the third of which, *Greenwich Village Follies of 1924*, bore no trace of his contributions by the end of the run.

By 1928, Porter was no stranger to the musical theater's two principles that composers must acknowledge, often begrudgingly: first, the show's the thing, and the score serves the show; and second, if a number must be dropped because it does nothing but add to the show's running time, lies beyond a performer's range, or fails to achieve the effect for which it was intended, check your stockpile of discards, eliminations, and rejects for a replacement before writing a new one. Three songs from *See America First* were eliminated before the New York premiere; eleven were dropped even earlier; two were replaced; one was interpolated from *The Pot of Gold*, which Porter wrote for his Yale fraternity, Delta Kappa Epsilon; and three from *Paranoia*, produced by the Yale University Drama Association the year after he graduated. If all the songs had been used, *See America First* would have seemed like a succession of musical numbers interspersed with snippets of plot—more like a revue with sketches than a musical. Porter had still not acclimated himself to the book musical with its (at least theoretical) integration of story and song. Revues were simpler: all he had to do was supply some songs.

Porter originally wrote twenty-one of them for *Hitchy-Koo of 1919*. Twelve made the cut; three were dropped before the New York opening; one was added to *Hitchy-Koo of 1922*, which never made it to Broadway; and six were never used. During the run of *Greenwich Village Follies of 1924* (September 16, 1924, to January 3, 1925), all of Porter's eighteen songs, including the standard, "I'm in Love Again," were removed at various times. Porter managed to salvage two of them. "I Love a Girl in a Shawl" was retitled "I Dream of a Girl in a Shawl" and interpolated into *Wake Up and Dream* (1929), then dropped before the London premiere but reinstated for the Broadway production; "Two Little Babes in the Woods" ended up in *Paris*.

GREENWICH VILLAGE FOLLIES (1924)

The cast—which included the Dolly Sisters, Georgia Hale (best known for her role as Georgia in Chaplin's *The Gold Rush* [1925]), and Vincent Lopez and His Orchestra—was typical of the series that John Murray Anderson created in 1919. For the 1924 edition, Anderson hired Porter to compose the score, which he did while residing in Venice at the Palazzo Barbaro. When Anderson, dissatisfied with some of the songs, asked for new material, Porter, who did not take the assignment seriously, either could not be reached or was incommunicado. What remained of the score was the work of Anderson, Irving Caesar, and Isham Jones, who, with lyricist Gus Kohn, composed the revue's best-known song, "It Had to be You."

Porter composed seven songs for Greenwich Village Follies of 1924:

"Brittany," in which boy pines for girl in Brittany;

"Two Little Babes in the Wood," which was dropped at some point before December 1924 and added to the score of *Paris* (1928)—a wonderfully cynical song about two orphan girls who, depending on which version one prefers (the Hans Christian Andersen or the John Murray Anderson), were either left in the woods to die by their cruel uncle (Hans Christian) or were found by a wealthy man who taught them that the fountain of youth "is a mixture of gin and vermouth" (John Murray);

"Broadcast a Jazz," the music to which has been lost, but the number was planned as the Act 1 finale and dropped shortly after the September opening;

"Wait for the Moon," a generic song about longing ("Just stay in my arms / And wait for the moon");

"My Long Ago Girl," another lost love lament;

"Make Every Day a Holiday," an exhortation to "give yourself a good time";

"I'm in Love Again," a vapid and repetitious swoon song that has enjoyed an afterlife in cabaret.

The only song with any wit is "Two Little Babes in the Woods," which may have irked Anderson because, in the alternate version of the orphans' fate, Porter refers to John Murray Anderson as a descendant of Hans Christian Andersen, who had to appeal to the "tired businessman" by having the orphans befriended by a Sugar Daddy who taught them the ways of the world.

Although one would like to have heard the jazz-inspired music of "Broadcast a Jazz," Porter's contribution to *Greenwich Village Follies of 1924* was negligible.

PARIS (1928)

In 1928, Cole Porter was known as a bon vivant in social circles and a world traveler, first; and as a composer, second. Eventually he struck a balance between his life and his art, but not until he was acknowledged as a composer of Broadway musicals. This had not yet happened at the time that *Paris* opened at New York's Music Box theatre on October 8, 1928, for a run of 195 performances. Unlike *Hitchy-Koo of 1919* and *Greenwich Village Follies of 1924*, *Paris* was a book musical in which Cora Sabot, a Massachusetts blueblood, travels to Paris to stop her son Andrew from marrying a French actress played by the star Irene Bordoni (1885–1953). Cora is so successful that the actress finds her soul mate in another performer; and Andrew, in a vacuous woman from his own class The book's point of departure seems to have been Henry James's *The Ambassadors* (1904), in which another

Massachusetts matron, also a widow, sends her fiancé to Paris to bring back her errant son. Then *Paris* moves into a world that would have been alien to James, whose Paris was the city where prodigal sons and their ambassadors are exposed to a world of genteel decadence and flexible morality, and return to America, sadder but wiser, with their Parisian lovers left behind. *Paris*, on the other hand, is gay Paree by way of Broadway, where the only authenticity comes from Bordoni's accent and names like Vivienne and Marcel. Porter was one of several songwriters, including Walter Kollo (music) and E. Ray Goetz (lyrics), Irving Berlin's brother-in-law, who was then Bordoni's husband and contributed two songs compared to Porter's eight, one of which was eliminated at the outset; another before the New York opening; a third replaced; and a fourth added to the score of *Wake Up and Dream*, reducing Porter's contribution to five.

Although Bordoni's *New York Times* obituary (March 29, 1953) gave Paris as her birthplace, she was Corsican-born but otherwise thoroughly Parisian. Neither a great singer nor a great dancer, Bordoni projected such an air of worldliness that it seemed Montmartre was her mentor, and her playbook was written in French. She was perfectly cast as Vivienne Rolland, the actress with whom Andrew Sabot is infatuated. Porter had originally written the ever popular "Let's Misbehave" as a duet for Vivienne and Andrew, in which she urges the proper Bostonian to get a past if he wants a future, which is best achieved by misbehaving, reminding him that even "bears have love affairs," thus giving an entirely new meaning to "misbehave." In 1928, Bordoni recorded "Let's Misbehave," a performance that can be heard on YouTube. Her rendition is somewhere between speech-song and recitation, expressively Gallic with faintly trilled "r"s and overly stressed syllables that makes it seem like a lesson in lovemaking. The lyrics themselves were mildly risqué (Bobby Short often sang all of them in his act at the Café Carlyle), but not naughty enough (at least as Bordoni sang them) for a scene in which the accomplished Vivienne instructs the callow Andrew in *la vie Parisienne*. Porter replaced "Let's Misbehave" with the even more popular and politically incorrect "Let's Do It, Let's Fall in Love," in which everyone ("Chinks," "Japs," "Laps," "Letts" et al.) and various fauna and flora do "it," which is not so much falling in love as making it. How else does one interpret "Sweet guinea pigs do it. / Buy a couple and wait." Wait for *what*?

On Film (First National—Warner Bros., 1929)

Warner Bros. was so encouraged by the success of its partial talkie *The Jazz Singer* (1927)—which utilized the Vitaphone sound system, in which the sound sequences were recorded on 16-inch, 33⅓ rpm shellac discs and synchronized with the picture—that, for a time, it made the musical a priority. Since stage musicals could be easily converted into film musicals, in 1929 Warner Bros. released the movie versions of Sigmund Romberg's *The Desert Song*, Jerome Kern's *Sally*, George M. Cohan's *Little Johnny Jones*—and Cole Porter's *Paris*. The studio decided that Martin Brown's book could make a smooth transition to the screen, but Porter's songs were too sophisticated for moviegoers to whom his name then meant nothing. Warner Bros.' handling of *Paris* was typical of the way Hollywood treated a Cole Porter musical: Porter's scores never reached the screen intact; sometimes they were winnowed down to a few numbers—one in *Something for the Boys* (Twentieth Century-Fox, 1944), the title song; none in *Mexican Hayride* (Universal-International, 1948). MGM showed more respect for *Kiss Me Kate* (1953) and *Silk Stockings* (1957), but truthfully, Cole Porter did more for Hollywood than it did for him.

Porter's name appears nowhere in the ads for *Paris*, which was marketed as an Irene Bordoni film:

Oo-la-la!
She Is Here!
Irene
Bordoni

Beneath "Bordoni" is a sketch of the star with a feathered head piece on which "PARIS" is inscribed.

In very small print "based on play by Martin Brown—a Clarence Badger Prod"

Hear Irene Bordoni sing! See the gigantic settings, gorgeous costumes and the fastest stepping chorus of beauties this side of life. Scenes in Technicolor.

A First National & Vitaphone Picture.

Brown at least got credit for the book, even though it was called a play. Badger was a prolific director of silent and early sound films, including another Warner Bros. film version of a stage musical, Vincent Youmans's *No, No Nanette* (1930).

CHAPTER 2

The List Song

Wake Up and Dream, Fifty Million Frenchmen, and *The New Yorkers*

"Let's Do It" is a list song in which the lyrics contain a musical enumeration of virtually anything: amours, acquisitions, activities, accomplishments, names, places, and so forth. The list song has a long tradition, the most famous examples coming from opera. In Mozart's *Don Giovanni*, Leporello, the Don's servant, informs Donna Elvira, one of the Don's former lovers, that she belongs to a long line of conquests, which he cites geographically and numerically, reminding her that while there were only ninety-one in Turkey, there were one thousand and three ("*mille tre*") in Spain. In Rossini's *The Barber of Seville*, Figaro comes on stage singing the famous aria "Largo al factotum," in which he describes the services he renders, from shaving and hair-cutting to advice to the lovelorn, regardless of age. Porter's first list song was "I've a Shooting Box in Scotland," written for the Yale University Drama Association's production of *Paranoia* and later incorporated into the score of *See America First*, where it was the penultimate number sung by Cecil (British actor John Heath Goldsworthy), the duke no longer in disguise, and Polly (Dorothie Bigelow, also British). Cecil describes himself as an inveterate collector of country places such as a shooting box in Scotland, a chateau, a chalet, a villa, and a hacienda, culminating in a list of all the illnesses brought on by his mania for collecting, including "malaria in Bavaria"—rhyme for the sake of rhyme rather than sense, which was typical of Porter who rhymed "sweeties" with "diabetes" ("The Physician's Song," *Nymph Errant* [1933]) and "Mae West" with "me undressed" (title song in *Anything Goes* [1934]). Stephen Sondheim was also a master of rhyme, but with him, rhyme is intrinsic to the meaning. In Sondheim's *Sunday in the Park with George* (1984), the pointillist painter Georges Seurat describes not just pointillism but art in general in "Putting It Together," noting that every detail is "part" of the "art"; that a mere vision is no "solution," but what matters is the "execution." The artistic process proceeds "bit by bit." Porter would have agreed, but would have added "with wit."

Porter regarded rhyming words or phrases in two ways: as more of an expression of cleverness than the kind of complementarity found in couplets where the second verse augments the first, resulting in a complete thought ("True Wit is Nature to advantage dress'd. / What oft was thought but n'er so well express'd" [Alexander Pope, *An Essay on Criticism*]); and as an evocation of a mood or emotion, as in "Night and Day" (*Gay Divorce*, 1932), in which the lover thinks of the beloved everywhere—both outside ("traffic's boom") and inside ("lonely room")

The list song, a Cole Porter perennial, may be bereft of depth—and sometimes, even of sense—but it brims with ingenuity. Some of the best include:

"The Physician" (*Nymph Errant*, 1933), in which the singer describes her doctor's reaction to her anatomy ("He did a double hurdle / When I shook my pelvic girdle");

"You're the Top" (*Anything Goes*, 1934), a mutual-admiration duet in which a couple trade superlatives, each comparing the other to historic places (the Coliseum), persons (Keats, Shelley), and things (Napoleon brandy). If all seven refrains are sung, the dizzying barrage of rhyming metaphors can leave the listener in a state of cerebral exhaustion. You come away with the feeling that rhymes run riot In Porter's fertile brain like daisies;

"Anything Goes," the title song, which celebrates a world turned upside down by changing mores where good is bad, black is white, day is night; and where no one raises objections to anything: four-letter words instead of better words, cars, bars, hymns, limbs, even "love affairs" with "young bears";

The delightfully bawdy duet "But in the Morning, No" (*Du Barry Was a Lady*, 1939), between She and He (Ethel Merman and Bert Lahr in the original Broadway production), in which She asks if He uses the breast stroke, does double entry, can ante up, and likes third parties—to which He replies in the affirmative, "but in the morning, no." The closest He ever gets to double entendre is asking if She would sell her seat to which she replies "gladly," "but in the morning, no."

"They Couldn't Compare to You" (*Out of This World*, 1950), clearly modeled after Leporello's "*Madamina, il catalogo*" in *Don Giovanni*, in which Mercury lists his lovers, mythological and historical, from Galatea, Medea, Circe, and Sappho to Lola Montez, Calamity Jane, Nell Gwynn, and Anne Boleyn;

The title song in *Can-Can*, which consists of an eight-line verse and seven twelve-line refrains, all ending with: "Baby, you can can-can, too." It is another giddy head-spinner insisting that the can-can is so easy that anyone can do it: Dapper Dans/Callahans, Louvre custodians/Grand Republicans, Anglicans/lesbians, ass/bass, as Porter skewers sense as if proclaiming, "No species left behind."

ON STAGE: *WAKE UP AND DREAM* (1929)

There are some list songs in *Wake Up and Dream*—such as "Which Is the Right Life?" sung by costar Jessie Matthews (the star was the great song-and-dance man, Jack Buchanan)—in which the singer is faced with dilemmas she cannot resolve, including the right kind of lifestyle as well as the right man (the latter resulting in the strained rhyming of Walt Whitman with Paul Whiteman). It was an odd revue which, despite mixed notices, ran for 263 performances in London and 136 in New York. Although the "book" of *Wake Up and Dream* is credited to John Hastings Turner, it is really a revue, a series of musical numbers and sketches united by a common theme summed up by the title song that encourages everyone to find their inner Peter Pan, promising that they will be alive when their detractors are dead. Among the dreamers are Columbus, Elizabeth I, and Lord Essex; the title characters in that most dreamlike of operas, Debussy's *Pelléas et Mélisande*; Carmen; the California forty-niners; the personifications of Art, Music, and Power; the Spirit of Magic in the person of the superb Viennese dancer, Toni (Anton) Birkmayer; and the folkloric Bluebird, enacted by the great dancer-choreographer Tilly Losch as the harbinger of spring that inspires hope in those who endured a winter of discontent.

Revues are designed for audience members who can appreciate inside references and topical humor. *Wake Up and Dream* was unusually cerebral in its juxtaposition of historical figures and operatic characters, as illustrated in the sketch "Operatic Pills," in which Jack Buchanan impersonated the conductor Sir Thomas Beecham, whose father, Sir Joseph Beecham, was a well-known pill manufacturer. Other performers appeared as Madame Butterfly; the title character from Charpentier's opera *Louise*; and Elsa and Lohengrin from Wagner's *Lohengrin*.

Understandably, *Wake Up and Dream* had a longer run in London than in New York. Even with such a cavalcade of history, myth, and opera, as well as a bit of Léo Delibes's ballet *Coppélia* and a sketch called "Gothic" danced by Tilly Losch and Ann Barberova to music by J. S. Bach, *Wake Up and Dream* had a respectable run in Broadway. Perhaps it could have lasted longer if the stock market had not crashed on "Black Tuesday," October 26, 1929, about two months before the show opened on December 30.

It is difficult to determine how many numbers were included in the Broadway transfer of *Wake Up and Dream*, since, reportedly, some of the original ones had been removed. One certainly was: "Let's Do It," interpolated from *Paris* (1928) for British audiences and in no need of a reprise in New York. According to one source, there were nineteen in the London production, and ten in the New York one, which seems unlikely. Another lists eleven numbers in Part 1, including the extended dream sequence with Columbus, Essex, Elizabeth I, and others; and eight in Part 2. An undated program, clearly dating from mid-January1930, for the Selwyn Theatre, where the New York production ran from December 30, 1929, to April 26, 1930, tells a different story: twelve in Part 1 and twelve in Part 2. As often happens in revues and even musicals, some numbers listed in the playbill may not have been performed at a particular performance. In my own theatergoing experience, Gwen Verdon did not perform a strenuous dance sequence in *New Girl in Town* (1957) at the June matinee I attended, but when I went back a month later, she did. I was at the performance of Richard Rodgers's *Rex* (1976) that starred Nicol Williamson as Henry VIII and Penny Fuller as Anne Boleyn, and the young Elizabeth I. Williamson, who was known for behaving erratically, decided not to do the scene that featured one of the show's best songs, "From Afar," resulting in *Rex* ending fifteen minutes earlier than scheduled. Also, the order of the numbers in the New Yok production of *Wake Up and Dream* may have been fluid, with twenty-four being the ideal but fewer at certain performances. A revue is not a book musical. It may have a theme, but not a plot. Thus the theme of *Wake Up and Dream*, as expressed in the title song, would not have been affected by a few omissions.

In the Selwyn Theatre playbill, the twenty-first number is one of Cole Porter's most famous, "What Is This Thing Called Love?" Elsie Carlisle performed it in the London production, and, briefly, Frances Shelley in New York. The undated Selwyn Theatre playbill has William Stephens singing it. Stephens had the equivalent of a costarring role (his name was in all caps); among other numbers, he performed "I Dream of a Girl in a Shawl," with Tilly Losch, and sang the playful lament "I'm a Gigolo." Frances Shelley's name does not appear in the playbill because she was no longer in the show. At some point, probably in early January 1930, she left the *Wake Up and Dream* company and joined the cast of *The Nine-Fifteen Revue*, which only ran four nights (February 11–15, 1930). Four months later, she was back on Broadway in *Mystery Moon*, which opened and closed on June 23, 1930, and proved to be her last New York credit.

Since both Shelley and Stephens sang "What Is This Thing Called Love?" the song is gender-neutral, recorded by major vocalists both male (Bing Crosby, Frank Sinatra) and female (Billie Holiday, Ella Fitzgerald). It is a soliloquy, meditative and deeply introspective, in which the singer, "a humdrum person," had been leading a similarly humdrum life until love entered it and then left. The closest one gets to the singer's image of love is something that "flies in" through a window, lingers, and flies out. Unlike the bluebird, love knows no seasons; an open window, like an open heart, may invite entry but also allows for a quick exit.

The verse establishes the ruminative nature of the song. The refrain continues in the same vein with a series of four two-line stanzas, the third functioning as a bridge and the only one that is not a rhetorical question. In stanzas one and two, the singer struggles to define the elusive "love," calling it is a "funny thing" and wondering if its mystery is solvable. The bridge consists of two short sentences—statements, not questions. The singer refers to a "You" whose heartlessness prompted the questioning, thus providing a context for the song: a one-sided relationship that left the lover pondering the nature of that undefinable love, which was given gladly but never returned. The final stanza is almost a prayer, in which the singer directs the question, the same as the song title, to "the Lawd." It is interesting that Porter originally used the spelling "Lawd," although it was later changed to "Lord" in the sheet music lyrics. "Lawd" is the African American vernacular for "Lord." Lyricist Ira Gershwin used that spelling in Porgy's final aria in *Porgy and Bess* (1935), "Oh, Lawd, I'm on My Way."

But there can be no answer to a rhetorical question, at least not verbally. The final line of the first and last chorus is the song title: "What is this thing called love?"

In *Wake Up and Dream*, the "What Is This Thing Called Love?" sequence was not a solo; it involved three performers: William Stephens as The Singer, Toni (Anton) Birkmayer as A Statue, and Tilly Losch as The Girl. From the reviews, it seems that the setting was vaguely African (hence, "Lawd"), intentionally exotic in keeping with Porter's claim that the song was inspired by a dance he once saw in Marrakesh. Birkmayer, a soloist at the Vienna State Opera, was a superb dancer, striking in appearance and naturally statuesque. In the Gold Rush sequence, he partnered with Tilly Losch in "The Flirtation Dance." One suspects that a renowned dancer like Birkmayer did more than impersonate an inanimate object. Losch interpreted the emotions expressed in the song through dance, so that, in *Wake Up and Dream*, "What Is This Thing Called Love?" was not an ordinary show tune but a union of words, music, art, and movement.

Porter's shows were enjoyably frivolous—theatrical baubles, all surface sheen. He never ventured into the dark side as Rodgers and Hart did in *Pal Joey* or Rodgers and Hammerstein in *Oklahoma!* and *Carousel*. The depth in a Cole Porter musical did not derive from the book, but frequently from the lyrics, particularly those that dealt with love.

ON STAGE: *FIFTY MILLION FRENCHMEN* (1929)

There was little depth in both book and lyrics of *Fifty Million Frenchmen*, which was another hit (254 performances, November 14, 1929, to July 5, 1930). Given its lineage, the show promised more than it delivered. The book was by Herbert Fields (Vincent Youmans's *Hit the Deck*, Rodgers and Hart's *A Connecticut Yankee*); direction by Cole's friend from his Yale days, Edgar M. Woolley, better known as Monty Woolley, who went on to a major film career; sets by the renowned Norman Bel Geddes, and choreography by Larry Ceballos, who began on Broadway (*Paris, No, No Nanette*) and then settled in Hollywood where he was dance director or choreographer for such films as *The Yellow Rose of Texas* (1944), *Copacabana* (1947), and *Valentino* (1951). The boy (wealthy)-girl (of moderate means) plot hinges on a bet: boy bets that he can last for a month in Paris without drawing on his funds and still manage to announce his engagement to a girl before midnight on the last day. Complications (including a winning horse race ticket) abound, but the boy wins both his gamble and the girl.

Fifty Million Frenchmen was gay "Paree" for New Yorkers at the dawn of the Great Depression, who might have been amused at the sight of a rich young man working odd jobs (and not very successfully) in order to survive in a city that frowns on ineptitude. Two songs celebrated "Paree," a far cry from the Paris Porter celebrated in the ode to his beloved city, "I Love Paris" (*Can-Can*). In the duet "Paree, What Did You Do to Me?" a couple describes the transformative effect of the city, which loosened their inhibitions and gave them a taste of the bubbly. The couple may think they know "Paree," but theirs is the tourist version. In "You Don't Know Paree," the star, William Gaxton, describes the flip side of Paris, which only those who have loved and lost, laughed, and cried truly know.

The oddest song in *Fifty Million Frenchmen* is "The Tale of the Oyster," a specialty number written for Helen Broderick as a raunchy buyer from New York. The oyster in question becomes luncheon fare for Mrs. Hoggenheimer, who, while returning on her yacht, experiences *mal de mer* and "up comes the oyster." It is a tricky number, which has to be sung with a mock gravity that cabaret singers, particularly Bobby Short, have been able to affect. Although Broderick had a true flair for comedy, her delivery offended the sensibilities of culture critic Gilbert Seldes, which was enough to warrant its removal early in the run. "The Tale of the Oyster" would appear tasteless only to those who cannot appreciate Porter's devilish irony that spares no one, not even the poor bivalve, who actually gets the last word. The oyster had a taste of high society, which in turn had a taste of the oyster—the use of one word, "taste," with two meanings, a trope that classical rhetoricians would have termed "antanaclasis."

That Porter could use figures of speech and various metrical forms with such ease was the result of an education that was heavily grounded in classical languages and English literature. "Brush Up Your Shakespeare: (*Kiss Me, Kate* [1948]) contains allusions to thirteen of Shakespeare's plays as well as his narrative poem, *Venus and Adonis*. Mercury's lovers in "They Couldn't Compare to You" (*Out of This World*, 1950) ranged from the muse of dance, Terpsichore, Euripides's Medea, Wagner's Brunnhilde, and Homer's Calypso, Circe, and Penelope to Sappho, Maeterlinck's Melisande, Beatrice d'Esty, Queen Isabella of Spain, Anne Boleyn, Nell Gwyn, and Lola Montez. Porter required neither a rhyming dictionary nor an encyclopedia. He absorbed much of what he learned—or what interested him, which were clearly the classics.

ON STAGE: *THE NEW YORKERS* (1930)

Porter's next musical, *The New Yorkers*, had a shorter run (168 performances, December 8, 1930, to May 2, 1931) but it was far more adventuresome, even audacious, in its disregard for conventions: a Park Avenue socialite marries a bootlegger, played by the star, Jimmy Durante, who furnished his own material, consisting of five specialty numbers and comic bits that generated laughs from their malapropisms and mangled pronunciation.

The book was again by Herbert Fields, based on a concept by the *New Yorker* cartoonist Peter Arno, who limned New Yorkers with a cynical and sometimes jaundiced vision, often rendering them so starkly that it would have seemed unnatural if he had added flesh to their frames. Some cartoons were darkly humorous: a wife in the bathroom sees her husband trapped in a flooded shower; the sweet-faced "Whoops" sisters who always speak in double entendre; a convict asking his visiting mother, "You mean to say there was a file in that cake?"; a plane in a downspin with the caption, "My God, we're out of gin!"

One of the songs in *The New Yorkers*, "I Happen to Like New York," echoes Arno's vision. Like Porter, he could say he liked "the sight and the sound and even the stink of it"—perhaps the sight and stink more than the sound. Arno's New York was neither a crucible nor a melting pot, but a mosaic in black and white representing New York's seemingly infinite variety: slinky ladies and fashionable matrons; elegantly dressed men and straphangers in a subway car; barflies and fastidious diners; lecherous bosses and their cornered secretaries. Arno was to cartooning what Porter was to the Broadway musical: the high priest of sardonic wit and unapologetic irreverence.

Arno's mosaic came to life in *The New Yorkers*, where nothing was sacred, including the wedding of the socialite and the bootlegger with bridesmaids armed with machine guns. Many of the songs defied convention. Don't woo a woman with candy or flowers, as tradition dictates, but rather "Say It with Gin." Forget nature and stay inside with a drink ("The Great Indoors"). If sinners must sing (as they are encouraged to do in the popular song "Sing, You Sinners"), let them celebrate one of our great penitentiaries ("Sing Sing for Sing Sing").

One number in *The New Yorkers* that was not satirical was "Love for Sale," a prostitute's sales pitch, direct and dry-eyed, "Love for Sale" was considered in such bad taste—especially since it was performed by a white singer, Kathryn Crawford, with an all-white trio in front of Reuben's Restaurant and Delicatessen, then located on Madison Avenue—that the setting was changed to the Cotton Club in Harlem, with the great Black artist Elizabeth Welch replacing Crawford minus the trio. Racism naturally dictated the change, but theatergoers who were fortunate enough to see Welch, who spent most of her career in Europe, especially in Paris and London, heard "Love for Sale" the way Porter wrote it.

CHAPTER 3

Ça c'est l'amour

The Cole Porter Love Song

Cole Porter was constantly striving for the right metaphor for love. "What Love Is" (*Paranoia*, 1914) occupies a significant place in the Cole Porter songbook as an early attempt to conjure up the right words to describe the emotion that haunted him throughout his life, recalling the speaker's search for *le mot juste* in T. S. Eliot's "Little Gidding": "the common word exact without vulgarity / the formal word precise but not pedantic." In "What Love Is," Porter goes through various metaphors, only one of which is satisfactory: "lotus of life. "Love is the lotus of life" is the alliterative maxim of a twenty-two-year-old expert.

Whether Porter thought of the lotus in Buddhist terms as the multivalent symbol of transcendence, enlightenment, and rebirth—a flower that grows in the earth, rising out of matter into the embodiment of ideal beauty, just as the seeker of the peace that surpasses understanding must rise above the material world to a higher state—is hard to determine.

He may also have been thinking of the lotus-eaters in Book 9 of Homer's *Odyssey*, for whom the plant acts as a drug that produces a state of tranquility, similar to a "high." When Odysseus's men eat the lotus, they lose any desire to return home, and Odysseus must force them back to the ship. Either at the Worcester Academy or Yale, he would also have read Tennyson's "The Lotus-Eaters," which imagines Homer's islanders living in an earthly paradise where "it seemed always afternoon" and where "all things always seemed the same." The lotus is an exotic opioid, leaving those who eat its fruit in a state of perpetual satisfaction with no desire to return to a world that cannot guarantee lasting bliss.

If love is the lotus of life, it is either the closest to perfection that one can achieve in an imperfect world or a sweet-tasting drug that makes the lover oblivious to life's slings and arrows. The song is titled "What Love

Is," not "What Is Love?" At twenty-two, Porter thought he knew, but as he grew older, he became less confident.

When he wrote "What Is This Thing Called Love?" (*Wake Up and Dream*, 1929) seven years later, Porter was at a loss to find the right metaphor for the "thing." Porter returned to the all-purpose "thing" in "You Do Something to Me" (*Fifty Million Frenchmen*, 1929), calling that "something" hypnotic and mystifying but at the same time "soothing"—adjectives in search of an essence. The "thing" in "You've Got That Thing" (*Fifty Million Frenchmen*)—whatever it is—can alter the natural order of things, causing birds to forget to sing, farmers to leave their farms, reformers to reform their reforms. And since this is another boy-girl duet, it has to end on a heterosexual note: "that thing" leads to something "any stork might bring." Thus, "that thing" is the procreative drive, or, as Porter defined it in "Paris Loves Lovers" (*Silk Stockings*, 1955), "the urge to merge with the splurge of the spring"—in other words, sex.

Cole Porter wrote two kinds of love songs: the perfunctory and the probing. He knew that, traditionally, musicals need at least one romantic ballad, which, depending upon the degree of inspiration and the nature of the show, he made sure to include. The result could be poetry in song or prose in stanzas. "I'm in Love Again" is the latter.

For *Greenwich Village Follies of 1924*, Porter added "I'm in Love Again" after the New York opening, but it was eventually dropped along with his other contributions. Although the song became a standard, it is perfunctory and prosaic—love reduced to populist rhymes ("comin'"/"strumm in'"/"hummin'"/; "springin'"/"ringin'") and the lover to behaving like "a lovebird singin'" and "a spring lamb springin'"—the latter a play on words that classical rhetoricians would have called "antanaclasis," in which a word is repeated in two different senses, but that Alexander Pope would have called "false wit."

Porter's least interesting love songs are the perfunctory, although some of them have a wistful romanticism that endears them to singers with a preference for ballads. *Out of this World* (1950)—a contemporary setting of the Amphitryon myth in which Jupiter takes a fancy to a mortal woman and assumes the form of her husband—did not need a love song, but Porter provided one for the unsuspecting wife: "I Am Loved," which is one extended cliché, in which the wife rhapsodizes on what a "wonderful" (repeated three times), "glorious," "beautiful" *thing* (that word again) love is. Love is just one of those *things* ("Just One of those Things," *Jubilee*, 1935). It is an onrush of emotion that cannot be permanent, because it is "too hot to cool down." And when it does, it is over because it was "just one of those things." One of what *things*? Porter conjures up metaphors: a bell that rings occasionally, a lunar flight. But bells stop ringing, and flights land. Love can be described adjectivally, metaphorically, or in terms of its effects.

Except for "the lotus of life," Porter was never able to come up with a suitable metaphor for love. It was a "thing," personified as a bird that flies in and out of a window ("What Is This Thing Called Love?"). It is a state that can make the lover regress and act like a child, and what rhymes with child? "Wild." ("I'm in Love Again"). Even physical attraction is a "thing" ("You've Got That Thing"). The modifier "certain" is no help. Love is a game, and two can be "grand" at it ("Easy to Love," aka "You'd Be So Easy to Love" [*Born to Dance*, MGM, 1936]). But the game of love is never serious. "Easy to Love" starts quietly, seductively, and then begins to soar, suggesting another heavenly trip. But the flight is aborted, and passenger lands in a cottage, married with children, and sitting down to a breakfast of eggs and bacon. There is something almost ludicrous about the domestic turn the song takes. It is as if, after the adoring and idolizing phase is over, nothing is left but eating and procreating. "Easy to Love" is the most heterosexual love song Porter had ever written. And the least credible.

Porter could write about love as a form of rapture that borders on possession, a force that insinuates itself into the lover ("I've Got You Under My Skin," *Born to Dance*, MGM, 1936) or is so overwhelming that one who is "so in love" will endure taunts, pain, deception, and desertion ("So in Love," *Kiss Me, Kate*, 1948). But these are extremes, more like passion than love—a kind of Dionysiac mania that beclouds reason, which those who have known both emotions can accept, even if they have never experienced subcutaneous burrowing or masochistic ecstasy.

"What is love? 'Tis not hereafter / Present mirth hath present laughter," Feste sings in *Twelfth Night* (Act 2, 3). Porter would agree. "What Is This Thing Called Love?" poses a question that is never answered. So does "At Long Last Love" (1938), whose refrain is a series of questions in which the lover is trying to find the right metaphor for love which is binary and admits of two extremes, high or low grade. Is it a sapphire or a charm, a rainbow or a mirage, real turtle soup or mock, the Lido or Asbury Park, a porterhouse or an ordinary steak? The song title is misleading. Porter simply does not know. The lover admits in "I Love You" (*Mexican Hayride*, 1944) that he cannot write a love song and instead enlists the help of nature, with the breeze, the hills, and the dawn declaring what he can only say in three words. Although "I Love You" is one of Porter's perfunctory songs, written for the male lead in *Mexican Hayride* (1944), musical comedy star

Wilbur Evans, it became enormously popular after it was recorded by Bing Crosby, Jo Stafford, and Perry Como, suggesting that listeners shared the same sentiments.

Porter has always been better at describing love's effects than love itself. It bores under the skin ("I've Got You Under My Skin") and insinuates itself into the lover's consciousness producing a "hungry yearning" within ("Night and Day"). It's a jolt, a thunderbolt, a fire to be kept bright and blazing ("I Am in Love," *Can-Can*, 1953). But does it last? First two people fall in love; then each finds someone else ("Weren't We Fools?, 1927," written for Fanny Brice). Sometimes worship is preferable to love, since worship reduces the object of veneration to an idol, awesome but lifeless ("I Worship You," *Fifty Million Frenchmen*, 1929). Even if one has found the ideal lover, the fear of loss broods over the relationship, which, should it end, is irreplaceable ("After You, Who?," *Gay Divorce*, 1932). Closeness is difficult, since the ground between lover and beloved is constantly shifting ("So Near and Yet So Far," *Gay Divorce* [1932]). Even in a romantic ballad like "In the Still of the Night" (*Rosalie*, MGM, 1937), the lover wonders if love is an illusion that will grow dim and disappear, leaving a chill in a night that was previously tranquil. Love is a dream, and when the dreamer awakens, it's time to say "goodbye" ("Goodbye, Little Dream, Goodbye," *Born to Dance*, MGM, 1936). The trick is to keep the dream alive, even if the love object can only be a fantasy figure for "dream dancing" ("Dream-Dancing," *You'll Never Get Rich*, Columbia, 1941). That Porter chose to hyphenate the song title suggests that the dancers can only partner in a dream, where the dancers and the dance are inseparable.

Porter rarely wrote songs celebrating the joys of love. "I'm in Love Again" has a bouncy banality typical of a young lover without a poet's vocabulary. "I Love You" draws on clichéd images from the world of nature that saves the lover the trouble of finding the right metaphors. "True Love" (*High Society*, MGM, 1956), a duet for Bing Crosby and, briefly, Grace Kelly, gives some indication of what true love is: an exchange of devotion ("I give to you and you give to me"). But human beings need an assist from above; "a guardian angel on high" facilitates the exchange. Although Porter, who would die eight years later in 1964, was not a particularly religious man, "True Love" implies that perfect love is not something that humans can achieve by themselves.

Porter is at his best either celebrating imperfect love or questioning its permanence. He can describe its effects, treat it playfully, take it seriously, or view it cynically. In "Ça, c'est l'amour' (*Les Girls*, MGM, 1957), Porter presents love as a kind of round robin: union-separation-reunion. A couple fall in love; then one leaves; the other grieves; the one who left returns, now even more desirable; and all is well unless the cycle repeats itself, and there is no guarantee that it won't. That's love—or rather, the other kind that is not for sale but only for lease. Porter was familiar with both. He had expressed similar sentiments in "C'est magnifique," one of the numbers in *Can-Can* (1953). When two people fall in love, it's *magnifique*. When one exits, it's *tragique*. When the errant partner returns, it's *magnifique* again—until it turns *tragique*. Like a carousel, *l'amour* is a cycle of starts and stops. There was only one still point in Porter's turning world: his wife, Linda.

As a gay man married to a woman who knew about his sexual orientation and whose approval he sought when taking a male lover, he was brutally frank when he wrote in "Love for Sale," "I know ev'ry type of love." Although the song is a prostitute's monologue, Porter understood her clientele, which, except for gender, was no different from men like himself who took their "trip to paradise" by a different route.

Linda Lee Porter understood his needs. What she could offer was admiration and unswerving love. She was the constant in his life, which had many variables. Porter was forever booking trips to his kind of paradise, yet he could claim, like the speaker in Ernest Dowson's poem "Non Sum Qualis Eram," that he had been true to Linda "in my fashion." Whether the shadow of Linda fell over Porter during those trysts, like the shadow of Cynara over the speaker in Dowson's poem when he was enjoying the kisses of a "bought red mouth," is doubtful. Linda knew her husband distinguished between love and sex, combining them in song but keeping them separate in his private life.

Porter once claimed that "Love for Sale" was his favorite song. From his experiences with male prostitutes, he knew, like the woman in the song, that love means sex, a commodity obtained for a price and not to be mistaken for "true love." That she cannot offer because she has been through "the mill of love" that grinds the soul into numbness, so that love/sex becomes a transaction between buyer and seller.

When set alongside Porter's own life, "Love for Sale" becomes a kind of impressionistic autobiography, with the woman as a stand-in for the men that he sought out for anonymous sex. While he and Monty Woolley were best friends, but never lovers, they were both gay and would drive around looking for men who, socially and culturally, were not of their class, such as truck drivers and sailors. They also had procurers who catered to their racial preferences, Blacks being less expensive.

Porter's relationships with men were complex. Paul Sylvain was more than Porter's valet and chauffeur; he was a trusted member of the household for whom Porter had an abiding, almost fraternal affection, and who delighted in handling Porter's luggage when he and Linda traveled abroad. During the Philadelphia tryout of *Out of This World* in September 1950, Porter requested a room with private bath for Sylvain at the Barclay Hotel on the same floor as his own suite. When the manager offered servant's quarters instead, Porter refused, insisting on a traditional guest room. When Porter had a nervous collapse in fall 1951 after cutting short his trip to Paris, Sylvain took care of all the arrangements for his convalescence and treatment, at Boston's General Hospital. Writing to Porter's close friend, Sam Stark, on October 7, 1951, Sylvain did not refer to the Porters by name but as "C. P." and Linda as "L. P.," adding that C. P. had been admitted under the name of "Paul Sylvain" to keep the press from getting wind of his condition, which required electric shock treatment. When Porter learned that Sylvain had died of cancer on July 21, 1959, he acknowledged his loss: "I shall never cease to miss him." Porter went beyond expressing his condolences. He arranged for Sylvain's wages to be paid to his widow and set up a trust fund for his two daughters.

The prostitutes, on the other hand, were short-term. They performed their service, were compensated, and went away. One doubts Porter even knew their names. Then there were men with whom he corresponded, expressing himself openly, which he could not do in his love songs. But those relationships—the ones of which we know—were never fully satisfying because they were rarely reciprocal. The precious lotus of perfection bloomed only in Linda, whom he described as "the most perfect woman in the world" in a letter written to Monty Woolley.

It certainly did not bloom in Charles Green Shaw (1892–1974), who was a year behind Porter at Yale, and whom he addressed as "Big Boy" and "Infinite Dimensions" because of his height. One can infer that they were lovers, at least for a time, from the tone of one letter, in which Porter berated Shaw for not writing, admitting how much he missed him. Whether this was love or infatuation is hard to know, since Porter often confused the two; the exception was Linda, whom he loved unequivocally.

Shaw was too obsessed with achieving fame in the arts to become romantically involved with anyone. From the letters, Porter appears to have been more enamored of Shaw than Shaw was of him. Shaw achieved a certain amount of eminence in his own right. He was an abstract painter whose work can be seen at the Metropolitan Museum of Art, the Whitney, and the Chicago Art Institute. He also wrote poetry, essays, and reviews. By 1959, Shaw was no longer "Big Boy." Porter now addressed him as "Dear Charlie," thanking him for his collection of poems, *Into the Light*.

Boris Kochno (1904–1990) was different. Porter seems to have met Kochno in Venice in 1922; it was as if Porter had discovered his dream lover. Kochno had been the lover of Sergei Diaghilev, founder of Ballets Russes, later his secretary, and finally scenarist for the company's experimental works. He went on to achieve international fame, creating ballets for George Balanchine, *Prodigal Son* being the most famous; Leonid Massine; and Roland Petit. One can understand Porter's attraction to Kochno, who had a dancer's form and an aesthete's face—the incarnation of Dorian Gray. "Je t'adore," Porter swooned, writing in French because Kochno's English was either faulty or nonexistent. Kochno certainly had "that thing": "I dream only of the moment when we will be reunited." "I embrace you." "You have completed my life." "Write me and tell me you love me as much as I love you." Kochno did not. Porter had yet to achieve fame as a composer of Broadway musicals, while Kochno was already known for his ability to create scenarios for ballets and had also provided Igor Stravinsky with the libretto of his one-act opera *Marva* (1922). Kochno was well along in his career; Porter was just on the first leg of his.

In *Anchors Aweigh* (MGM, 1945), Frank Sinatra sang the wistful ballad "I Fall in Love Too Easily," which pretty much describes Porter's condition. He was looking for the male equivalent of Linda who could provide the sexual fulfillment that Linda could not. The requirements were simple: a lover of the arts, handsome or at least not unattractive, compatible, and acceptable to Linda as his companion of the moment. Kochno satisfied the first two, but he seems to have tired of Porter's adolescent outpourings: "You are the only thing in the world that is dear to me"; "I want you in my arms"; "All day I lie awake thinking of you." It was not mutual, and by 1925, the affair was over.

Later came dancer-choreographer Nelson Barclift (1917–93). By then Porter had matured, and Barclift was then Corporal Barclift, who, with Sergeant Robert Sidney, choreographed the wartime musical revue, Irving Berlin's *This Is the Army* (1942) with an integrated cast, as Berlin insisted upon, consisting largely of soldiers, with Barclift as the principal dancer who, in one number, appeared in drag. In his letters, Porter generally addressed him by his last name, suggesting a more formal kind of relationship, During the Broadway run of *This Is the Army* (July 4, 1942, to September 26, 1942) Barclift was stationed at Fort Jay on Governor's Island in New York Harbor, making it easy for him to get to the theatre on Broadway and Fifty-third Street and see Porter as well. When Barclift shipped off to Italy in 1944, their correspondence continued, usually consisting of small talk (parties with movie stars like Merle Oberon and Joan Fontaine, film recommendations) except for a detailed letter Porter sent him describing his leg operations, which suggested something much stronger than physical attraction. There were no amorous effusions, no importuning, but just "I miss you like hell" and "We miss you," the "we" being himself and Linda, who was quite fond of him. It always pleased Porter when Linda showed affection for one of his companions, and Porter was especially happy about their cordial relationship. Yet Porter sensed that Barclift, who had been in the theater since 1939 and had not gotten his big break, was too career-conscious to be the longtime companion he was seeking. It was not so much a question of what he could do for Porter as what Porter could do for him, particularly since being stationed abroad had put his career on hold. In May 1945, Porter wrote to Barclift, addressing him as "Glitter boy" and summing up their relationship with unusual candor: "I actually miss you in spite of the fact that I realize perfectly that you are incapable of love, affection, loyalty, sentiment or friendship." Earlier, he had written similarly to Kochno, complaining that the pages of his letter were unnumbered and that he sounded like *"un vieux philosophe"* ("an old philosophe"). Porter also complained about the lack of reciprocity. His French, with its play on *recepteur* and *recevoir* (receiver and receive), leaves no doubt about the nature of their relationship: *"C'est que tu deviens un recepteur. Et moi, j'ai besoin de recevoir de mon côté aussi"* ("It's that you are becoming a receiver. For my part, I need to receive also"). Theirs was not "I give to you and you give to me" but rather "I give to you and you take from me."

Porter did not realize that, as artists, Kochno and Barclift were as narcissistic and self-absorbed as he was. Porter wanted an acolyte, who shared his interests, was not actively pursuing a career, and would be satisfied with companion status plus whatever else that entailed. This was not a job description for a careerist.

When Barclift was discharged with the rank of Sergeant in 1946, their relationship resumed briefly. On May 6, 1946, Porter wrote Barclift from Los Angeles: "Please go out of your way to be nice to Linda, since she likes you an awful lot." Then the affair abruptly ended, and Barclift went from lover to working professional when he was hired to choreograph the stage version of Jules Verne's *Around the World in Eighty Days* (1946), shortened to *Around the World*, a "musical extravaganza" with a score by Porter and a book by Orson Welles, who also directed, produced, and starred in it. The extravaganza, as outsized as Welles's ego, came in for some critical drubbing that also extended to Porter's score, which was dismissed as inferior. *Around the World* closed after seventy-five performances; it was also Barclift's last Broadway stage credit.

Whether any of Porter's affairs occasioned one of his love songs is conjectural. Barclift claimed that "You'd Be So Nice to Come Home To," one of the songs Porter wrote for the film *Something to Shout About* (Columbia, 1943), composed in 1942 and published in October of that year, was inspired by their affair, then in its early stage. That seems plausible, since Porter met Barclift at least a month before *This Is the Army* opened on July 4, 1942. In June 1942, Porter asked Barclift to call Linda, who was staying at their cottage in Williamstown "because I love you so much and I know that the more you know her, the happier you will be." Porter was then living at the Waldorf Towers, not far from the theatre where *This Is the Army* was playing. At the same time Porter was working on the score for *Something for the Boys* (1943), which included the song "I'm in Love with a Soldier Boy," specifically "an army man," which Corporal Barclift was, Porter was then in love with, or smitten by, Barclift. If Barclift was the inspiration for "You'd Be So Nice to Come Home To," it would not only be "nice"; it would also be "paradise," which marked the second time "paradise" furnished a rhyme. In "Love for Sale," Porter rhymed "price" with "paradise." With Barclift, there was no price tag.

For *Greenwich Village Follies of 1924*, Porter composed "I'm in Love Again," which was added shortly after the opening. Porter was then in Kochno's thrall, "love" is repeated ad nauseam, and the lover is totally helpless ("I can't rise above it," "I love, love, love it"). The banal lyrics are on a par with the gush that poured out of his letters to Kochno. Perhaps it is not coincidental that, three years after the end of their one-sided affair, Porter wrote "What Is This Thing Called Love?" (1929), one of his most introspective lyrics that is also a soul-searching attempt to make sense of a dead end relationship.

One might wonder if Linda was the inspiration of any songs. Although Barclift maintained that "You'd Be So Nice to Come Home To" was *their* song, Porter could have had Linda in mind, too. "You'd" is a contraction of "you would." "Would" implies a desire, in this case, to be with another. Barclift *was* with Porter in New York in 1942. Linda was not; she was in Williamstown, Massachusetts. Was Porter thinking of Linda as well?

"You'd Be So Nice to Come Home To" belongs to that catalog of World War II songs such as "You'll Never Know (Just How Much I Love You)," "I'll Be Seeing You," "We'll Meet Again," and "Apple Blossom Time" that conjured up an Edenic America that never really existed except in the lyrics of sentimental songs which held out hope that tomorrow would not just be another day but a better one. Porter may have had Barclift and perhaps Linda in mind when he wrote "You'd Be So Nice to Come Home To," but it was coopted by men and women serving their country who had their own special "you," which did not include Barclift or Linda.

It is impossible to know if Linda was the inspiration for Porter's two best love songs, "Night and Day" and "So in Love," both of which reject the venality of "Love for Sale," declaring that love—as opposed to mere sex—is offered freely. Taken together, "Love for Sale," "Night and Day," and "So in Love"—all with three-word titles—form a trilogy: the first describes love in purely physical terms—a transaction that offers momentary pleasure but nothing more, certainly not "true love" of which the seller is incapable; the second, love as passion on a grand scale, so overwhelming that it permeates every moment of the lover's existence; the third, love as a force so powerful that the lover is willing to endure anything to make it last. Porter found this kind—"love is not love / Which alters when it alteration finds," as Shakespeare wrote in *Sonnet 116*—only with Linda. Even when they were apart, as they often were, one can imagine Porter thinking of her "night and day."

THE LOVE TRILOGY

"Love for Sale" (*The New Yorkers*, 1930)," "Night and Day" (*Gay Divorce*, 1932), and "So in Love" (*Kiss Me, Kate*, 1948) are not merely show tunes; they are carefully crafted poems, not verse like so many of Porter's songs where the imagery is generic rather than emotionally precise. A songwriter who is also a poet paints pictures with words and evokes moods with music, so that the listener both hears the emotion expressed and sees in his or her imagination the concomitant image. "You'd Be So Nice to Come Home To" (*Something to Shout About*, Columbia, 1943) is verse; the lover imagines the "you" sitting by the fire, under winter stars, or under an August moon. Fireplaces, stars, and moons could be sofas, skies, and suns for all it matters. The song's sentiments and soothing melody made it a wartime hit, not its imagery.

In "Love for Sale," the verse sets the mood with the moon gazing down on an empty street, its smile changing to a smirk—the prostitute's cue to start plying her trade. The eight-line verse is classically structured without calling attention to itself: two four-line stanzas, each made up of two ten-syllable lines; one four-syllable line; and one two-syllable line. The A-A-B-A rhyme scheme is as direct as the prostitute's monologue: **street/ feet, cop/shop, down/town, smirk/work**. No off rhymes, no internal or identical ones—just a prostitute's job description, with Porter's signature minor to major key shifts.

The refrain does not follow any metrical scheme. It consists of five stanzas, each introduced by "love for sale," which is repeated five times. Metrically, the third is the most interesting: a four-line stanza with the rhymes now internal (**thrill/mill, new/true**) and each line ending with "love." Porter the songwriter disappears into the woman's unconscious, allowing her to sing in jagged verse, scoffing at poets who celebrate love and reminding the potential buyer that she knows more than they—"ev'ry type of love," to be exact. For a price there's a trip to paradise: it's on a back street and upstairs.

"Love for Sale" is both the first and last line of the song, the alpha and omega of her profession. The title is repeated three other times in the refrain, but Porter does not rhyme "sale" with another word, even though rhymes are prevalent throughout the song. "Sale" is the equivalent of a price tag, which does not require rhyme to be understood. "Love for Sale" does not need an alternate verse; it is a poem, a sung monologue with verse and refrain in which the vocal line is closer to speech than to song,

The verse of "Night and Day," which also consists of eight lines, describes the effect the beloved has on the lover in the form of a relentless succession of sounds—a tom-tom's "**beat beat beat**"; a clock's "**tick tick tock**"; the rain's "**dip drip drip**"—that reverberate in the lover's consciousness, making it impossible to think of anything other than "**You You You**" as if the beloved has now become part of the triad of sounds. Strong chord progressions complement the steady rhythm of the of the tom-tom, the clock, and the rain, creating a triptych of sound and image, so that one can visualize the tom-tom, the clock, and the raindrops with their distinctive sounds and hear the music that weaves them all together.

The fifteen-line, three-section refrain begins and ends with "night and day," which is repeated three more times plus twice as an inversion, "day and night." The phrase "night and day" also serves as a bridge between the first two sections of the refrain and returns to close out the third. The first section, in which the lover thinks of the beloved everywhere, consists of four lines, with terminal rhymes only in lines three and four (**"far"/"are"**). The second section is, metrically, more traditional. The lover is specific, yearning for the beloved whether on a noisy street or in a silent room. The rhyme scheme is standard A/A/B/B (**"so"/"go"**, **"boom"/"room"**). The third section is modified A/A/B/B. The A/A rhymes in the first two lines are internal: the juxtaposed "**yearning burning**" in line two; and "**hide of me**" in line one balanced by "**inside of me**" in line two. Lines three and four are typical B/B: "**through**"/"**you.**" "Night and Day" is everything a poem should be: rhythmically and, in this case, metrically varied with sound wedded to sense; exact in its imagery; and striking in its treatment of a conventional subject—the longing of one person for another—so that one could echo Alexander Pope and say that Porter succeeded in describing "what oft was thought but n'er so well express'd."

"So in Love" lacks a verse, as do four other songs from *Kiss Me, Kate* ("Why Can't You Behave?," "I Hate Men," "I've Come to Wive It Wealthily in Padua," and "Another Op'nin', Another Show"). Instead of a verse, "So in Love" is preceded by a bit of dialogue that leads into the song, putting it in context. Lilli Vanessi is costarring with her ex-husband, Fred Graham, in *Kiss Me, Kate*, a musical version of Shakespeare's *The Taming of the Shrew*, which Graham is also directing. He had flowers sent to a featured member of the cast which are accidentally delivered to Lilli, rekindling the love she once felt for him, especially since the flowers are identical to those of her wedding bouquet. The flowers provide the motivation for "So in Love," which, like most of Porter's songs, falls into sections—three this time: the first two consisting of quatrains with lines 1 and 2 ending in identical rhyme (**dear/dear**) and three and four in a/a rhyme (**sky/I**) in section 1; **you/you/why/I** in section 2.

Identical rhyme is unusual in poetry, but not unprecedented. Walter De La Mare's "Autumn" is a three-stanza poem, in which the first two lines of each stanza end with "was." "Bad for Me" (*Nymph Errant*, 1933) is different. In print, "Bad for Me" may look like a series of identical rhymes, with thirteen lines of the refrain ending with "me." But these are really internal rhymes with the rhyming words occurring *within* the lines, so that it's not "me/me" but "**bad for me**"; "**new for me**"/"**stew for me**"; "**swell for me**"/"**hell for me**."

"So in Love," on the other hand, has no inner rhymes but only identical ones at the end of the first two lines of each section—**dear/dear, you/you**, with a/a rhymes in the third and fourth The bridge is the traditional A/B/A/B: **mysterious/there/delirious/care**. The third section is unusual. Like the first two sections, lines 1 and 2 end with "**me**"; since the third ends with "**die**," one expects the fourth to end with "I." But Porter tacks on a three-line coda: "**So in love, / So in love / So in love, with you, my love, am I.**" Now "die" in line 3 gets its mate, "I," in line 7. And Porter gets to use love in two different meanings—another use of one of his favorite figures of speech.

The melody changes in the bridge, in which Lilli rhapsodizes about love's mysterious powers that are so great that one can embrace the other even in the other's absence. The melodic line rises and falls in rapturous bliss as she recalls their first meeting on a "**night mysterious**," balanced by a "**dream delirious**." That Porter was thinking as a poet is clear from his use of anastrophe, the change of normal word order that can turn prose into poetry, or at least into a poetic rhythm. "Mysterious night" is unmusical. In "**night mysterious**," the last two short syllables suggest the night's shadowy softness.

Porter's best lyrics are poems—metrically and rhythmically varied and studded with word pictures. It is not surprising that he is included in the Library of America's American Poets Project, along with, among others, Edna St. Vincent Millay, Walt Whitman, William Carlos Williams, Theodore Roethke, and John Berryman.

CHAPTER 4

La vie est gai

Gay Divorce

Gay Divorce (1932) had a strange genesis. It originated as an unproduced play by J. Hartley Manners, best known for *Peg O' My Heart* (1922), which brought stardom to Laurette Taylor, whom Manners married and for whom he wrote other plays. Laurette had previously been married to Charles Taylor, by whom she had a son, Dwight, and a daughter, Marguerite. Dwight Taylor was a respected screenwriter (the Fred Astaire-Ginger Rogers musicals *The Gay Divorcee*, the retitled *Gay Divorce*; *Top Hat*; and *Follow the Fleet*; and the melodramas *I Wake Up Screaming, Nightmare, Conflict,* and *Pickup on South Street*); he also wrote the books for two Porter musicals, *Gay Divorce* and *Out of this World.* Taylor based his *Gay Divorce* book on his stepfather's unproduced play. The book apparently needed improvement, resulting in an adaptation by Kenneth Webb and Samuel Hoffenstein, the latter a poet and screenwriter. Hoffenstein had a gift for adaptation and, as a former drama critic, press agent, and published poet, knew how to improve a work, as he showed in his film adaptation of Robert Louis Stevenson's *Dr. Jekyll and Mr. Hyde* (Paramount, 1932), in which he created two women, the virgin and the whore, neither of whom existed in the original—the former for Henry Jekyll, who desires her; the latter for his alter ego, Mr. Hyde, who kills her. He improved *Laura* (Twentieth Century-Fox, 1944) by transforming Waldo Lydecker from the overweight slob that he was in Vera Caspary's original into the trim and urbane Clifton Webb, who invested the role with imperious disdain. Kenneth Webb (no relation) was the brother of orchestrator-composer Roy Webb, who composed the scores for most of Val Lewton's RKO horror films (*Cat People, The Leopard Man, I Walked with a Zombie, The Curse of the Cat People, The Body Snatcher,* and *Bedlam*). He also orchestrated several Broadway musicals, the most famous being Rodgers and Hart's *Peggy-Ann* (1926) and *A Connecticut Yankee* (1927). Kenneth, who was less well-known, started as a writer of silent scenarios and later turned to playwrighting. He had a modicum of success on Broadway with *One of the Family* (1925), which featured three excellent character actors: Georgia Backus, Beulah Bondi, and Grant Mitchell; and *Houseboat on the Styx* (1928), a cavalcade of figures from the Bible (Delilah, Queen of Sheba, Noah, Adam, Eve), classical mythology (Helen of Troy, Charon), history (Nero, Shakespeare, Ponce de Leon, Henry VIII and his six wives, George Washington, Napoleon), and fiction (Sherlock Holmes) that enjoyed a respectable run of 103 performances.

Hartley's play seems to have been a bedroom (as opposed to drawing room) comedy, in which the characters do not commit adultery but have affairs either in boudoirs, not bedrooms, or in hotel suites, not rooms. In short, infidelity upgraded and euphemized. In Taylor's version, commercial novelist Guy Holden (Fred Astaire) has fallen in love with the enigmatic Mimi (Claire Luce), unaware that she is married and seeking to rid herself of her boring husband. Her lawyer, who is also Guy's friend, has arranged for a "co-respondent" to pose as her lover, thus constituting grounds for divorce. Complications arise when Guy is mistaken for the co-respondent. The husband is at first reluctant to divorce Mimi, until a waiter, an amateur geologist, recognizes him, addressing him as Professor Brown, whom he had for geology (and who has been leading a double life). When Mimi asks the waiter if she resembles Mrs. Brown, he replies in the negative. Professor Brown is shown the door, and Guy and Mimi are now free to marry.

The musical offered a new take on divorce: no acrimony or haggling, just stylish deception, bubbly and buoyant, too airborne to be sullied by dirty hands. For this carefree romp, "gay" was the right word. To quote a phrase from another Porter lyric, "Easy to Love," Ted and Mimi are "grand at the game," which apparently is easy to learn.

In the musical, "gay" does not have a homosexual connotation, although Porter may have known that it could. Gertrude Stein seems to have used "gay" as code for homosexual in her short story "Miss Furrer and Miss Skeene" (1922), which Porter might have read. By 1941, if not earlier, Porter was well aware of the other meaning when he wrote "Farming" (*Let's Face It!* [1941]), which satirized celebrities who have embraced the outdoor life, noting that George Raft's cow has never calfed because his "bull is beautiful, but he's gay." In *Gay Divorce*, "gay" turns up in three numbers, in which it means nothing more than insouciant and light-hearted: "feeling far from gay" ("After You, Who?"), "gayer set" ("What Will Become of Our England?"), and "gay enough" ("I've Got You on My Mind"). As Porter grew more audacious in his use of double entendre, "gay" ceased being unequivocal.

Gay Divorce has been dismissed as a one-song show, but that song, "Night and Day," is arguably the best Porter ever wrote. It is certainly the most deeply personal. But there is another song that made Fred Astaire agree to do the musical after Porter played it for him. Astaire's sister and dancing partner, Adele, had married Lord Charles Arthur Francis Cavendish in 1932, after which the couple moved to Lismore Castle in County Waterford, Ireland. Astaire felt insecure about appearing in a musical without her. But Porter knew that while Astaire was not an outstanding singer, he could handle music that lay comfortably within his middle register. Astaire could make a number sound like speech set to music, a kind of musical parlando. Gene Kelly could do the same. Listen to Kelly sing "You Were Meant for Me" to Debbie Reynolds in *Singin' in the Rain* (MGM, 1952). It's not speech-song, which Rex Harrison made famous in *My Fair Lady* (1956), but speech sung.

"After You, Who?" was a perfect fit for Astaire with its simple rhymes: **you/blue, try/qualify, laughter/after.** Astaire always sang with stylish sincerity, devoid of histrionics. He may not have been able to mine the poetry of "Night and Day," but he could sing it, as did others, as a love song, although it is really one of infatuation and obsession, which are often mistaken for love.

"NIGHT AND DAY"

In the verse, the lover feels the presence of the unnamed beloved, identified only as "you," in a tom-tom's beat, a clock's ticking, and rain dripping. Each sound is repeated three times—beat/ beat/beat, tick/tick/tock, drip/drip/drip; and an inner voice repeats "you" three times. This type of parallelism, in which groups of words balance each other, represents sheer craft. There was nothing fortuitous about this arrangement, which illustrates what Horace in *Ars Poetica*, 290 calls *"limae labor,"* literally the toil of the file—a metaphor that suggests writing is a form of verbal smoothening and polishing, as if words were rough objects that need furbishing before they can be forged into sentences. As Stephen Sondheim wrote in "Putting It Together" (*Sunday in the Park with George*): "Art isn't easy."

"Night and Day" is unusual in its succession of repeated notes, replicating the intense longing the lover is experiencing for the "you" and complementing the repetitive sounds that the lover hears from objects (tom-tom, clock) and from nature itself (raindrops). It is as if we have descended from the outer world of sounds and things to the inner world of boundless "longing" and then back to the only reality that the lover knows: "torment" that will only cease with the possession of the "you."

"Night and day," the first and last three words of the refrain, are musically the same, implying that there is no difference between them We seem to be in an age before the world's creation when day and night have not been separated, and time is a continuum. Whether it's night and day or day and night does not matter. The same is true of the outer and inner worlds which become one, or at least concentric, with ordinary sounds evoking an extraordinary response. It's not night 'n' day, but night *and* day.

TO STRESS OR NOT TO STRESS

As a devoted opera lover, Porter knew that a succession of stressed syllables is common in opera There are long one-note segments in Don Basilio's "La Calumnia" aria in Rossini's *The Barber of Seville*. "Che gelida manina" ("How cold your little hand is") are the first words of Rodolpho's Act 1 aria in *La Bohème*; each syllable of *gelida* and *manina* is stressed, whereas in spoken Italian only the first syllable of *gelida* and the second of *manina* would be. The aria begins in D flat major, traditionally associated with slowness (e.g., Debussy's *Claire de lune*); the measured opening, in which each of the seven syllables consists of the same note, expresses Rodolpho's reaction to the touch of Mimi's hand, which he proceeds to warm. The syllabification is dictated by an emotional response, in this case to a cold hand, and reinforced by the accompanying music—the same combination that is at the heart of "Night and Day."

Stresses can—and often do—fall differently on syllables in sung lyrics than they do in ordinary discourse. Added syllables, for example, are common in chanted liturgical texts. In the Roman Catholic high mass, the celebrant adds another syllable to "vobiscum" ("Dominus vobiscum," "The Lord be with you"), so that it becomes vo-*o*-biscum. In "Sursum corda" ("Lift up your hearts"), each word acquires two added syllables: "Su-*u*-ursum co-*o*-orda."

From his Latin studies, Porter learned that words are accented differently in Latin poetry than in everyday speech. In the verb *cano* ("I sing"), the accent falls on the first syllable, but in the first line of Virgil's *Aeneid*, *Arma virumque cano* ("I sing of arms and the man"), the accent falls on the last (*ca-no*) for the sake of the meter, dactylic hexameter. Similarly, in English, if-èd is added to "fix," the è makes "fixed" disyllabic. It is no longer **fixed** (one syllable) but **fixed** (two) as in: "Or fill the **fixèd** mind with all your toys

(Milton's *Il Penseroso*). The extra syllable is necessary to fill out the iambic pentameter; otherwise, the line would have had nine syllables instead of ten.

Porter was adept at shifting accents. In *Can-Can*, to get "lesbian" and "Anglican" to rhyme with the second syllable of "can-can" (the title song in the show), Porter shifts the accent from first to the last syllable: lesb**ian**, Angl**ican**. In the second and last lines of each refrain in "Siberia" (*Silk Stockings*, 1955), "Siberia" gets two extra syllables ("Siberi-eri-a"). Siberia will indeed seem eerie for Communists who have discovered the joys of capitalism in Paris. In "They Couldn't Compare to You" (*Out of this World*), "Gallipoli" has to be sung as if it were pronounced Galli-**ippo-lippy** for the sake of the meter.

Porter would also modify words for the sake of rhyme. In "Katie Went to Haiti" (*Du Barry Was a Lady*), Katie doesn't meet a native, she meets a "**natie**." To get a rhyme for "Raft" (the actor George Raft), he changed the spelling of "calved" to "**calfed**" ("Farming," *Let's Face It!*). "Trop," as in the French *de trop* ("too much"), is pronounced "tro." But in order for "trop" to rhyme with "top" ("You're the Top," *Anything Goes*), the "-p" is sounded. In "Nobody's Chasing Me" (*Out of this World*) to get a rhyme for "Debussy," which has to be sung with the accent on the second syllable (De-***bus***-sy), Porter changes "goose" to "goosey," which serves another purpose: he can end the segment not with "nobody's chasing me," as he did the others, but with "nobody's goosing me," a bawdy touch in an extremely bawdy show.

Although Porter knew prosody from his readings of Latin, English, and French poetry, his lyrics are not metrically uniform. He never wrote a text that could be labeled as, say, iambic pentameter (a Shakespearean sonnet) or iambic tetrameter (Wordsworth's "Written in Early Spring"). He knew that what matters is rhythm, the succession of stressed and unstressed syllables, which, depending on the length of the lines, can produce a variety of meters within the same poem, as is the case with "Night and Day," which scans but not the same way that Shakespeare's *Sonnet 29* ("When in disgrace with fortune and men's eyes") does—as fourteen pentameters.

"NIGHT AND DAY" AS SUNG BY FRANK SINATRA AND DEANNA DURBIN

If performed as written, "Night and Day" requires an artist who can approach it as musical poetry with fidelity to both the words and the music, each with its own rhythms that at times diverge, so that a word like "matter," which should have a stress only on the first syllable, acquires another on the second. A true artist will study the song the way a conductor or an opera singer studies a score to discover the composer's intentions. Frank Sinatra first sang "Night and Day" in *Reveille with Beverly* (Columbia, 1943), in which he omitted the verse and began with the refrain. Without the verse, "Night and Day" becomes a ballad that can be crooned, purred, or jazzed. With the verse, it becomes a soul-baring confession. Sinatra brought real ardor to the lyrics. There is a youthful urgency in his delivery, as if he were importuning the "you" to listen to his *chanson de coeur*. Sinatra was not at a stage where he could make the song into a *cri de coeur*, something that came from somewhere deep within him, but as a *chanson*, a song that was nonetheless heartfelt.

His 1957 version is the exact opposite. He had become Sinatra the swinger, and "Night and Day" is a track on an album appropriately titled *A Swingin' Affair*. There is a jauntiness, even a recklessness about his rendition, which is supported by an arrangement that allows him the freedom to swing with swagger and slang (burnin', yearnin', makin') and substitute "baby" for "darling" ("no matter, baby"). Then, a few years later, he recorded the song as Porter had written it, complete with verse, for the album *Sinatra and Strings* (1962). He pays close attention to the repeated notes in the verse, so that the sounds of the tom-tom, clock, and raindrops have the measured beat of a metronome. Sinatra had recorded the song several times, but this is the definitive rendition.

Another—and less known—rendition is not by a popular vocalist, although she did record a number of songs for Decca Records. It is by Deanna Durbin, who enjoyed great popularity during the decade she starred in films at Universal (1936–48). Durbin was a true lyric soprano who could have had an operatic career if she chose that path, although she did sing arias in many of her films. In *Lady on a Train* (Universal, 1945), a screwball mystery, she played an amateur sleuth attempting to track down a murderer. At one point she has to impersonate a nightclub singer, which gave Durbin the opportunity to show off her lustrous soprano with "Night and Day," sung in its entirety. Her careful phrasing makes the song seem like an operatic aria on the order of the "Habanera" in Bizet's *Carmen*, which is preceded by a *recitative*, making the aria similar to the traditional verse-refrain format; or "Celeste Aida" in Verdi's *Aida*, which is preceded by a *recitativo* that reveals Radames as eager for victory on the battlefield as he is for Aida. In concerts, both arias are often sung without their introductions, just as "Night and Day" is frequently performed without the verse. The "Habanera" and "Celeste Aida" can produce the same effect when performed alone as well as in context. The same is true of "Night and Day."

You do not need to have seen either *Gay Divorce* or *The Gay Divorcee* to get caught up in the song's powerful undertow, as Durbin's 1945 and Sinatra's 1962 renditions prove.

"NIGHT AND DAY" IN CONTEXT

In *Gay Divorce* (Act 1, 2), Guy and Mimi encounter each other at a seaside hotel. He recognizes her as the elusive woman he had been seeking, but Mimi doesn't want him to know she is married.

> GUY: Mimi, before you say something, some little thing, I can—
> MIMI: Keep from thinking of me—
> GUY: Thinking of you.

According to the stage directions, "She looks at him. For a moment they stand gazing into each other's eyes. She wavers, and he seizes her and draws her to himself. They almost kiss but go into the NUMBER instead." After the NUMBER, they kiss. At first Mimi is responsive, but then, remembering that she is married and believing that Guy is the co-respondent, slaps him once on each cheek and exits "almost in tears." We will never know how Fred Astaire and Claire Luce performed "Night and Day" on Broadway. However, one can assume that the way Astaire and Ginger Rogers, who replaced Luce, performed it in the movie version, *The Gay Divorcée*, at least approximated the original. Astaire admitted that Luce was his muse; it was she who inspired him to work out the details in the routine they did after he sang "Night and Day" to her, which explains why Astaire wanted Luce as his costar in the film, but RKO preferred Rogers, one of the studio's contract players. Whatever inspiration Luce provided paid off, winning the praise of *New York Times* drama critic Brooks Atkinson, who noted in his review (November 30, 1932) that "in the refulgent Claire Luce, Fred Astaire has found a dancing partner who can match him step for step." He was also impressed by Luce's ability to "glide over the furniture . . . without missing a beat." However, he was well aware of their limitations as singers, writing that they are "singers only by necessity" who treat the songs as "perfunctory items."

In *The Gay Divorcée*, there is no furniture to glide over, only a couch on which Astaire puts Rogers down gently after their dance.

Although Hermes Pan was the film's (uncredited) assistant dance director and choreographer, it's hard to imagine anyone other than Astaire recreating the elaborate dance routine that followed "Night and Day." Astaire had a light baritone, soothing but not honeyed, a bit ethereal without sounding disembodied, but without the fervor that Sinatra at his best brought to the song, tempered by emotional restraint that kept it from turning into a self-pitying soliloquy. Astaire's diction is phonetically precise; he sings "near" as if it were pronounced "neah," with the slightest hint of an "r." In *Gay Divorce*, "Night and Day" is not an eleven o'clock number; it does not even bring the curtain down on Act 1. Even if Astaire had Sinatra's voice, he could not have sung it with the passion of a disconsolate lover, which would have been at odds with the context: a romantic interlude between a man and a woman, designed as a showcase for performers who were not known for their singing. Astaire's delivery is musical Art Deco: sleek and streamlined; his is not the ardor of a moonstruck swain but of an impeccably attired wooer.

"Night and Day" is not a stand-alone number; in *The Gay Divorcee*, it is the prelude to a breathtaking dance sequence that eclipses it, making the song a segue into something bigger than itself. The number is not so much a courting dance as "an elegant evocation of seduction and ecstatic consummation." Astaire makes the first move; Rogers reacts with virginal coyness but yields. They dance together, gliding across the floor. They dance apart. They do a bit of contra and a bit of ballroom before dancing with abandon in the dizzying finale. As the sexless seduction nears its end, she falls into his embrace, looking up at him as he looks down at her—he pleased with the outcome, she dazed by the encounter. He then eases her onto a couch and asks, "Cigarette?" Katharine Hepburn reportedly said of Astaire and Rogers, "He gave her class, and she gave him sex." In the "Night and Day" sequence, Astaire was supplying the sex, and Rogers was responding to it.

"Night and Day" is too good for a musical confection like *Gay Divorce*. If sung as written with fidelity to the repeated notes with their trip-hammer intensity and the vivid imagery that calls for vocal coloring, "Night and Day" should have been in a musical either about a doomed romance or an unfulfilled one. The problem is that Porter wrote neither. Thus it is best sung in concert or cabaret by artists who can perform it the way Porter conceived it.

If "Night and Day" seems so out of place in *Gay Divorce*, one reason may be the circumstances that allegedly inspired it: Porter's affair with the architect Edward Tauch (1905–54), whom Porter had commissioned to build a house for himself and Linda in Beverly Hills. But Linda, who was plagued with pulmonary problems, felt that the climate would only aggravate her condition. The house was never built, but Porter acquired a new lover and traveling companion—for a time. If the inspiration was Tauch, "Night and Day" is a revelation of Porter's state of mind while in the throes of another relationship, this one more tortuous than the others, leaving the composer enmeshed in love's coils with release coming only with the end of the affair.

CHAPTER 5

An Errant Nymph and an Ex-Evangelist

Nymph Errant and Anything Goes

ON STAGE: NYMPH ERRANT (1933)

Nymph Errant was never produced on Broadway, although it was performed at New York's Equity Theatre on Manhattan's West Side in 1982. However, a recording was made of a live concert version at London's Drury Lane on May 21 1989, at which the score was sung by such musical theater stalwarts as Kaye Ballard, Lisa Kirk, Andrea McArdle, Liliane Montevecchi, Patrice Munsel, Larry Kert, and the great cabaret artist Elizabeth Welch, who had appeared in the original London production in 1933 and returned fifty-six years later to reprise her show-stopping number, "Solomon." She sang it as if it were a folk tale set to music, which softened the perverseness of the lyrics. "So——olomon had a thousand wives" and dispatched them with a thousand knives when he learned of their infidelity. Then "So——olomon no longer had a thousand wives."

The above-mentioned recording did not inspire a New York production the way Columbia's 1950 studio recording of Rodgers and Hart's *Pal Joey* (1940), with Vivienne Segal and Harold Lang, led to the celebrated 1952 revival with Lang and Segal, the latter reprising the role she created in the 1940 original. *Nymph Errant* was not in that category; it only racked up 154 performances (October 6, 1933, to February 17, 1934) at London's Adelphi Theatre despite its source. Romney Brent adapted James Laver's popular 1932 novel of the same name as a vehicle for Gertrude Lawrence, who was the main attraction.

Nymph Errant was thoroughly British in tone, with propriety prevailing whether the heroine is in an English garden, a Turkish harem, or a desert. It is as if Noel Coward had rewritten William Makepeace Thackeray's *Vanity Fair* in the style of *Private Lives* and changed Thackeray's Becky Sharp into Evangeline Edwards, sending her on a series of adventures that threaten to compromise her virginity but manage to leave it intact, much to her chagrin Evangeline had been scheduled to return to her aunt's home in Oxford after spending four years at a Swiss finishing school. The chemistry teacher, Miss Pratt, encourages the graduates to "experiment" while they are still young, urging them not only to seize the day but also the apple, no matter how high it hangs on the bough. In short, let your reach exceed your grasp.

"Experiment," the opening number, gives *Nymph Errant* a distinctly 1920s sensibility that links it to Porter's next musical, the *echt* American *Anything Goes*, in which the title song could serve as the credo of the experimenters, who, once they found that their reach could exceed their grasp, plucked the apple and moved on to the next level of nonconformity, sloughing off social codes and antiquated mores and inhabiting their own world where everything is the reverse of what it is in polite society. In *Nymph Errant*, Evangeline is thrown into that world when, on her way back to Oxford, she encounters Andre de Croissant (perhaps an emblematic name) who promises to make her a star at his *Folies de Paris*. When Andre becomes too paternalistic, Evangeline transfers her affections to an Italian count who whisks her off to Venice. When the count becomes more interested in Henrietta Bamberg, one of Evangeline's classmates who is also experimenting, he passes Evangeline off to a Greek business tycoon, who is later killed by Turks.

Evangeline's next stop is a Turkish harem where she does not pass muster as a concubine. Finally, she returns to her aunt's home in Oxford, a *virgo intacta* in spite of herself. *Nymph Errant* has come full circle, beginning and ending in the same garden. Experimentation has brought Evangeline no fulfillment but only involvement in a series of escapades that have left her no wiser than she was before. As the final curtain is about to descend, Evangeline is alone in the garden, musing on her transcontinental odyssey and realizing that she never plucked the apple from the bough. At that point the aunt's gardener offers her an apple—a sentimental ending to a decidedly unsentimental musical.

Nymph Errant contains two standout numbers, "The Physician" and "Solomon," which have little to do with the plot except to stop it for a display of virtuosity by Gertrude Lawrence and Elizabeth Welch, respectively. When a eunuch in the harem asks Evangeline if she had ever been in love, she replies with a catalogue song, in which she bemoans the fact that her physician was more in love with her anatomy than with her. It is an unusual catalogue number because it is in the form of a tale, in which she describes his reaction to her various anatomical parts, ending with a punch-line admission: When she wants to pay him, he replies. "Why, don't be funny, / It's I who owe you money."

"The Physician" is mosaic of wit and rhyme with three refrains, each consisting of two five-line narrative segments bridged by a middle part, in which Evangeline voices her frustration, followed by a five-line coda. Each refrain has twenty-one lines, the last of which is always the same: "But he never said he loved me." The rhyme scheme of the first is typical: A/B/C/C/B (**entrancing/glee/larynx/pharynx/me**); each middle part is comprised of six lines with the same ABC rhyme scheme: **doubt/me/soul/out/me/whole**.

To appreciate Porter's lapidary art, one has only to look at the printed text of "The Physician" in the Library of America edition and marvel at the way each refrain is structured both rhythmically and metrically. The first line of each refrain is a perfect iambic pentameter; the last, a perfect iambic tetrameter: "He said my cerebellum was brilliant. . . . But he never said he loved me." Between the first and last lines, the length varies, usually between seven and nine syllables. The meter may not be consistent, but the rhythm is. Seven-syllable lines are followed by eight-syllable ones, couplet fashion.

Gertrude Lawrence's rendition of "The Physician," which she recorded in 1933, can be heard on YouTube, providing a good example of how she sang it on stage. Lawrence had a small voice, delicate and attenuated, that made up in clarity for what it lacked in volume; she sang as if her vocal cords were made of gossamer and as if *Nymph Errant* was an operetta, which, in a sense, it was. She toyed with the lyrics, hinting at their naughtiness while at the same time sounding girlishly demure, rather like a convent-educated coquette.

Lawrence's rendition was appropriate for 1933 British theatergoers, but Lisa Kirk's in the 1989 concert version was more in keeping with what American audiences would expect to hear if *Nymph Errant* is ever resurrected, even in concert form. Kirk, who created the role of Lois Lane in *Kiss Me, Kate*, had a smoky contralto, clear but not crystalline, sultry but not smoldering. She knew there was a subtext in "The Physician," which had more to do with sex than physiognomy. When Kirk gets to "He murmured 'multo bella' / When I sat on his patella," she doesn't so much sing it as tease it, so that even if you know that the patella is the kneecap, you would think it was located elsewhere. Kirk's sly delivery makes the physician in question more of a voyeur than an anatomist.

"The Physician" was followed by "Solomon," which also does not advance the plot but at least fits the context. A Black American woman, Haidee Robinson, is making the grand tour and visits the harem where Evangeline is saying. One of the concubines lets out a melismatic wail, holding onto one syllable which she sings in different notes. Haidee upstages her with "Solomon," beginning with a melisma, in which she does a run of notes on the "So-" before singing last three syllables, "olomon." She approaches the rest of the song as if she were telling a spiced-up story. No one who saw *Nymph Errant* in 1933 ever forgot Welch's smart and sassy delivery in her only scene.

Naturally there were great anticipation at the Drury Lane on May 21, 1989, when Elizabeth Welch (1904–2003), then eighty-five, was about to reprise the song she introduced more than half a century earlier. She did not disappoint her admirers. She handled the melisma effortlessly, intoning "So——olomon" at the beginning and end of each of the four stanzas and approaching the text if it were an ancient tale jazzed up for a generation that likes its stories short and sassy. Porter wrote "Solomon" for Welch after hearing her sing "Love for Sale" when she auditioned for Kathryn Crawford's replacement on Broadway in *The New Yorkers*. "Solomon" is not a Black vernacular song as such, despite expressions like "jazzin'" and "massa," but it requires a performer who can combine a preacher's moral authority with Broadway razzamatazz, so that the song becomes a perversely ironic parable. Despite all the luxuries that Solomon lavished on his thousand wives, they all cheated on him. Seeking vindication, he sent his eunuch to procure a thousand knives to rid himself of the unfaithful lot. When Welch gets to the last stanza, she does not so much sing it as belt it, hitting the notes as if she were inflicting blows ("he slashed their gizzards / and gashed their muzzles"). As a result, Solomon no longer had a thousand wives.

The rest of *Nymph Errant* is lesser Porter, as the recording of the 1989 concert makes clear, but it is worth hearing for Lisa Kirk's "The Physician" and Elizabeth Welch's "Solomon."

ON STAGE: *ANYTHING GOES* (1934)

On October 21, 1930, theater history was made when George and Ira Gershwin's *Girl Crazy* opened at the Alvin Theatre, now the Neil Simon. Just before the Act 1 finale, Ethel Merman in her Broadway debut as "Frisco Kate," a performer at an Arizona dude ranch, sang "I Got Rhythm" as a clarion song of the self, astonishing audiences with her Olympian voice and achieving instant stardom when, as she wrote in her autobiography, "I held the C note for sixteen bars, a whole chorus, while the orchestra played the melody." When Merman added that "the audience went a little crazy," she was being modest. It was an eruption of both applause and approbation, the kind reserved for occasions when something out of the ordinary has occurred. "Reportedly, she did about ten encores." It was not that *Girl Crazy* was a great show. There was nothing particularly distinguished about John Bolton and John McGowan's book, in which a father sends his playboy son to Arizona to develop a sense of responsibility by managing the family ranch, which instead he turns into a dude ranch with professional entertainers. Apart from "I Got Rhythm," three other standards emerged from the score: "Embraceable You," "Bidin' My Time," and "But Not for Me." Although Ginger Rogers in the lead role introduced "Embraceable You," she was never identified with it the way Merman was with "I Got Rhythm," which she reprised so often on television and in concerts that hers became the definitive rendition.

While Ethel Merman was a champion belter, she knew how to handle a ballad with a beat ("Do I Love You?" from *Du Barry Was a Lady*) and reach a level of poignancy ("Make It Another Old-Fashioned, Please" from *Panama Hattie*, which is heartbreak stoically rendered). But it is as a belter than Merman is chiefly remembered. Her voice still came from on high in 1970, when she was the last to play Dolly Gallagher Levi in Jerry Herman's *Hello, Dolly!* If you were at the box-office window purchasing tickets during a matinee when the show was in progress, you could still hear her. Enrico Caruso's voice might have been able to shatter glass, but Merman's could come through closed doors.

Merman's first of five Cole Porter musicals was *Anything Goes* with a book originally by Guy Bolton and P. G. Wodehouse but revised so substantially by Howard Lindsay (who also directed) and Russel Crouse that it became *theirs*. The team devised a corkscrew plot with twists and counter twists—a cross between madcap operetta and French farce. In the New York Public Library for the Performing Arts' Special Collections, there is a carbon copy of a typescript attributed to Lindsay and Crouse, which reads like an early draft of their book. Additions, deletions, and corrections were made in pencil; also written in pencil on the title page is the following: "This is rare, never having been printed." The typescript shows that they sketched out the main plot points which they continued to refine until the final draft. Disguises are donned and doffed; a stowaway is mistaken for Public Enemy No. 1; and a cuddly gangster (Public Enemy No. 13) and his moll pass themselves off as a minister and a missionary—all this aboard an ocean liner with cabins in lieu of the doors that figure so prominently in French boulevard comedy. By the show's end, everything is neatly resolved. Billy Crocker, the stowaway, who is also a Wall Street broker, pairs off with Hope Harcourt, who had been engaged to Lord Evelyn Oakleigh. Reno Sweeney, the trumpet-voiced ex evangelist (who can still work the revival circuit, as she shows with a rousing "Blow, Gabriel, Blow"), had set her sights on Lord Evelyn and now has him to herself. And the avuncular gangster, "Moonface" Martin of the emblematic name, is declared "harmless," which was obvious from the way Victor Moore played him—as a sweet-natured small-time con man.

The typescript suggests that, initially, Lindsay and Crouse envisioned Reno as a gold digger. When Billy asks one of the passengers, "Did Reno make the boat?" she replies, "Make the boat? She made the captain." When Reno meets Lord Evelyn, she's immediately attracted to him because of his looks and his title: "I'm nuts about him. If I play my cards right, I think I can make him. That would make me a lady." The double entendre was not very subtle, and Lindsay and Crouse had enough sense to soften her character, showing that beneath the brassy persona was a lady who is by no means a tramp: a lady who behaves like a "dame" and in certain circles might be considered a "broad," but who is a generous, caring human being.

In the final version, Reno admits that she is still drawn to Billy, who is only interested in Hope. And she does not set out to "make" Lord Evelyn. They discover each other as passengers normally would on an ocean liner. Happy ending with two couples headed for the altar: Reno and Lord Evelyn, and Hope and Billy.

The 1987 Lincoln Center revival with a revised book by Timothy Crouse (Russel's son) and John Weidman (book writer for Stephen Sondheim's *Pacific Overtures* and *Assassins*), with Patti LuPone as Reno Sweeney and the delightfully goofy Bill McCutcheon as Moonface, set the standard for subsequent productions, including the 2011 New York revival with Sutton Foster as Reno and the ageless Joel Grey as Moonface. Crouse and Weidman reworked the original, retaining enough of its plot points to keep the names of Lindsay and Crouse in the credits. Except for the first scene which takes place in a bar, the action is set aboard the *SS American*, while in the original, there was also a scene late in the second act in which Billy, Reno, and Moonface, dressed in Chinese attire, pay a visit to Lord Evelyn's uncle, informing him that they will disclose his nephew's indiscretion with a young Chinese woman, Plum Blossom, unless Lord Evelyn agrees to marry her. To avoid scandal, the uncle settles with them, this freeing Hope to marry Billy. Admittedly, the scene is contrived; Lindsay and Crouse's imagination must have flagged at this point. "Plum Blossom" is not a character, but only a name. Lindsay and Crouse apparently chose to leave it at that so Lord Evelyn could marry Reno. They also could have improved the scene if they modeled it after Shakespeare's *Much Ado About Nothing* (Act 5, 4), in which Claudio, having been told that his beloved Hero is dead, is about to marry Leonato's "niece," her face covered by a veil. When the "niece" removes the veil, it is really Hero, who in the previous act had collapsed after being wrongly accused of infidelity. Similarly, if Lord Evelyn were forced to marry Plum Blossom, he could have discovered that he had really married the veiled Reno.

That is how Crouse and Wideman rewrote the scene: Billy, Reno, and Moonface, all in Chinese dress, arrive in time to interrupt the shipboard wedding of Lord Evelyn and Hope, alleging that Lord Evelyn had seduced Plum Blossom (Reno in disguise). Hope insists that Lord Evelyn do the honorable thing and marry Plum Blossom, and she, in return, she will marry Plum Blossom's relative (Billy in disguise). The trio drop their masks, resulting in the union of not two but three couples, a favorite Shakespearean resolution (e.g., *The Merchant of Venice*, *Measure for Measure*, *A Midsummer Night's Dream*): Hope and Billy; Reno and Lord Evelyn; and Hope's mother, Evangeline (someone seems to have been familiar with *Nymph Errant*) and Billy's employer, the Wall Street banker Elisha J. Whitney.

The 1987 revival introduced another novelty that was also repeated in later revivals: interpolations. It was as if audiences couldn't get enough of Cole Porter. "Friendship" (*Du Barry Was a Lady*), "Easy to Love" and "Goodbye, Little Dream, Goodbye" (both from *Born to Dance*), and "It's De-Lovely'" (*Red, Hot and Blue*) were added to the score, totaling twenty-five musical numbers, including reprises.

On the surface, *Anything Goes* is just another Cole Porter musical that enjoyed a run of 420 performances during the 1934–35 season. Neither the lover-as-stowaway setup nor the shipboard setting was original. In Jerome Kern's *Sunny*, the title character is an American circus performer working in Britain, who falls in love with an American tourist and stows away on the ocean liner on which he is returning to the States. The action of Gilbert and Sullivan's *H.M.S. Pinafore* (1876) takes place on board the eponymous ship, whose captain has promised his daughter Josephine to Sir Joseph Porter, First Lord of the Admiralty. Josephine, however, prefers a lowly sailor, Ralph Rackstraw, who in the denouement is revealed to be high-born. The finale is the uniting of not just Josephine and Ralph, but also the captain and Little Buttercup; and Sir Joseph and his cousin Hebe—a time-honored way of achieving closure. Perhaps Crouse and Weidman were inspired by *H.M.S. Pinafore* when they were reworking the book of *Anything Goes* and decided to add a third couple to the original two.

What is unique about *Anything Goes*, in terms of Porter's musicals at this point in his career, is the placement of the songs within the story. There is better integration in *Anything Goes* than in any of his previous shows. In *The New Yorkers*, there is no reason for Kathryn Crawford and the Three Girl Friends to sing "Love for Sale" in front of Reuben's, or for Elizabeth Welch to sing it at the Cotton Club when the location was changed to Harlem. Kennedy and Welch were not characters; they just came on stage to perform "Love for Sale" and then exited. They could have sung "What Is This Thing Called Love?" for that matter; "Night and Day" added nothing to the plot of *Gay Divorce*—it was simply an occasion for Fred Astaire and Claire Luce to do some spectacular dancing. No song could compete with two dancers gliding over furniture.

The songs in *Anything Goes* either reveal something about a character or derive from something in the plot. Reno and Billy are old friends, but she would prefer a different relationship, which she reveals in the show's first number, "I Get a Kick Out of You," "kick" being the only emotion she's left with from an attraction that is not mutual. Reno gets no kick from champagne or a plane—just Billy, who thinks of Reno only as a friend and ally able to strike up a relationship with Lord Evelyn so that he might lose interest in Hope.

The title song marks the end of Act 1, in which Reno reveals to Billy that Lord Evelyn is falling in love with her, proving that today "anything goes." But the song has even greater significance in terms of another disclosure: Billy has been traveling with the passport of Snake Eyes Johnson, Public Enemy No. 1. When Billy is mistaken for Snake Eyes, he becomes a celebrity in the eyes of the passengers. In 1934, American moviegoers had seen some of the early crime films—*Little Caesar* (1930), *The Public Enemy* (1931), and *Scarface* (1932), in particular—in which criminals were portrayed as colorful individuals, especially when played by such charismatic actors as Edward G. Robinson, James Cagney, and Paul Muni. These were not gangsters as such but upwardly mobile men who, despite being criminals, had the same aspirations as everyone else: starting low (petty crimes) before going big time (bank heists)—each stage often marked by a costlier wardrobe with better tailoring, as in *Little Caesar*. The passengers' elation when they realize that Public Enemy No. 1 is on board is understandable; it is as if Caesar Enrico Bandello (*Little Caesar*), Tommy Powers (*The Public Enemy*), or Tony Camonte (*Scarface*) were in their midst.

When Reno agrees to divert Lord Evelyn's attention from Hope to herself, Billy and Reno express their admiration for each other in "You're the Top," in which they heap superlatives on each other. "Blow, Gabriel, Blow" comes out of the passengers' request for a revival ceremony from Moonface, who is posing as a minister. Confusion results when Billy confesses he is not Public Enemy No. 1, and Moonface admits that he is Public Enemy No. 13. Reno tries to restore order by launching into "Blow, Gabriel, Blow," a jazz-inflected revival rouser, with "blow" and "low" each getting an extra syllable. Porter did the same with another revivalist parody, "Climb Up the Mountain (And Lay Your Burden Down)" in *Out of this World*, in which mountain receives an additional syllable (mou-unt-ain), as if often the case in hymns ("A-maz-i-i-ing grace," "Jesus Christ is risen today / A-a-lei-ei-ei—lu-u-u-u-ia"),

Porter was a master of the song of resignation, in which losers in the game of love are too clear-eyed and hardened by life's slings and arrows to succumb to self-pity. "I Get a Kick Out of You" is carefully crafted with a seven-line verse in A/A/B/C/C/C/B: **told/cold/case/spree/ennui/see/face**. The verse depicts Reno's present state: jaded and apathetic—until she sees Billy's "fabulous face."

The sixteen-line refrain follows: four quatrains, the third as middle part or bridge; and the first, second, and fourth ending with "I get a kick out of you." Quatrains one, two, and four are A/B/C/C, with internal rhyme in the second lines of each. The first quatrain is representative: **champagne/all/true/you**. The second line, "Mere alcohol doesn't thrill me at all," is a perfect pentameter, with internal rhyme (**alcohol/at all**) and balanced phrases of four syllables each (**mere alcohol/thrill me at all**).

The bridge is the most personal part of the song; Reno resigns herself to Billy's indifference, expressed in an A/A/A/A quatrain (**see/me/me/me**). Unlike the other quatrains that end with "I get a kick out of you," the third begins with "I get a kick," which Reno still does, repeating "me" three times to emphasize her resignation to a platonic relationship. Porter had used repetition before, but so have other poets to achieve a feeling of mounting intensity by repeating a word or phrase. Each of the first four stanzas of Sir Thomas Wyatt's "A Supplication" begins and ends with "forget not yet." The last begins with "forgot not then" and ends with "forget not this"—"then," the love that the poet felt in the past; "this," the love that he still feels in the present. In the final stanza of John Keats's "Happy Insensitivity," the first three lines end with the same word, "it"—the opposite of the bridge in "I Get a Kick Out of You," in which the last three lines end with the same word, "me."

"I Get a Kick Out of You" represents Porter's subtlest use of rhyme. Even the first words of the first lines of stanzas one, two, and four rhyme: **champagne/cocaine/plane**. Reno gets no kick from **champagne** (line 1, stanza one), **cocaine** (line 1, stanza 2), or a **plane** (line 1, stanza 3), She only gets a "kick" out of **you**.

Wordsworth used similar and equally subtle end rhymes in "London 1802." The last words of the first lines in stanzas one and two rhyme:

> O friend! I know which way I must **look**. (line 1, stanza 1)
> Or groom! We must go glittering like a **brook**. (line 1, stanza 2)

The last word of the third stanza is "**expense**." One expects the complementary rhyme to come in the first line of the fourth; instead, it comes in the second: "Is gone; our peace, our faithful **innocence**." Wordsworth, like Porter, created a pattern of interconnected rhymes: two A/B/B/A quatrains; one A/B/B/ tercet; and one A/B/A tercet—the B ("**innocence**") providing the link with the A ("**expense**)" in the other tercet.

THE ARCHITECTURE OF "ANYTHING GOES"

The title song is meticulously crafted, consisting of a verse and three refrains—the last two of which are either dropped in revivals or performed without references to celebrities like Sam Goldwyn, Anna Sten, and "Missus R" (Eleanor Roosevelt) well known in Porter's day but not to a twenty-first century audience. In the 2018 revival, the first refrain was followed by an elaborate tap dance number led by Sutton Foster (Reno) in naval attire, ending with lines from the first refrain that were readily understandable: "When ev'ry night the set that's smart is in- / Truding in nudist parties in / Studios / Anything goes."

The eight-line verse begins dramatically: "Times have changed," an arpeggiated chord (one that is broken down into individual notes in descending or ascending order—here descending, "changed" has to be drawn out, taking on an additional vowel sound—another long **a** [cha-**anged**]). The first four lines set the tone: what was the norm once is the reverse today. The last four, introduced by "if today" (to-**day-a**)—the same arpeggio but in a different key—provides an example: If any pilgrims tried landing on Plymouth Rock, Plymouth Rock would land on them.

Each refrain consists of three A/A/B/B quatrains (e.g., **stocking/shocking/knows/goes**). The song title is the equivalent of a proposition; the refrains offer the proof with both general (good is bad, day is night, wrong is right) and particular illustrations; the latter are dated, but the reference to movie mogul Sam Goldwyn instructing his discovery, the Ukrainian actress Anna Sten, in diction can still draw a smile from those familiar with Goldwyn's malapropisms, such as, "Include me out."

A seven-line bridge separates the second and third quatrains of each refrain. The first six lines of each bridge end with the same word: **like** in bridge 1, **today** in bridge 2, **got** in bridge 3; the seventh, with a word that rhymes with "**goes**," the last line of each refrain. On the printed page, the first six lines of each bridge look like identical rhyme—a string of likes, todays, and gots. But it's really internal end rhyme—not just **like**, but "if driving **cars you like** / if **low bars you like**. The internal end rhyme scheme continues in the other two bridges—all of them celebrating an age where every preference can be indulged: **cars, bars, hymns, limbs, bears, chairs**.

"Anything Goes" is mathematical in its construction:

an eight-line verse, four of which are generalities; the other four, specific examples (Sam Goldwyn, Anna Sten, Nelson Rockefeller),

three eight-line A/A/B/B refrains, each with a seven-line bridge with internal end rhyme in the first six and the seventh ending with a word that rhymes with "**goes**."

carefully balanced phrases such as **smart is/parties** and **-trud/nud-** (Porter originally had the smart set "indulging in nudist parties." Then he realized he could get an internal rhyme if he used "intrude," hyphenating it so that one line ends with **-in,** and the next begins with **-trude**, which would rhyme internally with **nud-**.)

syncopation that makes the syllables bounce along the line as words either lose their accents or shift them, resulting in groups of unstressed syllables buoying up the lines that have been liberated from the strictures of conventional prosody (**looked on**, two stressed syllables; **stocking**, two stressed syllables). Everything goes, including traditional accentuation.

ANYTHING GOES: THE LINDSAY AND CROUSE BOOK

In his superb analysis of *Anything Goes*, Geoffrey Block raised an important question about the relationships between Reno, Billy, Lord Evelyn, and Hope Block. The stars of the original were Ethel Merman (Reno) and William Gaxton (Billy)—in the language of the theater, leading lady and leading man; one might even assume that were also "the romantic leads." But in the first scene, the writers make it clear that Reno's feelings for Billy are not reciprocated, and that the love of Billy's life is Hope, who is engaged to Lord Evelyn. Now the plot path lights up: Reno and Lord Evelyn, Billy and Hope. This is an unusual resolution for the book of a musical: Reno and Billy are the leads; Sir Evelyn and Hope, supporting cast. In the original production of Frank Loesser's *Guys and Dolls* (1950), billed below the title were the names of Robert Alda (Sky Masterson), Vivian Blaine (Miss Adelaide), Sam Levene (Nathan Detroit), and Isabel Bigley (Sarah Brown). Yet the parts were evenly distributed, and no one could rightly be called the "lead." If one wanted to think in terms of "romantic leads," there are two sets—one younger (Sky and Sarah); the other older (Nathan and Miss Adelaide).

A rare example of the lead actor ending up with a featured cast member occurs in Rodgers and Hart's *On Your Toes* (1936), which starred Ray Bolger as a former vaudevillian-turned-music teacher; and Tamara Geva in the non-singing role of a fiery-tempered Russian ballerina. It seems unlikely that rubber-legged Bolger would find his soul mate in Geva, whose primary function is to provide a plot complication and partner with him in the *Slaughter on Tenth Avenue* ballet, the show's highlight and the chief reason for its successful 1983 revival. Bolger's love interest is his student, Frankie Frayne (Doris Carson in the original), who gets to sing "Glad to Be Unhappy," which tells us as much about her character as it does about Larry Hart.

Carson at least had a solo, one of the best the team ever wrote. In the original production of *Anything Goes*, Sir Evelyn didn't sing a note, yet we are asked to believe that Reno, who has been given the best numbers in the show, could possibly have something in common with a featured actor with whom she does not even share a duet.

Crouse and Weidmann must have sensed the incongruousness of their relationship. In the 1987 Lincoln Center revival, Sir Evelyn is given Hope's number, "The Gypsy in Me," which turns into a wild dance suggesting that within his prim exterior was an active libido that led to his fling with Plum Blossom. In the 2011 revival, British-born Adam Godley proved such an effective Sir Evelyn that he was nominated for a Tony as Best Featured Actor in a Musical.

Porter indicated musically that Reno and Billy were a better match than Reno and Sir Evelyn by composing a duet for them, "You're the Top," a classic of one-upmanship in which Reno and Billy try to outdo each other in hyperbole, each calling the other everything from "the pants on a Roxy usher" and "Inferno's *Dante*" to a "Ritz hot toddy" and "a Botticelli." Perhaps some 1934 audiences reimagined the denouement by concluding that, if Reno and Billy could regard each other as "the top," they were, to use a familiar phrase, "made for each other"—if not on stage, then in their mind's eye.

ANYTHING GOES (PARAMOUNT, 1936)

The second movie version of a Porter musical fared slightly better. Unlike *Paris*, which arrived bereft of score, *Anything Goes* could lay claim to two numbers, exclusive of the title song which was sung over the credits and then heard no more. Moviegoers were at least treated to Ethel Merman's ballad of resignation, "I Get a Kick Out of You," in which she acknowledged her affection for someone who prefers another. Unfortunately, Lewis Milestone, a fine director with little feeling for musicals, kept cutting away from Merman (Reno) seated on a crescent moon as she glides over tables at a nightclub, to focus on Bing Crosby (Billy Crocker), who is paying no intention to a song that is meant for him. He is more intrigued by the mysterious Ida Lupino, who is traveling against her will to marry Lord Evelyn (Arthur Treacher). It made no difference that Crosby and Lupino had never met. Gallantry knows no bounds. She is a damsel in distress; he, her knight errant; and Merman, the go-between, with considerable help from "Moonface" Martin (a sadly miscast Henry Travers), who manage to get him a change of clothes, a state room, and a passport that belongs to Public Enemy No. 1, Snake Eyes Johnson. Then it's the brig, a dockside exit with "Moonface" and Crocker disguised as Asians, and Crocker and Lupino safely ensconced in a limo with Lord Evelyn and Reno peering through the window as a Paramount News camera records their exit for posterity. If this self-reflective touch is the studio's way of marketing Paramount News, which boasted of having access to "the eyes and ears of the world," it might have been put to better use than announcing the wedding of an heiress to a commoner. Rarely has so much been made of so little.

The script by several hands was basically a scissors-and-paste job similar to storyboarding or *decoupage*, in which the plot essentials are rendered in comic strip fashion, each designated as a separate action: Crocker is attracted to mystery woman; Crocker stows away on board; Crocker gets help from Reno and Moonface; Crocker dons a disguise; Crocker lands in the brig; Crocker and Moonface play strip poker with Koreans and win their clothes; Crocker and Moonface elude authorities; and Paramount considers the ocean crossing important enough memorialize it in a newsreel. In case anyone is wondering what happened to Ethel Merman, she was billed over Crosby, who had most of the songs, none of which could compare with Porter's score.

Paramount did not pay $100,000 for a score by Cole Porter. The studio paid it for a movie starring its Golden Boy who sang one Porter song, "You're the Top," downgraded to the point of gibberish. Instead, Crosby was given material by other—and lesser—composers, whose melodic gifts did not matter as long as Crosby sang the lyrics. Who cared about Ethel Merman in small-town America? Who even knew who she was?

Merman was no more meant for the screen than Crosby was for the stage. She was Broadway and brassy. She could never adapt to the confines of the screen, which was too restricted for a voice without boundaries. In *Anything Goes*, Crosby crooned, and Merman clowned, doing their best with the revised lyrics that were Paramount's idea of Porter for Dummies. But they were also pros who knew that the only way to sell a picture, regardless of its quality, was to make it seem as if everyone in the audience believes you are singing only for them.

CHAPTER 6

A Cole Porter Primer

Prosody and Figurative Language

Every student at some point learns a few figures of speech, the most common being simile, metaphor, and personification; and perhaps even synecdoche (substitution of the part for the whole) and metonymy (substitution of a more descriptive color, word, or phrase for an ordinary one, such as *brass* for army officials, *take the veil* for becoming a nun). Shakespeare knew considerably more. The Tudor rhetoricians classified two hundred figures of speech under the headings of **grammar** (proper usage); **logos** (an appeal to reason through figures like simile and metaphor that require the ability to discern similarities and differences in comparisons); **pathos** (an appeal to the emotions with a figure like *auexis*, which is similar to hyperbole—exaggeration for effect, as in Marc Antony's description of Caesar's assassination [*Julius Caesar*, 3, 2], with Caesar's heart bursting and his blood running down the pedestal of Pompey's statue—a vivid account by someone who was not present); and **ethos** (an appeal to character—*comprobatio*, in which a speaker seeks audience approval by appearing as a person of integrity, as Brutus [*Julius Caesar*, 3, 2] does by calling himself a man of "honor," who participated in the assassination not because he loved Caesar less, but because he loved Rome more—a neat antithesis but no match for Antony's oratory).

Although Shakespeare learned many of the figures in grammar school at Stratford where rhetoric was emphasized, he absorbed most of them through his reading of Latin authors, especially Cicero, Ovid, Horace, and Virgil: "When Shakespeare began writing plays, he had a grasp of a rhetorical system (the one codified by the Tudor rhetoricians). From rhetoric he derived literary construction and literary criticism. Rhetoric gave him the theory and practice of imitation. His knowledge of the classics he derived from grammar-school sources."

Porter did not know two hundred figures, but through required courses in Latin, Greek, French, and English literature at Worcester Academy, he acquired a knowledge of considerably deeper than simile, metaphor, and metonymy. He fell under the influence of Dean Daniel Webster Abercrombie, who also taught Greek and who, by Porter's own account, showed him how he could match the rhythm of his words with that of his music. "Words and music are so inseparably wedded to each other that they are like one." Porter's lyrics were naturally musical, so much so that, if one did not know the actual notation, reading the lines aloud would provide an approximation.

In Porter's day, poetry was taught as a literary form that adhered to the principles of versification, the art of creating verbal music through meter (the regular succession of stressed and unstressed syllables) and melody (the regular succession of vowel and consonant sounds). Students learned to scan poetry by dividing the syllabic line into feet such as the *iambic* (an unstressed syllable followed by an stressed one, **amid**); *trochaic* (the opposite, **doleful**); *anapestic* (two unstressed syllables followed by a stressed one, **at the cor**-ner); and *dactylic* (one stressed syllable followed by two unstressed ones, **murmuring**). An iambic line admits of substitutions such as the *pyrrhic* (two unstressed syllables, **by the**), *trochee* (stressed/unstressed, **coldly**), and *spondee* (two stressed syllables, **birds sang**). There were other types of meters, and perhaps Porter learned the Alcaic and Sapphic in his Latin poetry classes. Then students would have been taught the Latin method of scanning English verse: **u** placed over the short syllable; the macron (-) over the long. Today it is more common to speak of stressed and unstressed syllables and to use the marks ʹ above stressed syllables, and **x** above unstressed ones.

Porter was never a strict metrician whose lyrics followed a specific meter like the iambic pentameter. Rather, he would alternate meters within a lyric. No music survives of "At the Dawn Tea" (1913), written when he was a junior at Yale. It's a two-stanza lyric, the first consisting of five lines; the second, of six:

> At the dawn tea, at the dawn tea
> Disregarding the cold daybreak,
> If you're then there,
> You'll see men there
> All lit up like a birthday cake.

At first glance—and without reading the stanza aloud—lines one, two, and five are octosyllabic. Lines three and four are quadrisyllabic—two iambic dimeters. While there is no metrical uniformity, there is consistency: three tetrameters (lines 1, 2, 5) and two dimeters (lines 3, 4).

Now, if read aloud, a slightly different rhythm emerges. The text suggests that **dawn tea** is a trochee (stressed/unstressed), but the voice says spondee (stressed/stressed). The same is true of **then there, men there, daybreak,** and **-day cake**. If you stress the last two syllables of each line—**dawn tea, daybreak, then there, men there, -day cake**—you can hear the music in the words. You can also hear the rhythm that Porter was hearing.

The second stanza is similar:

> At the dawn tea, at the dawn tea,
> It's a party
> That is jaunty.
> It's a place where they all talk
> Conversational small talk—
> The Prom dawn tea.

If you stress the last two syllables of each line—**dawn tea/party/jaunty/ all talk/small talk/dawn tea**—and leave the others unstressed, as if they were running to meet up with the stressed ones, you will experience the rhythm that Porter intended. By deviating from ordinary accentuation, Porter was experimenting with syncopation, in which the regular pattern is disrupted to achieve a different kind of rhythm either by accenting a word that is ordinarily unaccented or vice versa. If you recite lines four and five, stressing only the last two syllables (**all talk/small talk**), and let the tongue skip over the first five (**it's a place where they/ conversational**), it sounds like jazz with notes given a beat that they ordinarily do not receive.

This is not a great lyric, but it does show that Porter knew the difference between meter and rhythm, and how rhythm can create an alternate meter that, when a line is read aloud, rearranges the scansion on the printed page to accommodate the human voice. Even though a poem is written in a particular meter, when recited, it may deviate from it. If asked to scan the first line of Christopher Marlowe's "The Passionate Shepherd to His Love," "Come live with me and be my love," one might say it consists of four perfect iambs. Yet the poem is an exhortation. No passionate shepherd would say, "Come live (unstressed/stressed)—with me (same)—and be (same)—my love (same)." The shepherd would only stress **me** and **love**. Hamlet urged the players to deliver their lines "trippingly on the tongue" (Act 3, 2). The same is true of reciting poetry. In recitation, "come live with" would come off as three unstressed syllables; "and be," as two unstressed ones. Scansion is a branch of prosody; recitation is performance.

THE FIGURES

"True wit is nature to advantage dress'd," Alexander Pope wrote in *An Essay on Criticism*. Words are naked, but when the right word is dressed in the right image, the word is appropriately clothed, not ostentatiously or shabbily but properly. Figurative language provides the attire.

Beginning at Yale and continuing throughout his long career as a composer of Broadway and Hollywood musicals, Porter used figurative language freely. For example:

Alliteration: The Repetition of Consonants

"**d**euced, **d**ull, and **d**eadly" "My Houseboat on the Thames" (*The Pot of Gold*, 1912 Delta Kappa Epsilon fraternity show);
"At the **R**ainbow / The **R**ainbow / The **R**ainbow / The **R**ain **R**ainbow Hotel" (*The Pot of Gold*, 1912);

Assonance: The Repetition of Vowels or Vowel Sounds

"Far over the p**oun**ding / s**oun**ding / b**oun**ding / Over the b**oun**ding sea" ("Rolling, Rolling," *Cora*, 1911 Delta Kappa Epsilon fraternity show);
"Such as b**o**nds, and st**o**cks, and Paris fr**o**cks" ("Two Little Babes in the Wood," *Paris*, removed from *Greenwich Village Follies of 1924*);
"**Do do** that Voo**doo** that you **do** so well" (*Fifty Million Frenchmen*, 1929);

Anaphora: The Repetition of the Same Word or Group of Words at the Beginning of Successive Lines

Nine of the ten lines of "What Love Is" (*Paranoia*, 1914) begin with "love is." Many of the lines in "Let's Not Talk about Love" *(Let's Face It!*, 1941) begin with "let's." There are numerous other examples, one of the best being "I Love Paris" (*Can-Can*, 1953), in which each of the first five lines of the refrain begins with the song title; and one of the worst being "Drink" (*The Seven Lively Arts*, 1944), in which "drink" is the first word of practically every line;

Antithesis: The Juxtaposition of Opposites

"You bill and coo! / You fret and stew!" ("When a Body's in Love," 1916, dropped from *See America First*);
"The young fall, the old fall" ("They All Fall in Love," *The Battle of Paris* [Paramount, 1929]);
"At Long Last Love" (*You Never Know*, 1936) is a series of antitheses in question form ("Is it a rainbow or just a mirage?");

Epistrophe: End Repetition

"Down in a Dungeon Deep" (*Paranoia*) is the title of the song as well as its last two lines.
There are many other examples such as "I concentrate on you, / I concentrate / And concentrate / On you" ("I Concentrate on You," *Broadway Melody of 1940*); "Tell me where. / Oh, where, / Oh, where" ("Where, Oh Where?," *Out of This World*, 1950);

Epanalepsis: Repetition of the Same Word at Both the Beginning and End of a Line

This was not a figure Porter favored, although "with a fol, with a fol / With a hey, with a hey" ("A Member of the Yale Elizabethan Club," *The Kaleidoscope*, a 1913 production of the Yale Drama Association) comes close. Better is "the leopard's chasing the leopard," "the llama's chasing the llama" ("Nobody's Chasing Me," *Out of This World*);

Anadiplosis: Repetition of the Last Word of a Line in the First Word(s) of the Next Line

"Hear me calling / Calling for you ("Maid of Santiago," *The Kaleidoscope*)
"I think of you night and day / Day and night" ("Night and Day," *Gay Divorce*); "You've got that thing / That thing . . .," ("You've Got That Thing," *Fifty Million Frenchmen*);
"I'm always doing something / Something for the boys" (*Something for the Boys*, 1943).

Paranomasia: Play on Words

Double entendre was Porter's specialty. The *Du Barry Was a Lady* lyrics abound in sexual innuendo. In "But in the Morning No," performed on stage by Ethel Merman and Bert Lahr, Merman asks Lahr if he likes third parties, can ante up, fill an inside straight, perform double entry, and do the breast stroke, to which Lahr replies in the affirmative: "But in the morning, no." The last line of "Katie Went to Haiti" is "and practically all Haiti had Katie."

Porter's most popular—and charmingly risqué—double entendre song is "My Heart Belongs to Daddy," which Mary Martin introduced in *Leave It to Me* (1938). "Daddy" is a term of endearment for the "sweet millionaire" to whom the young woman has given her heart. "Play" is innocuous; "make a play for the caddie" is sexual. "Asking for more" does not mean another helping of finnan haddie. Athletes talk of "making the team." When Mary Martin flashed her demure smile and insisted she never dreamed of "making the team," it was clear that she did not aspire to the majors. She may have had an errant libido, but her heart belonged to Daddy.

One doubts that Porter knew all the technical names for the figures that crop up in his lyrics. The same can be said of President John F. Kennedy, who, in his inaugural address, proclaimed: "Ask not what your country can do for you; ask what you can do for your country." He was using the figure *antimetabole*, in which words are repeated in reverse grammatical order. In the first part of the sentence, "country" is the subject of the clause, and "you" is the object of the preposition "for"; in the second part, "you" becomes the subject; and "country," the object. Porter used the same figure in the "Anything Goes" verse, comparing the Pilgrims landing at Plymouth Rock in 1626 with what would happen if they arrived today: "'Stead of landing on Plymouth Rock / Plymouth Rock would land on them." Anyone with a penchant for figurative language will experiment with grammatical structure, seeing if a point can be made more vividly—or, in poetry, an image can be conveyed more gracefully—by an inversion or an unusual comparison.

"Mark the music" (Shakespeare, *The Merchant of Venice*, Act 1)

A lover of language—and Porter was enamored of it—does not need a poetry handbook to locate its wellsprings. Even one who knows little or nothing of meter can weave language into patterned sound, with stresses falling naturally on certain syllables, leaving others softly unstressed. The ear functions as the poet's arbiter in matters of rhyme and rhythm. Syllables have always been sacrificed for effect. If "it will" flattens the rhythm of the line, try "'t'will," as Porter did in the title song in *Can-Can*. "'T'will be so easy to do" is euphonious; "it will be so easy to do" sounds so leaden that it implies the opposite of ease. Porter uses "'cause" frequently—four times in "They Ain't Done Right by Our Nell" (*Panama Hattie*, 1940).

Syllables are not sacrosanct; sometimes their addition or subtraction can improve the tempo. "Another opening, another show" sounds like a maxim; "another op'nin', another show" sounds like the beginning of a song, which it is (the opening number *in Kiss Me, Kate*). A handbook of rhetoric would call "op'nin'": an example of **syncope**, in which a syllable is removed from the middle of a word. But the ear is oblivious to handbook definitions; it only knows what it hears.

Since Porter understood that rhyme is harmonious sound, he would often shift accents, alter spellings, or invert word order to achieve it. The title song in *Can-Can* is a series of accent displacements so that words ending in -**can** will rhyme with **can**. Thus in "Michigan," the accent is transferred from the first syllable to the last ("If a lass in Michi**gan can**"); similarly, with "pelican" and "Anglican" ("If a clumsy peli**can can**"; "If a gangly Angli**can can**").

The catalogue number, "Brush Up Your Shakespeare" (*Kiss Me, Kate*), is rife with deliberate misspellings and mispronunciations in the interests of rhyme and characterization. It is sung by two low-level mobsters with a knowledge of, if not Shakespeare's plays, at least of their titles: not "ambassador" but "embassida" to rhyme with "Cressida" (as in *Troilus and Cressida*); not "Othello" but "Othella" to rhyme with "fella"; not "Cleopatra" but "Cleopaterer" to rhyme with "flatter/'er"; not "MacDuff" but MacDuffy to rhyme with "huffy."

Anastrophe, an inversion of the usual word order, is a common figure in both poetry and prose. "To dig I am not able; to beg I am ashamed" (Luke 16:3, Challoner-Rheims Version) is nicely balanced, with a succession of unstressed and stressed syllables. If the steward in Luke's Gospel, accused of squandering his possessions, had said to his master, "I am unable to dig and ashamed to beg," it would merely be a statement of fact. But the inversion, and particularly the change of verbs (dig, beg) to infinitives (to dig, to beg) gives his words an aphoristic quality, making them memorable and, for generations, quotable, like "to err is human, to forgive, divine" (Alexander Pope, *An Essay on Criticism*).

Poets frequently invert either to maintain metrical consistency or rhythmical uniformity. William Wordsworth's "Yarrow Visited September 1814" consists of eleven stanzas in iambic tetrameter. In the second stanza, the poet recalls the incomparable beauty of Yarrow: "Not have these eyes by greener hills / Been soothed, in all my wanderings." The meaning is clear: these eyes have never been soothed by greener hills. To turn that prosaic sentiment into poetry, Wordsworth splits the verb in two, placing "have" in the first line along with the phrase "by greener hills"; and "been soothed," at the beginning of the second—all in accordance with the metrical form he has chosen.

Even in his Yale days, Porter was deviating from standard word order. The second verse of "Antoinette Birby" (date unknown but prior to 1913) begins: "Arrived in the city, this maiden so pretty / Did walk down Chapel Street." Likewise, "And when this I'd gotten" ("The Prep School Widow," *Paranoia*, 1914); "Years have I waited for someone adorable" ("Oh, What a Lovely Princess," *Paranoia*).

Porter used inversions frequently in *Kiss Me, Kate* (1948) to impart a faux Elizabethan tone to the lyrics:

"A group of strolling players are we" ("We Open in Venice");

"I hate men / Though roosters they, I will not play the hen" ("I Hate Men").

PORTER AND RHYME

Prosody to Porter was like an acrostic—a composition that required careful planning so that one rhyme could set off a chain reaction of others either in succession or at intervals as if they were pieces of glass in a mosaic that had to be carefully inlaid to create the desired pattern. With Porter, structure was everything. Nothing fortuitous, nothing ad libitum.

The lyrics that Porter wrote between 1909 and 1914 reveal his mastery of the verse-refrain form, his metrical dexterity, and especially his love of rhyme—not just end rhyme but also remote and internal:

Remote Rhyme: Rhymes at a Distance from Each Other.

The seventh line of the refrain of "Llewellyn" (*And the Villain Pursued Her*, 1912, Yale Dramatic Association) ends with "**you**," but its complement ("**do**") does not appear until the fourteenth. Similarly, in "When the Summer Moon Comes Along," "**spoon**" (verse 1, line 5) does not get a rhyme until "**moon**" (verse 1, line 10); in "It's Awfully Hard When Mother's Not Around" (*The Pot of Gold*), "**wrong**" (refrain, line 5) doesn't get its mate until line 10 ("**along**").

Porter experimented with remote rhyme throughout his career. "**Pleasin'**" (verse 1, line 2 of "You'd Be So Nice to Come Home To" (*Something to Shout About*, 1943) has to wait until line seven for "**season**"; it's the same in verse 2: "**own up**" (line 2), "**sewn up**" (line 7). In "Who Said Gay Paree?" (*Can-Can*), "**fun**" in the first line of the refrain is paired with "**sun**" in the sixth; in the same musical "**odds**" ("I Am in Love," refrain, line 17) finds a rhyme in "**gods**" (line 21).

Internal Rhyme: Rhyming pairs either in the same line or two separate lines

"**neglect your**"/"**architecture**" ("Exercise," *The Pot of Gold*, 1912);
"**sandwich/Land which**" ("In the Land Where I Was Born," *The Kaleidoscope*, 1913);
"**Hand in hand, we'll make for the land**" ("Come We to Bohemia," *And the Villain Pursued Her*, 1912);
"**Run for shelter, helter-skelter to the Yale Hope Mission**" ("Beware of the Sophomore," *The Kaleidoscope*, 1913);
"**O'er the foam we can roam 'neath the star-bedizened dome**" ("On My Yacht," *The Kaleidoscope*).

Porter was especially fond of internal rhyme which generates its own kind of rhythm, with the rhyming words linked together by a chain of syllables in a different meter. Poets have also altered the rhythm within a long line to lighten the weight brought on by a preponderance of stressed syllables, as Gerard Manley Hopkins has done in the twelve-syllable line, "A **care kept—Where** kept? Do but tell us where kept, where—" ("The Leaden Echo and the Golden Echo"). Except for "A." the first and last segments of the line consist of clusters of long syllables ("**care kept—Where kept**" and "**where kept, where**"), variegated by a group of four short syllables ("*Do but tell us*") to keep the line from sagging under its spondaic weight.

Similarly, in "So deep in my **heart**, you're really a **part** of me" ("I've Got You Under My Skin," *Born to Dance*, 1936), "heart" and "part" are linked by a four-syllable chain ("**you're really a**") that differs rhythmically and metrically from "**So deep in my heart**" (iamb, anapest; x '/x x ') and "part of me" (dactyl; ' x x) "*You're real-ly a*" is an iambic interval: an iamb (x ') and a pyrrhic (x x), speeding up the twelve-syllable line that the stressed monosyllabic **deep** and **heart** slowed down, and then resuming with the dactylic "**part of me**" (′x x).

Scanning the line makes one appreciative of Porter's art.

x ′/x x ′/x ′/x x/ ′x x

The second foot (**in my heart**) is an anapest: x x ′; the fifth, **part of me**, is the reverse, a dactyl: ′ x x. With Porter nothing is fortuitous. *Pas de chance.*

Porter was also not averse to using *Imperfect or Off Rhyme*, the partial correspondence of sounds:

"**shining**"/"**entwining**" ("She Was a Fair Young Mermaid," *The Pot of Gold*);
"**walk**"/"**New York**" ("Longing for Dear Old Broadway," *The Pot of Gold*);
"**clamor**"/"**melodrama**" ("The Lovely Heroine," *Cora*, 1911);
"**morning**"/"**marathoning**" (*The Kaleidoscope*).

By 1914, Porter had mastered the rudiments of his craft. All that remained was their perfection.

CHAPTER 7

Strange Bedfellows

Cole Porter and Moss Hart's *Jubilee*

Until *Kiss Me, Kate*, the musicals that followed *Anything Goes* never enjoyed Broadway revivals, but were only performed in concert or off-Broadway. For twenty years, from 1998 to 2018, *Musicals Tonight* functioned as a theater museum where small-scale productions of one hundred musicals—the near forgotten (*Three Wishes for Jamie, Let It Ride, Louisiana Purchase*) and the well-known (*Anything Goes, Bells Are Ringing, The Boys from Syracuse*)—were presented in off-Broadway venues, most often on Theater Row, Forty-second Street, off Ninth Avenue. Lovers of the Broadway musical, especially those of a certain age, supported the company which, despite a makeshift set, a minimum of props, and a piano or a few musicians in lieu of an orchestra, provided an opportunity to savor the score and hear the dialogue, dated perhaps, but delivered by young professionals too stage-struck to sound jaded. *Musicals Tonight* brought back some of Porter's lesser shows such as *Jubilee, Panama Hattie, Du Barry Was a Lady, Mexican Hayride*, and *Out of this World*. While most of Porter's musicals between 1935 and 1947 were successful, *You Never Know* (1938) and *Around the World* (1946) were not. Yet most could lay claim to at least one song—sometimes more—that went on to become a standard (see table 1).

Table 1

Jubilee (1935)	"Begin the Beguine,"
	"Just One of Those Things"
Red, Hot and Blue (1936)	"It's De-Lovely"
You Never Know (1938)	"At Long Last Love"
Leave It to Me (1938)	"My Heart Belongs to Daddy"
Du Barry Was a Lady (1939)	"Do I Love You?"
	"Friendship"

Panama Hattie (1940)	"Let's Be Buddies,"
	"Make It Another Old-Fashioned, Please"
Let's Face It! (1941)	"Let's Not Talk about Love"
Something for the Boys (1943)	Nothing, not even the title song
Mexican Hayride (1944)	"I Love You"
Seven Lively Arts (1944)	"Ev'ry Time We Say Goodbye"
Around the World (1946)	Nothing

The shows themselves were either so firmly rooted in their era that they would need an overhauling for a successful revival (*Let's Face It!*, *Something for the Boys*); star-driven vehicles that would be difficult to cast (Ethel Merman, Jimmy Durante, and Bob Hope in *Red, Hot and Blue*; Merman and Lahr in *Du Barry Was a Lady*; Merman in *Panama Hattie*; Bobby Clark in *Mexican Hayride*); operettas (*Jubilee, You Never Know*) that would prove too artificial for contemporary audiences, unless staged as period pieces— and even then would not attract tourists whose idea of a musical is *Chicago*, *Hamilton*, and *Moulin Rouge*. Unless *Musicals Tonight* is resurrected or a similar company is formed to revive the lesser gems of the American musical theater, they will be known through original cast recordings (if such were made) or in the works of theater scholars who have found a way of bringing them back to life on the printed page.

ON STAGE: *JUBILEE* (1935)

The book and score of *Jubilee* were written by Moss Hart and Porter during a four-and-a-half-month cruise around the world on the *Franconia* from early January to the end of May 1935. In addition to Hart and Porter, the other passengers included Linda and the ubiquitous Monty Woolley. The title of the musical was inspired by George V's twenty-fifth anniversary as king of England in the Jubilee year of 1935. The book had nothing to do with that jubilee, but with one in operetta-land Britain, whose royal family consists of King Henry and Queen Katherine, affectionately called Kate, who have nothing in common with Henry VIII and Katherine of Aragon; their nephew, Prince Rudolph (changed to Prince James before the Broadway premiere); their daughter, Princess Diana; and their son, Prince Peter (the fifteen-year-old Montgomery Clift in his second stage role). With Melville Cooper as the whimsical King and Mary Boland, the embodiment of flightiness, as the Queen, no one would never regard them as stand-ins for King George and Queen Mary of England. The Queen addresses the Prime Minister as "Fruity" and is enthralled by an Olympic swimmer turned actor, Charles Rausmiller (think Johnny Weissmuller, Olympic star and cinema's favorite Tarzan), known to the public as Mowgli, the character he played in a series inspired by Rudyard Kipling's *The Jungle Book*, in which Mowgli, like Tarzan, had unique survival skills, which included the ability to communicate with members of the animal kingdom.

Jubilee gets off to a slow start, with everyone making suggestions for the entertainment. The Queen wants Mowgli so he teaches her the Australian crawl; Prince Rudolph wants Karen O'Kane, the American performer appearing at the Café Martinique, to dance the beguine; and Princess Diana wants Eric Dare, a phenomenally talented playwright-actor-composer whose latest play is *Scheme for Dying* (think Noel Coward, whose *Design for Living*, with the Lunts and himself, was a hit of the 1932–33 season).

Hart's book is a mix of satire and *à clef* which turns serious, as operettas often do, when the royals take a break from palace life and spend a week living like ordinary people. Actually, they have no other choice when the princes, eager to see Radio City, perhaps meaning the Music Hall, and then travel west to see real cowboys, throw a rock through a window with a message threatening the family with violence unless they vacate the palace by midnight. Sensing an insurrection is brewing, they flee to Feathermore (think Balmoral Castle), where there is nothing to do but listen to the radio or to the rain. They decide to leave Feathermore for a weekend incognito at Rockwell Beach (think Brighton) where they encounter the flamboyant Elsa Standing (think celebrated party giver and Porter's close friend, Elsa Maxwell), who joins their circle.

Although Hart and Porter worked independently of each other, Porter may have suggested that Hart consider centering the book around a royal family that takes a vacation from life at court to explore the outside world. Porter's first musical, *See America First*, involved a titled Brit, who, like the King in *Jubilee*, seeks a respite from a life of privilege and sets out for California, along with similarly minded young men eager to escape from the strictures of their class. Since the royal-in-disguise is a familiar character in operetta (Prince Karl in Sigmund Romberg's *The Student Prince*, Robert Misson in Romberg's *New Moon*, Prince Franz in Victor Herbert's *Sweethearts*), Hart, perhaps encouraged by Porter, has the royal family not only revel in civilian life but also return to their kingdom once the prime minister reveals that the "insurrection" was a hoax devised by the princes who were desperate to see America. Oddly enough, so were the King and Queen, who fancied what it would be like touring the United States as Mr. and Mrs. Smith.

The masquerade must end, and the Jubilee Year festivities begin. The King and Queen have no intention of giving up their newly acquired entourage. It is as if Shakespeare had Prince Hal bring Falstaff and his drinking buddies to court after becoming Henry V. If Hal must disown Falstaff, it follows that the King and Queen should do the same with their coterie. But this is musical comedy where "anything goes." Since Hart revealed his flair for satire in *Once in a Lifetime* (1930), coauthored with George S. Kaufman—a hilarious sendup of a frazzled Hollywood transitioning from the silent to the sound era—.it must have been his idea to model the hostess, the swimmer-movie star, and the multifaceted playwright after real celebrities and work them into the finale. Rausmiller (Mowgli) is named Commissioner of Aquatics (translation: the Queen's personal swimming instructor); Elsa Standing is named Commissioner of Royal Functions (translation: hostess/party-giver). Eric Dare is in the audience looking slightly forlorn. Previously he told Princess Diana that a relationship was out of the question because he is too vain and selfish. Karen O'Kane, who is presented to the King and Queen, looks longingly at the prince, whose eyes, according to the stage description, "are positively glowing." Karen doesn't get a title, but one assumes she will soon become the prince's consort. Prince Peter is too young for a romantic partner, and Diana will find another multitalented beau who is neither vain nor selfish. As in Shakespeare's *Twelfth Night*, a world is turned upside down, and confusion reigns until it's denouement time when order is restored, the fog of ignorance is lifted, and everyone is wiser for the experience.

Unlike *Anything Goes*, with its profusion of hit songs, *Jubilee* had two perennials, "Begin the Beguine" and "Just One of Those Things." The former was first sung by June Knight as Karen—who had appeared in several stage musicals including Porter's *Fifty Million Frenchmen* as a member of the chorus—and then danced by Charles Walters and herself. Walters was a masterful dancer who went on to MGM, first as a dance director and then as a film director whose specialty was the musical (*Good News*, *Easter Parade*, *Summer Stock*, *High Society*).

The "Begin the Beguine" lyrics have the sinuous eroticism of "Night and Day" but not the rich imagery. Porter has given conflicting accounts of the first time he heard a beguine, a dance common to the West Indies incorporating elements of the waltz and the rumba and composed in 4/4 time. Whether Porter heard a beguine in Paris in the 1920s or at some South Seas stopover during the round-the-world cruise in 1935 is irrelevant. Porter, who loved wordplay, was intrigued by the off rhyme of "begin" and "beguine," and it was probably that combination that led him to compose "Begin the Beguine" in 4/4 time, as marked in the score.

As an accomplished singer who was playing one in *Jubilee*, June Knight needed a song; Charles Walters as Prince James, who has become attracted to Karen, needed a dancing partner, which he found in Knight, who could sing, dance, and act.

Like "Night and Day" in *Gay Divorce*, "Begin the Beguine" is first sung, then danced. It is the sort of song that one might hear in a smoky club, performed by a singer in a sequined gown. It is a memory song of an affair that began on a night of "tropical splendor"; then the fire that once burned bright became an ember. At first the singer does not want to hear the beguine again because of its association with a dead-end affair. Then she relents and demands to hear it, convinced that it will bring the stars back to the sky, along with the "rapture serene" and a promise never to part—or so she hopes. It's clearly a song of mixed emotions and mounting anxiety: neurosis set to music in 4/4 time. In terms of popular culture, "Begin the Beguine" is a lesser "Night and Day," seductive in its rhythms but colorless in its lyrics.

"Begin the Beguine" was performed midway in Act 1; "Just One of Those Things," near the end of the show, when it seems that Karen's romance with the prince was just "one of those crazy flings." The eighteen-line refrain falls into two sections, the first eight lines celebrating their romance as a "fabulous" flight, "a trip to the moon on gossamer wings." The first section is metrically traditional: A/A/A/A/B/B/A/A (*things/flings/rings/things nights/flights/wings/things*). The second section is somewhat more intricate, as if something that had been knitted together is now unravelling: A/A/B/C/C/B/D/D/E/E (*bit/it/town aware/affair/down amen/then/***fun/one** *of those things*)—the only internal rhyme in the song. By choosing to close with an internal rhyme, Porter can end with a trochee (*one of*, - x) and a spondee (*those things*, ′ ′); musically, an expression of finality—but not for Karen and the prince.

Jubilee has been revived in concert form and in small venues, but never on Broadway. The score only has two standouts, several name-dropping numbers, and a first-act finale that takes place at a costume ball where a masque, "The Judgment of Paris," is performed; the only part of the masque that has survived are the lyrics to "Aphrodite's Dance," performed by June Knight as the goddess with a double chorus chanting in quasi-classical Greek. The men call Aphrodite "Aphroditah" and "kalah," rather than *kalle*, the correct form of the adjective *kallos* ("beautiful"). Porter may have thought that "Aphroditah" and "kala" were more euphonious than *Aphrodite* and *kalle*, in which the final -e is the Greek eta and pronounced like a long -a. The women call Aphrodite "miara" and "kourga," harlot and prostitute, respectively, according to Porter's glossary. Close, but *miara* is the feminine of the adjective *miaros*, meaning foul or polluted; *kakourga* is evildoer (feminine). One should recall that Porter was an excellent Greek student at Worcester Academy, and in "Aphrodite's Dance," used soundalikes instead of the correct Greek words, presumably in the interests of melody.

The masque was a sendup of high culture and bourgeois style, and could be dropped In revival, but that would leave the other songs, which are not vintage Porter and which include an unusually large number of name-droppers. Karen and the prince sing a duet, "A Picture of Me without You," in which each compares the other to various figures without their complements (Ogden Nash without rhyme, Paul Revere without a horse, and Clifton Webb without his mother Mabel)—five eight-line refrains, the first six beginning with "Picture X without Y." Clever, topical, and overlong. Even the entire company gets a catalogue song, "Gather Ye Autographs While Ye May," an octet which the King, Queen, Prince Rudolph/James, Karen, Princess Diana, "Mowgli," Eva Standling, and Eric Dare sing at the beginning of Act 2. In "Mr. and Mrs. Smith," the King and Queen envision themselves as commoners with one of the commonest of surnames, setting sail for New York and anticipating a visit to Coney Island and a ride in the Goodyear blimp; then proceeding to California for a glimpse of Greta Garbo and Fred Astaire. The veneer of jollity cannot cover over the poignancy of the royal couple's pipe dream of taking a mythical journey to an equally mythic America—which they will never see once the insurrection is dismissed as bogus.

CHAPTER 8

Triple Threat

Ethel Merman, Jimmy Durante, and Bob Hope
in *Red, Hot and Blue*

ON STAGE: *RED, HOT AND BLUE* (1936)

Jubilee ran for 169 performances; *Red, Hot and Blue*, for 181. The latter starred Ethel Merman, Jimmy Durante, and Bob Hope with Merman and Durante's names intersecting with Hope's in the ads, implying that no one was the star. It also contained one of the weakest books of any Ethel Merman musical, perhaps with the exception of *Happy Hunting* (1956). The writers were again Howard Lindsay and Russel Crouse, who downgraded the character they created for Merman in *Anything Goes* from an evangelist-turned-entertainer to a former manicurist, nicknamed "Nails," whose millionaire husband died, leaving her a fabulously wealthy widow. We are asked to believe that "Nails" is so obscenely rich that she becomes a philanthropist who, because her father had been a felon, convinces a prison warden that she can rehabilitate ex-convicts and parolees by employing them as butlers, and young women from reform school as servers at her parties. Her chief ally is the captain of the prison's polo team (it must be a progressive prison), "Policy Pinkle" (Durante), who is so enamored of prison life that whenever he is released, he does something to guarantee his return. Now for the kicker: "Nails" also has a crush on lawyer Bob Hale (Hope), who cannot forget his childhood love, known only as "Baby." When Hale was six and living on Riverside Drive in New York, he tried to steal a kiss from four-year-old "Baby" while her mother was making waffles. In trying to push him away, "Baby" came down on the waffle iron, leaving her with a singular mark of identification. Like Reno Sweeney, who took it upon herself to help Billy Crocker win Hope, good-hearted "Nails" devises a plan to find "Baby" for Bob, even though it will mean the end of their relationship. She has her staff of parolees flood the country with lottery tickets, the winner being the one who can produce "Baby." What Nails does not know is that Peaches, one of the young women in her employ who had been sent to reform school for "corrupting the morals of an adult," is "Baby." Hale discovers her identity first; Peaches becomes so aggressively flirtatious that he puts her over his knee and starts spanking her, only to recoil in shock when he sees her unique ID.

Hale has now lost interest in the lottery, but some senators from the Finance Committee, who had been thinking of a lottery as a way of avoiding a tax hike, have not. When they heard about the love lottery, they decided to try their luck and, not surprisingly, won. Since the senators have found "Baby," Hale will have no other choice but to marry her—and on the White House lawn, no less. Meanwhile, "Policy Pinkle" has become a public figure, so admired that an interior decorator has been hired to redo his cell. Just when it seems the situation is hopeless, the Supreme Court rules that the lottery is unconstitutional because "it might benefit the American people." Pinkle can go back to his beloved prison, Hale and Nails can head for the altar, and Peaches can embark on the world's oldest profession.

The writers served Durante and Hope far better than they did Merman. They clearly understood that Hope's brand of comedy consists of setup and punchline. Give Hope a cue line like "They say two's company," and Hope can come back with "And three's the result." Give Durante a set piece like a conversation with an interior decorator suggesting a color scheme for his cell, and it becomes sketch comedy and the funniest scene in the show. That leaves Merman with nothing to do but sing and misuse words, saying "laxative" when she means "lax." Merman interacted well with Durante, but she had no rapport with Hope, who, even in the *Road* movies with Bing Crosby and Dorothy Lamour, was a standalone comic playing alongside two other performers. Merman and Hope were stars in their own firmaments, which were always meant to be separate.

The book is a mashup of the improbable, the impossible, and the satirical—all skewered to the point that they leave the audience no other choice but to take comfort in Porter's score, which included two big numbers for Merman and a duet with Hope, "It's De-Lovely," the best-known song in the show.

"Down in the Depths (on the Ninetieth Floor)" is a character song that Merman sang in a gold lame gown early in Act 1, recounting the frustration of being in love with someone in love with someone else—namely Hale, who, at this point, is still pining for "Baby." Merman has always been able to add a poignancy to lyrics, which she did memorably in "I Got Lost in His Arms" in Irving Berlin's *Annie Get Your Gun* (1946) and unforgettably in "Everything's Coming Up Roses" in Jule Styne's *Gypsy* (1959); she does the same in "Down in the Depths." But with the rehabilitation program and the love lottery, one wonders if "Nails" had any time to face tomorrow alone with her sorrow. And if living in a penthouse on the ninetieth floor only intensifies her malaise, move to a lower floor. The song says more about Porter than it does about Merman's character. Porter never seemed satisfied. The life of a world traveler was far more adventuresome than one defined by name and address. And "Nails" would never describe her living quarters as a "regal eagle nest." That kind of internal rhyme is pure Porter.

Porter wrote "You're the Top" in *Anything Goes* as a duet for Reno and Billy, implying that given their mutual admiration, they would end up together in a mind's eye production or one in an alternate universe of perfectly matched couples. He did the same for "Nails" and Hale with "It's De-Lovely," in which, after two verses and five refrains, it is evident that, at some point, "Baby" will be nothing more than a plot point.

"It's De-Lovely" is one of the most ebullient songs Porter has written. The notes bounce around like champagne bubbles. On the surface, the number seems as if Porter is casting a cold eye on young love; the duet is cynical and a bit goofy, but ever so subtly it becomes a five-part tale of a couple who start out taking a walk on a spring evening, followed by courtship, then marriage, and finally the birth of their first child, a boy who grows up to be so handsome that he lands at MGM.

Like practically all of Porter's songs, "It's De-Lovely" is mathematically structured. Each of the five refrains consists of sixteen lines, the third and sixth of which are always the same: "It's delightful, It's delicious, it's de-lovely." Each refrain ends with "it's de-lovely," except for refrain 4, the baby refrain, in which "He's" replaces "It's." The last five lines of each refrain, 13 -15, are outbursts of gleeful nonsense, as if they were competing with each other to see which can include the most outrageous words, even doggerel and portmanteau, beginning with de-:

Refrain 1 delectable, delirious, dilemma, delimit, deluxe

Refrain 2 divine, diveen, de-wunderbar, de-victory, de-vollop, de-vinner, de-voiks

Refrain 3 de dreamy, de-drowsy, de-reverie, de-rhapsody, de-regal, de-royal, de-Ritz

Refrain 4 is the exception. The "d's" are replaced by "p's" as the couple reacts to their child: pollywog, paragon, Popeye, panic, pip—words found in any English dictionary but weirdly inappropriate.

Refrain 5 brings the duet full circle, ending the same as refrain 1.

Any composer writing for Ethel Merman must fit the songs to her persona: a wise-cracking, brassy, slangy, but essentially moral dame who feels deeply but only expresses it when no one is around to hear; or if anyone is, like Billy in the first scene of *Anything Goes*, it is as if he isn't there. "Down in the Depths" is intended only for the audience who should know that for all her wealth, she lacks the one commodity that "cash in the bank galore" cannot buy: Bob Hale's love. Merman can go swagger or soft; she can lower the decibels or raise them. She can also sing plaintively, although less so in Porter's shows than in Irving Berlin's ("I Got Lost in His Arms"; "Moonshine Lullaby" in *Annie Get Your Gun*; "Marrying for Love" in *Call Me Madam*) and Jule Styne's ("Small World" in *Gypsy*). But it is in the clarion mode that Merman excels, revealing her unique ability not just to break—but explode— into song so naturally that it becomes a heightened form of expression. When "Nails" realizes that Bob Hale is finally hers, she bursts into "Ridin' High," proudly proclaiming her indifference to Barbara Hutton's wealth, Katharine Hepburn's nose, Marlene Dietrich's legs, Dorothy Parker's wit, and Simone Simon's figure. "Ridin' High" is one of Merman's—and Porter's—less well-remembered songs, but it comes at a crucial point in the plot, which explains its placement and appropriateness.

Red, Hot and Blue may never see a Broadway revival, but "It's De-Lovely" has survived as an interpolation in the 1994 and 2011 revivals of *Anything Goes*.

Porter's musical is not to be confused with (although it has been) the 1949 Paramount film of the same name with Betty Hutton and Victor Mature. That film is a mixture of comedy, crime, and music, with Hutton as an aspiring stage actress who becomes involved in a murder. It is considered a musical because (a) that genre was Betty Hutton's specialty, and (b) she sang five songs by Frank Loesser, the best of which is "Now That I Need You." Ironically, if Paramount wanted to make the movie version of *Red, Hot and Blue* in 1949 with a change of "Baby's" distinguishing mark, Hutton would have been the perfect "Nails." She proved that she could handle the intricate lyrics of "Let's Not Talk about Love" in the film version of Porter's *Let's Face It* (Paramount, 1943).

CHAPTER 9

1938, A Year to Remember— *You Never Know* and *Leave It to Me*

On October 24, 1937, Porter was seriously injured when he was horseback riding on Long Island. The horse for some reason bolted, throwing him to the ground and then coming down on him, crushing both legs. Porter was quite graphic about his injuries in a letter to Monty Woolley (December 2, 1937). He sustained a compound fracture of his left leg ("that means that the bones went through the skin"). "The right leg was smashed to such a pulp from below the knee to the ankle" that the doctors informed Linda that his legs might have to be amputated, which eventually happened but not for quite a few years. Despite the excruciating pain which was alleviated by delirium-inducing drugs, Porter accomplished the impossible: he had two shows on Broadway the following year—one a failure, the other a hit.

ON STAGE: *YOU NEVER KNOW* (1938)

You Never Know, which opened on September 31, 1938, at the Winter Garden Theatre, was not really a "Cole Porter musical," since he was not the sole composer and lyricist. But it did not matter. Porter had to get back to the only activity that could ward off the specter of permanent invalidism and the curtailment—or termination—of his insatiable love of travel.

You Never Know had a long gestation period.

It began life as *Bei Kerzenlight* (*By Candlelight*, 1927), a three-act boudoir comedy by the Viennese writer-actor Siegfried Geyer. After the Vienna premiere, it arrived on Broadway September 30, 1929, as *Candle Light* in a translation by P. G. Wodehouse that starred Leslie Howard, Gertrude Lawrence, and Reginald Owen for a run of 128 performances, surpassing the mere seventy-eight of *You Never Know* nine years later. The movie version *By Candlelight*, with Paul Lukas, Elissa Landi, and Nils Asther, was released by Universal Pictures in 1933.

The film, which was a faithful replica of the play with additional characters, was high-gloss infidelity in a world of chilled champagne, late-night suppers, and an impeccably made bed that a valet just has to turn down to give his amorous employer easy access to it. This is also a world in which a bogus countess, really her maid in disguise (Elissa Landi), mistakes a valet (Paul Lukas) for his employer, Prince Alfred (Nils Ashter), who is having affair with *her* employer, Countess von Rischenheim (Dorothy Revier). When Prince Alfred arrives unexpectedly, he has no other choice but to assume the role of the valet. It's the typical operetta formula of mistaken identity, deception, romantic intrigue, and happy ending. The valet and the maid become a couple; the prince goes on philandering; and the countess, flirting. Director James Whale, who converted horror into gothic in *Frankenstein* (1931) and *Bride of Frankenstein* (1935), turned *By Candlelight* into operetta without music

In 1937, Austrian composer Robert Katscher turned *By Candlelight* into a four-character chamber operetta, which the Shuberts thought could become a full-scale musical comedy, but it was not a smooth translation. Contractually, there was the title song by Katscher, which had to be retained, plus another song, "No (You Can't Have My Heart)" with music and lyrics by Dana Suesse, which was interpolated into the score. Five songs had lyrics by other writers. Nine of Porter's songs were cut during the extensive tryouts, the longest of any Porter show: New Haven, Boston, Washington, DC, Philadelphia, Pittsburgh, Detroit, Chicago, Des Moines, Indianapolis, Columbus, Buffalo, Hartford. By the time it arrived at the Winter Garden on September 21, 1938, the songs that had words *and* music by Cole Porter amounted to twelve.

You Never Know is more in the tradition of French boulevard comedy than *By Candlelight*. Paris has replaced Vienna as the setting of the lovers' roundelay. Josef the valet has been renamed Gaston (Clifton Webb); the prince is now a baron (Rex O'Malley); the countess, Madame Baltin (Libby Holman), the wife of a cheating entrepreneur; and her maid, formerly Marie, is Mimi (Lupe Velez), who calls herself Maria when pretending to be Madame Baltin while carrying on an affair with Gaston, who is posing as the baron, who is having a rendezvous with Madame Baltin. When the masquerade is over, everyone has a good laugh except Madame Baltin, who is forced to admit that she also took a ride on love's merry-go-round while her husband was off on his own. And what would be a more civilized ending to this *ronde d'amour* than Gaston, Mimi/Maria, the Baron, and

Madame Baltin sitting down to a candlelight supper? "Lord, what fools these mortals be!" (*A Midsummer Night's Dream*, Act 3, 2). Love's folly that reduces mortals to love's fools is a tradition that extends from Shakespeare to Oscar Wilde, Noel Coward, and classic screwball comedy (*Trouble in Paradise, The Shop Around the Corner, Midnight*). Unfortunately, *You Never Know* lacked the wit and incisiveness of Wilde and Coward, and Valez's outrageous behavior toward Holman garnered more attention than the show, which closed after two months.

It was not Porter's best score. One song became a standard, "At Long Last Love," introduced by Clifton Webb, who probably sang it with a kind of ironic detachment, since a probing reading would have been both out of character and out of place. "From Alpha to Omega," a duet for Webb and Valez, was a lesser "You're the Top" ("From Alpha to Omega, / From A to Z, / From Alpha to Omega, / You're made for me").

You Never Know underwent another revision by Paul Lazarus for a production at the Pasadena Playhouse in California that opened on May 26, 1991. Three songs that had been cut from the score, including Porter's own version of "By Candlelight," "I'm Back in Circulation," and "I'm Going In for Love," were restored; four were interpolated: "I Happen to Be in Love" from *Broadway Melody of 1940*, which was unused; "Ridin' High" from *Red, Hot and Blue*; "Let's Not Talk about Love" from *Let's Face It!*; and "Let's Misbehave," which was replaced by "Let's Do It" in *Paris*. Unfortunately, the Pasadena Playhouse production did not lead to a Broadway revival, although Lazarus's revision is available through Samuel French Inc.

ON STAGE: CLEAR ALL WIRES! (1932)

Like *You Never Know*, *Leave It to Me* originated as stage play. Bella and Sam Spewack's *Clear All Wires!* (1932), their third Broadway collaboration, which starred Thomas Mitchell as a likable but unscrupulous reporter who invents when the facts prove dramatically dull. Like their other two efforts, *Clear All Wires!* was not a hit and ran for two months during the 1932–33 season. The Spewacks converted *Clear All Wires!* into a screenplay for MGM, which filmed it in 1933 *sans* exclamation point. The fast-talking Lee Tracy was cast as Buckley Joyce Thomas, the self-aggrandizing correspondent and exponent of fake news long before President Trump made it into a buzz word. The Spewacks, who had been Moscow correspondents for four years, 1922–26, based their play on their own experiences in the Soviet capital. They realized they had to open up the single-set play, in which all three acts took place in a Moscow hotel room, and dramatize incidents that had been narrated in the stage version, resulting in such overplotting that, when the denouement is finally reached, it is rushed and unconvincing. Yet the Spewacks added a great deal of local color to their screenplay, beginning with the opening sequence in Morocco where Thomas is having tea ("Two lumps, please") with the leader of a band of rebels seeking independence from France. Thomas promises to tell the story of their fight against French imperialism. Instead, he files a tale of his capture and mistreatment by the rebels and his eventual rescue by the French Foreign Legion. But that is Thomas's theory of journalism: when the facts lack color, use the typewriter as your palette. He had previously had himself kidnapped—and ransomed—in Paris. Anything for a story that sold papers and himself. Thomas is a precursor of the amoral Chuck Tatum (Kirk Douglas) in Billy Wilder's *The Big Carnival* (1951), who lets a man stay trapped in a cave-in to keep the story fresh so it can grow into a series of articles.

Thomas's publisher at the *Chicago Globe* has a "protégé" by the name of Dolly Winslow (Una Merkel), who calls him "Daddy," although he claims he is only interested in furthering her career as an opera singer—in spite of the fact that she sounds worse than Susan Alexander in *Citizen Kane* (1941). Knowing that Dolly and Thomas had once been an item, the publisher sends Thomas to Moscow to cover the fifteenth anniversary of the Russian Revolution. The unprincipled Thomas takes over the hotel suite of a rival correspondent and has Lefty, his Man Friday (James Gleason), steal his ticket to a military parade. As a result, Thomas is fired for "conduct unbecoming a gentleman." Meanwhile, Dolly arrives in Moscow, hoping to rekindle her romance with Thomas. Sensing trouble, Thomas has Lefty put Dolly on a train to Siberia.

When Thomas cannot get an interview with Stalin or the head of the secret police, he decides to stage an attempted assassination of a prince, dubbed "the last of the Romanovs," although the prince had only a minor connection with the dynasty. The attempt backfires, and Thomas gets grazed in the arm

The incident arouses the suspicions of the secret police, and Lefty and Thomas are confined to the same cell block as a counterrevolutionary, who will admit involvement in the abortive assassination if Thomas tells his story to the world: the next revolution will prove that "communism is not Marxism"—which, ideologically, is true. Buckley is freed, given a raise, and dispatched to China, this time with Kate (Benita Hume), an ace reporter (and his true love), whose commitment to the truth counterbalances his indifference to it. Once in China, Thomas gets himself captured and ransomed again—proving that fake news is always the same, differing only in time, place, and details.

The film is blatantly pre-Code. When Dolly sees Thomas's hotel suite, she complains that the bed is too small, obviously expecting to share it with her ex-lover. The prince, who has married one of Thomas's old flames, admits that theirs is a marriage in name only and offers her to him. Both the play and the film skirt the issue of Soviet totalitarianism, except for their portrayal of the head of the secret police whose ruthlessness is covered over by a veneer of urbanity. Both play and film work as romantic melodrama, with muted political and muffled satiric overtones. The question now arises: could the Spewacks, who converted their play into a film, now turn it into the book of a Cole Porter musical? The answer is "yes," but with a major overhaul.

ON STAGE: *LEAVE IT TO ME* (1938)

In *Clear All Wires!*, Buckley Joyce Thomas controlled the narrative both by the schemes that he concocted and situations that he used to his own advantage. An unregenerate heel is not the kind of leading man that audiences expect in a musical comedy. In *Leave It to Me*, Buckley is now "Buck" Thomas (William Gaxton), a reporter but less of a fabulist than his predecessor. The Spewacks realized that it would be a great idea to reteam Gaxton with Victor Moore, his costar in George Gershwin's Pulitzer Prize-winning musical *Of Thee I Sing* (1931), in which Gaxton played John P. Wintergreen, and Victor Moore, Alexander Throttlebottom, running for president and vice president on the Love ticket—a gimmick expected to provide a distraction from the woes of the Great Depression with its *amor omnia vincit* message (one of the many great songs in the show is "Love Is Sweeping the Country"). Throttlebottom, as portrayed by Moore, is a genial bumbler, whose name nobody can remember but who ascends to the presidency after Wintergreen relinquishes it because he has become the father of twins.

The Spewacks envisioned the reworked *Clear All Wires!* as a political satire that would not lampoon the Supreme Court and the Senate, as did *Of Thee I Sing*, but Stalinist Russia, at which they threw a few darts—none lethally. "Buck" Thomas (Gaxton) would still be a reporter, more of a romantic lead than a Machiavel, who eventually finds his soul mate, as Buckley did in *Clear All Wires!* Moore is a new character, the meek

Alonzo "Stinky" Goodhue. His wife, Leora, was the Red Hot Mama herself, Sophie Tucker, whose outsized persona more than compensated for Moore's undersized one. Together they are Big Mama and Little Daddy.

Stalinist Russia was an odd choice for a 1938 musical. It was more than evident in the 1930s that the Soviet Union had become both xenophobic and antidemocratic. The show trials of 1934 made it clear to all but the politically naïve that Stalin was attempting to rid himself of real or perceived enemies. The famine in Ukraine tragically proved the folly of collective farming. When the Spanish Civil War broke out in 1936, the Soviet Union allied itself with the Loyalists fighting to preserve the republic that had been voted into existence and prevent Spain from falling back into the hands of the army and the Church. Actually, the Soviet Union planned to subvert the Loyalist cause and turn the republic into a Communist state, which, if it succeeded, would have made Spain one of the Soviet Socialist Republics, the first Communist country in Western Europe. The war ended in 1939 with a victory for Franco's Nationalists and thirty-five years of totalitarian rule. Stalin was actually a minor character in *Leave It to Me*, but after the Soviet Union signed a nonaggression pact with Nazi Germany on August 23, 1939, blurring the distinction between communism and fascism, he was written out of the plot.

Soviet-style communism, as opposed to Stalinism, can be the subject of satire, as Charles Brackett, Billy Wilder, and Walter Reisch proved in their brilliant screenplay for Ernst Lubitsch's *Ninotchka* (1939), with Greta Garbo as a committed Communist who addresses a waiter in a Paris bistro as "little father" and orders a meal of raw carrots and beets, prompting the waiter to say in exasperation, "Madame, this is a restaurant, not a meadow." That kind of wit is absent in *Leave It to Me*, which works better as farce than satire.

When reading the Spewacks' book, one cannot help but imagine *Leave It to Me* as a Chaplin comedy, with the Little Tramp blundering his way through Moscow as the United States ambassador to Russia, which is precisely what happens to Alonso "Stinky" Goodhue, who was given the ambassadorship because of his wife's generous contributions to Franklin Roosevelt's presidential campaign. J. H. Brody, the publisher of the paper for which Buck Thomas works, sought the position for himself and dispatches Thomas to Moscow to write a series of articles that will prove Goodhue's incompetence. Instead, they bond when Goodhue confesses that he would do anything to return to Topeka and feast on banana splits and sarsaparilla.

Everything Goodhue does to disgrace himself in the eyes of the Soviets backfires. Instead of being denounced when he extols capitalism, he is praised; instead of being reprimanded for kicking a Nazi dignitary, he is lauded. When he mistakenly shoots a radical instead of a duplicitous prince, as had been planned, he is designated "Comrade Alonzo." Buck finally comes up with a surefire scheme to get Goodhue recalled: advocating a confederation made up of France, Germany, and Russia that would be a microcosmic United States of America on European soil.

The Spewacks managed to transfer two characters from *Clear All Wires!* and their stories to *Leave It to Me*. Kate, the reporter, has been renamed Colette to account for the accent of the Russian-born Tamara Geva, who danced the *Slaughter on Tenth Avenue* ballet with Ray Bolger two seasons earlier in Rodgers and Hart's *On Your Toes* (1936). Dolly Winslow is back, still promising fidelity to her "Daddy," but eager to reconnect with her old flame, Buck, in Moscow. Since there is no Lefty to pack her off to Siberia, Dolly ends up there on her own. And midway in the second act, Mary Martin performed a genteel striptease while letting her hips move to the rumba beat of "My Heart Belongs to Daddy," the precursor of "Always True to You in My Fashion" from *Kiss Me, Kate*—another song about qualified fidelity. Dolly's audience consisted of five Eskimos, one of whom was Gene Kelly, in awe of the creature who arrived at their railroad station in a fur jacket and little else under it. Mary stopped the show, made the cover of *Life*, and attained instant stardom.

Leave it to Me ends with Dolly going back to her "Daddy," and Buck getting fired over Goodhue's proposal to unite three countries with a history of hostility toward each other in an attempt to promote world peace. But this time he does not go off to China. Goodhue has bought a Chicago newspaper and names as executive editor Buck, who immediately starts dictating a letter to Colette. Curtain.

It was neither a great show nor a great score. Apart from "My Heart Belongs to Daddy," another favorite of cabaret performers is "Most Gentlemen Don't Like Love (They Just Like to Kick It Around)," the opening lines of each of the four refrains. It was sung—or rather declaimed—by Sophie Tucker, who described men as irresponsible, unfeeling, and unfaithful. The number is raucous, slangy ("So I know what I'm talking of"—*of* to rhyme with *love*, rather than the more common *about*), and meant to be sung by an expert on the ways of the wayward male.

In his *New York Times* review (November 10, 1938), Brooks Atkinson called "My Heart Belongs to Daddy" "the bawdy ballad of the season," while commending Mary for singing it with "mock innocence." But it was precisely her demure look and sly ingenuousness that made the number titillating. The bawdy ballad—or rather duet—of the season would be in

Porter's next show, *Du Barry Was a Lady* (1939). "But in the Morning, No" is neither titillating nor risqué; it's unapologetically ribald with double entendres that are only meant to be taken one way (breast stroke, third parties, ante up, sell one's seat). Dolly has a roving eye; she may "make a play," "adore his asking for more (finnan haddie, that is)," and "never dream of making the team," but her *heart* belongs to "Daddy."

CHAPTER 10

Porter's Bawdy

Du Barry Was a Lady

ON STAGE: *DU BARRY WAS A LADY* (1939)

A synopsis of Herbert Fields and B. G. DeSylva's book of *Du Barry Was a Lady* would read like an absurdist operetta—were it not for the fact that the Theater of the Absurd had yet to arrive. It might also be called a surreal operetta, except that it never reaches the sublimely giddy heights of surrealistic art. It was simply an attempt to unite a great clown, Bert Lahr, billed first, and a great performer on her way to becoming a Broadway legend, Ethel Merman, in a musical that would showcase what each does best: Lahr, doing burlesque shtick including getting an arrow in his buttocks; Merman, singing, delivering the lyrics with crystalline clarity but here underserved with a trite love song, "Do I Love You?" ("Doesn't one and one make two?"), which is better suited to her romantic partner, who later gets a chance to sing it; "Give Him the OO-LA-LA"—that being the special quality women possess to snare the unsuspecting male; the suggestive "Katie Went to Haiti" near the end of the show; and two duets with Lahr, the eyebrow-raising "But in the Morning, No," and the finale, "Friendship," the musical's best-known song and another tribute to the durability of platonic relationships like "You're the Top," in which loyalty matters more than sex.

Du Barry Was a Lady has never had a Broadway revival, although in 2018 it was modestly staged off Broadway at Theater Row by the now-defunct *Musicals Tonight*, whose noble mission was to preserve the legacy of the American musical. The main reason for its neglect is the plot.

Louis Blore (Lahr), a former men's room attendant at a nightclub and now a sweepstakes winner, is in love with singer May Daly (Merman), who loves the unhappily married Alex Barton (Ronald Graham), whose sister Alice (Betty Grable) is in love with Harry Norton (Charles Walters).

To distract Alex, Charley (Benny Baker), Louis's replacement, convinces Louis to offer Alex a spiked drink, although what that would accomplish is never explained except to send Louis off to dreamland when the glasses get switched. Louis drinks the spiked one, which has him imagining that he is King Louis XV of France; May, Madame La Comtesse du Barry (lower case "d"); Charley, the Dauphin; Alice, La Marquise Alisande de Vernay; Harry Norton, Captain of the King's Guard; and Alex, a poet who composed the title song, in which he declares his love for France and attributes its ruin to Madame du Barry, which brings about a death sentence. Madame du Barry/May is sympathetic to the poet (he is, after all, Alex in eighteenth-century garb) and is vindicated when the chorus proclaims it is Louis who caused the ruin of France, bringing down the curtain on Act 1. Although it is a great ensemble with recitative, Alex singing "Do I Love You?"—meaning France—and a climactic chorus, it does not make much narrative sense; except for the final scene, the second act takes place at Versailles, where King Louis continues to pursue Madame du Barry, who will never become his mistress, unlike the historical Comptesse du Barry, who was Louis XV's third.

Now the significance of the fantasy, which takes up most of the musical, becomes clear: even if Louis Blore were Louis XV, true love would still elude him. Madame du Barry is no more destined to be the consort of a former men's room attendant parading around in a powdered wig, coat, waistcoat, and breeches than May Daly is to be the wife of Louis Blore. The historical Madame du Barry was Louis XV's third and last titled mistress, who was accused of treason during the Reign of Terror and guillotined in 1793. Louis XV died of smallpox the following year. The true story of Louis XV and Madame du Barry is the stuff of opera, not musical comedy.

In the final scene, we are back at the club. The drug has worn off, and Louis realizes that May is meant for Alex, to whom he gives the rest of the sweepstakes money for a divorce. He and May will remain friends, which they announce in the exuberant duet, "Friendship."

Another duet that has its highs and low—and Porter could reach some lows that border on the gross—is "Well, Did You Evah!," refitted for Bing Crosby and Frank Sinatra in *High Society* (MGM, 1956), who were only given the choicest lyrics which, in their freewheeling and slightly boozy delivery, became the film's highlight. In *Du Barry Was a Lady*, the duet is sung by Betty Grable and Charles Walters as their fantasy figures, the Marquise and the Captain of the King's Guard, who mock the vacuous "have you heard . . .?" conversation of the court. Some of the "have you heards?" are genuinely witty, but for every "have you heard that Mimsie

Starr / just got pinched in the Astor Bar?" there is "have you heard that Captain Craig / breeds termites in his wooden leg?" In a duet with four refrains, every couplet cannot be worthy of Alexander Pope. But audiences and critics loved it. Betty Grable made the cover of *Life* and went off to Twentieth Century-Fox, where she reigned as the studio's leading box-office attraction of the 1940s. Charles Walters also went West to MGM, where he became a major director of musicals.

One can only speculate about what prompted Fields and DeSylva to write a book for a musical, the bulk of which would be a fantasy with the main characters transported to the court of Louis XV of France. Possibly their inspiration was the popular but commercially unsuccessful *Marie Antoinette* (MGM, 1938) with Norma Shearer as the ill-starred Queen, John Barrymore as Louis XV, and Gladys George as Madame du Barry. Perhaps they thought theatergoers were ready for a parody of high bourgeois costume drama.

More likely it had to do with another MGM film that appeared in the same year as *Du Barry Was a Lady*. From the outset, *Du Barry Was a Lady* was planned as a vehicle for Bert Lahr, with Ethel Merman as costar—their names above the title, hers after his. Lahr was a late addition to the cast of *The Wizard of Oz*. It was lyricist E. Y. "Yip" Harburg's idea to bring Lahr to producer Arthur Freed's attention, convinced that he would be perfect for the Cowardly Lion. On July 25, 1938, Lahr joined the cast, although production did not begin until October 13. Lahr worked on the film for six months.

In July 1938, when Fields and DeSylva learned that Lahr had been cast as the Cowardly Lion, they must have conceived the idea of a plot similar to that of *The Wizard of Oz*, in which characters in the Kansas sequence—except Aunt Em and Uncle Henry—assume other identities when the action shifts to Oz. The misanthropic Miss Gulch (Margaret Hamilton) becomes the Wicked Witch of the West; the farmhands Hank (Ray Bolger), Hickory (Jack Haley), and Zeke (Bert Lahr), the Scarecrow, the Tin Man, and the Cowardly Lion, respectively; and Professor Marvel (Frank Morgan), the Wizard. It hardly seems coincidental that, just as a cyclone brings Dorothy to Oz, where five characters we have already met appear in other guises, a spiked drink in *Du Barry Was a Lady* turns Louis Blore into Louis XV and whisks five characters back in time to his court. *The Wizard of Oz* opened in New York on August 17, 1939, two days after its West Coast premiere. *Du Barry Was a Lady* opened on December 6, 1939. Bert Lahr fans could have seen him as a lion and a king in the same year; it is, however, as the former that he is better known.

When *The Wizard of Oz* opened in New York, the world was two weeks away from global war. When *Du Barry Was a Lady* opened at the

Forty-sixth Street Theatre (now the Richard Rodgers), World War II was in its second month; the show was still running six months later when, on June 21, 1940, France surrendered to Nazi Germany.

Du Barry Was a Lady had a healthy run of 408 performances. In his *New York Times* review (December 7, 1939), Brooks Atkinson expressed his displeasure with Fields and DeSylva's book that reached "a dead level of obscenity that does not yield much mirth," adding that "the performers supply more pleasure than the authors and composer." Although "But in the Morning, No" is designed to provoke a leer rather than a smile, it does possess a certain amount of wit—not in the lyrics, but in the music. The duet is scored in ¾ time as a minuet, creating a disparity between the stateliness of the musical form and the bawdiness of the lyrics. If there is such a thing as a raunchy minuet, "But in the Morning, No" comes close.

ON SCREEN: *DU BARRY WAS A LADY* (MGM, 1942)

MGM was the studio that produced most of the screen versions of Porter's musicals: *Panama Hattie* (1942), *Du Barry Was a Lady* (1943), *Kiss Me, Kate* (1953, without the comma), and *Silk Stockings*, the last two being the most faithful to the originals. *Panama Hattie* and *Du Barry Was a Lady* were cut to fit the screen image of Red Skelton, who inherited Bert Lahr's role. Skelton was one of the great clowns of film; he also made a successful transition to television, where he had his own show from 1953 to 1971. His background in vaudeville made him a master of anything-for-a-laugh slapstick. He did not consider it beneath his dignity to distort his face, contort his body, or take pratfalls. He knew how to use his push button eyes for comic effect; when he did a double take, they looked as if they might drop out of their sockets. Like Lahr, he had the kind of face that could elicit a smile before he uttered a word; like Lahr's, Skelton's face was malleable, capable of looking goofy, puzzled, tender, or even poignant.

The credits are deceiving: "Based on the play [*sic*] produced by Buddy DeSylva. Written by DeSylva and Herbert Fields. Words and Music by Cole Porter." "Book" would have been more accurate, but no matter. Yes, Cole Porter did write the words and music for the *stage* production, but only three songs from it were used: "Do I Love You?," "Friendship," and a laundered "Katie Went to Haiti," which had no relation to the plot but was a specialty number performed by the Pied Pipers with Tommy Dorsey and His Orchestra. MGM was primarily interested in the book, particularly the dream episode, which would allow Skelton to romp around in eighteenth-century finery, chase Madame Du Barry around her boudoir, get hit in the backside with an arrow, engage in a sword fight, and awaken before he is killed.

MGM's handling of *Du Barry Was a Lady* was not uncommon. Once a studio purchased the rights to a musical, it became a property, one of the most familiar terms in the Hollywood lexicon; the transfer of ownership allowed the studio to do with the property what it wished. MGM bought the rights to George and Ira Gershwin's *Lady, Be Good!* (1923), changed the punctuation to *Lady Be Good* (1941), discarded the old plot about a brother and sister in favor of one about a songwriting couple, and retained two Gershwin songs; the others were provided by Nacio Herb Brown, Ralph Freed, and Roger Edens. Nor was MGM the only studio to purchase a musical purely for the book or a few songs—or even no songs. Twentieth Century-Fox bought Porter's *Something for the Boys*, tweaked the book, kept the title song, ditched the rest, and released the movie version in 1944. Universal-International did the same with Porter's *Mexican Hayride* (1944), which was made into a 1948 Abbott and Costello comedy. Since neither comedian was a singer, the entire score was scrapped.

Screenwriter Irving Brecher began with the trio of Louis (Skelton), May (Lucille Ball), and Alec (Gene Kelly), and changed the characterizations. Louis advanced from men's room to coat room attendant. May was still the main attraction at the Club Petite, as evident from the opening number, which was a burlesque routine for the supper club elite. Ball (courtesy of voice double Martha Mears) and the chorus in abbreviated eighteenth-century dress designed for ample leg exposure and wearing puffed wigs of various colors that looked like cotton candy sang the title song by Roger Edens and Ralph Freed. Brecher also hardened her character; May is wary of marrying for love as her parents did, only to spend their lives in poverty. She plans to marry for money; then she meets Alec, no longer a married man but a single songwriter, who has composed a love song for her, which happens to be Porter's "Do I Love You?" Kelly was an extraordinarily versatile dancer but not much of a singer. Still, he could spin off the lyrics softly and move up to a wispy falsetto without crooning.

The plot then goes on break so the floor show can continue. The Three Oxford Boys cleverly mimic the distinctive—and now bygone—sounds of the bands led by Kay Kyser, Fred Waring, Harry James, and Guy Lombardo, all as a lead in to the real thing: Tommy Dorsey and His Orchestra performing Dorsey's theme song, "I'm Getting Sentimental Over You." The next attraction is Kelly (Alec apparently is a performer as well as a songwriter), who dashes on to an onyx-black circular platform and taps away to "Do I Love You?," which bursts into swing for the frenetic windup. (Apparently,

"Do I Love You?" was orchestrated in record time.) After half an hour of what seems like a list of bulleted plot points, all we know is that Louis is secretly in love with May, who is truly in love with Alec, who lacks the bank account of his rival, a millionaire who frequents the club regularly because of May.

Brecher knew that the dream sequence could not constitute the bulk of the film. On Broadway, it began in the third scene of the first act and continued throughout almost all of the second, becoming the musical's centerpiece. There were also seven numbers in the sequence that had already been eliminated, leaving a gap in the middle of the fantasy that would not be filled with seven new songs. Therefore, the Louis-May-Alec plot had to go on for a longer time than it did on stage—for an hour, in fact. As in the original, Louis wins the Irish sweepstakes, which makes him May's ideal kind of husband. At this point, one can appreciate the way Brecher made May into a woman who would choose money over love. Now she has to decide between Louis and Alec. To add another twist to an already knotted plot, Louis informs the press that he will be marrying "Du Barry," indicating that he has identified May with her character, which makes the fantasy more plausible than it was in the original. If May is Madame Du Barry, Louis must be Louis XV. Brecher kept the drugged drink switch, which is still far-fetched. A concussion would have been more natural, or even an ordinary dream. He was also true to Fields and DeSylva's book, in which characters from the main plot become eighteenth-century figures in the fantasy. In the film, the fantasy goes on for half an hour, which is enough for the subplot of a musical without any memorable musical moments. What redeems the silliness is the hilarious duet between Skelton and Ball, Burton Lane and Ralph Freed's "Madame, I Love Your Crepes Suzettes," in which Louis informs Du Barry that he doesn't "mean to be rude" but is "not in the mood for food." What he is in the mood for becomes evident when he chases her around the bedroom.

When Louis (now Louis Blore) regains consciousness, he realizes that May and Alec are meant for each other and offers them $10,000 toward their wedding—big bucks in 1943. May, no longer a fortune-hunter, turns down his gift. Louis, who had earlier gone on a spending spree, discovers he owes the IRS some $80,000. So it's back to the coatroom, but not before the finale, in which the principals sing "Friendship," originally a duet for Lahr and Merman. If one listens closely, it is evident that this time Ball is doing her own singing, sounding just like Lucy Ricardo.

CHAPTER 11

The War Years

Panama Hattie, Let's Face It!, Something for the Boys, and Mexican Hayride

Just as Herbert Fields and B. G. DeSylva tailored *Du Barry Was a Lady* to Bert Lahr's persona, they did the same for Ethel Merman in *Panama Hattie*. By then, the Ethel Merman character was a gal pal eager to change her status to fiancée who must

- help the man to whom she is attracted win the woman he loves who is engaged to a British Lord whom she is supposed to entice but for whom she eventually falls (Reno Sweeney in *Anything Goes*);
- help a lawyer with whom she is in love locate his childhood sweetheart, only to discover that the sweetheart has grown up to be a lady of questionable virtue ("Nails" O'Reilly Duquense in *Red, Hot and Blue*); and;
- find a way to deal with her love for an unhappily married man who cannot afford a divorce (May Daly in *Du Barry Was a Lady*).

In none of these musicals did her character guide the plot toward its resolution. In *Anything Goes*, it is a group effort with Reno, "Moonface," and Billy dressing up as Asians to make it possible for Billy to pair off with Hope; and Reno with Lord Evelyn. In *Red, Hot and Blue*, Bob Hale discovers that his childhood dream girl is little more than a hooker, sending him back to "Nails," his personal welcome mat. In *Du Barry Was a Lady*, it is Louis's generosity that enables Alec to get a divorce so he can marry May. The Merman figure exists to serve, not to be served. Vocally, she can blast any male out of the room. Dramatically, she either does for men what they cannot do for themselves or she depends on men to do for her what she cannot do for herself. In either case, she is not her own woman.

Ever since Lindsay and Crouse gave Reno the surname "Sweeney," the Merman character became Irish: "Nails" Duquense (formerly O'Reilly) in *Red, Hot and Blue*; May Daly in *Du Barry Was a Lady*; and in *Panama Hattie*, Hattie Maloney. Merman herself was not Irish. Her father, Edward Zimmerman, was German; her mother, Agnes Gardner Zimmerman, Scots. Contrary to popular belief, Merman was not Jewish; she was raised as an Episcopalian and was often seen at services at St. Bartholomew's on Park Avenue and Fiftieth Street in New York. Possibly the writers felt that an Irish Merman would suggest the down-to-earth quality of a dame who was really a lady at heart.

ON STAGE: *PANAMA HATTIE* (1940)

In *Panama Hattie* (1940), Merman is a club owner and entertainer in the Panama Canal Zone, engaged to a captain in the US navy—Nick Bullett, a divorced man from a distinguished Philadelphia family with custody of his eight-year-old daughter, Geraldine, whom Hattie must win over. The thinking behind her characterization is sadly patriarchal. Hattie is a successful businesswoman in a profession that would not pass muster with bluebloods to whom she would not appear a "lady." A club owner-performer is *déclassé*.

The setup is clear: upper-class male, lower middle-class female who has to impress her fiancé's daughter—not the other way around. Hattie's idea of a lady is a woman (over)dressed to the nines. The *Panama Hattie* Playbill for the week of September 22, 1941, shows Merman as Hattie in her ladylike regalia. She is in virginal white: tight-wasted jacket with lace-trimmed bodice and sleeves; white skirt discreetly hemmed; white shoes with exposed toe and white ankle ties; a choker of oversized fake pearls; a white hat with an avian motif that looks as if a dove had landed on it; and a white parasol that she uses as a walking stick. The daughter sees her and laughs. Failure no. 1.

Hattie's rival for her fiancée's affections is Leila Tree, an admiral's daughter, who suggests to the unsuspecting Hattie at a banquet that she present the admiral with a flower-filled cup. The flowers trigger the admiral's allergy, and the banquet is a fiasco. Failure no. 2.

Hattie, mocked by her potential stepdaughter and considered persona non grata after the cup incident, must somehow redeem herself. Fields and DeSylva have been following the familiar protagonist-up-the-tree template, which they modified for a two-act musical: get protagonist up the tree in Act 1; keep protagonist there in Act 2; and bring the protagonist down in Act 3. The debacle with the daughter sent Hattie up the tree; the cup incident kept her there; now it is time for her descent.

In 1940, the Panama Canal was considered a potential target for saboteurs intent on disrupting shipping. Leila Tree has a friend, Mildred, who is in league with saboteurs planning to set off a bomb in the control room. Hattie exposes the plot, returns to the admiral's good graces, and is free to marry Nick and be a loving stepmother to his brat. One would think that, for once, the Merman character, effected the resolution. Not exactly. To avoid suspicion, Mildred was planning to have Geraldine leave the package with the bomb on her father's desk. Hattie overhears the plot and disposes of the bomb herself. It was only by chance that she heard of the plot, but that's enough for a triumphant denouement.

The writers may have conceived the idea of the bomb from Alfred Hitchcock's *Sabotage* (1936), in which a terrorist sends his nephew across London to deliver a package containing a time bomb. The boy encounters delays, and the bomb goes off on a bus, killing him. Obviously, the writers had no intention of having Geraldine suffer a similar fate, but the idea of recruiting a child for such a nefarious enterprise is still unnerving. But this is musical comedy, not Hitchcock's world in which nothing is what it seems.

Fields and DeSylva seemed to be prescient. In 1943, Germany embarked on Operation Pelikan, a detailed scenario for bombing the canal. But word leaked out, and Operation Pelikan was abandoned. Fields and DeSylva make no mention of the saboteurs' politics—or Mildred's, for that matter. Obviously they were fifth columnists, probably in league with Nazi Germany. The year before *Panama Hattie* premiered, Warner Bros. released *Confessions of a Nazi Spy* (1939), which dramatized the activities of German spies operating out of the Yorkville section of Manhattan. Fields and DeSylva did not develop the sabotage plot point, assuming that only theatergoers concerned about domestic espionage would care about the politics of the would-be saboteurs.

Merman had three good songs, one of which, "Let's Be Buddies," Hattie's attempt to bond with Geraldine, would have been embarrassing had it not been for Merman's deeply sincere rendition, available on a disk that also includes twelve songs from *Call Me Madam*. In the duet, recorded in December 1940 with Joan Carroll, who originated the role of Geraldine, Merman adopts the kind of voice that adults use with when talking to youngsters—enunciating with exaggerated clarity. She has to ask Geraldine if she could try to "go for this moll," referring to herself by using the slang expression for a female lowlife, which Hattie certainly is not. Hattie tries desperately to be Geraldine's "buddy." Hattie to Geraldine: "Then would you let me get you a cute little dog?" Reply: "Would you make it a bear?"

Another self-deflating number is "I've Got My Health," in which Hattie admits she's a loser at heart but "I've still got my health so what do I care?" But the lyrics belie the characterization. Hattie is not a failure at what matters most: success in the entertainment business, something not easily achieved. But like many successful women, she would prefer to be a success in marriage—at least, that how the writers have defined her.

After the disastrous banquet, Hattie, who had given up drinking, is about to go off the wagon, explaining in the verse of "Make It Another Old-Fashioned, Please" that life has become so difficult that it calls for a drink. Porter wrote the number for Merman, not her character. Hattie would never sing of living high in a castle that was struck by lightning or owning a treasure that has turned to trash; these are metaphors for dashed hopes. She also sings it early in Act 2, not in a bar but alone in the Sant'-Ana Plaza in Panama City; in fact, the only scene that takes place in a bar is the second scene of Act 1.

"Make It Another Old-Fashioned, Please" is a monologue in which a member of life's "disillusioned crew"—and that would include Hattie—is seated at a bar, preparing to drink away her disappointments. The song has two refrains, the first six lines of each being identical. She asks the waiter for another old-fashioned, repeating the request—the repetition indicating her need to numb the pain. When she's ready for the third round, she doesn't ask for the traditional cocktail: no cherry, orange, or bitters: "Just make it a straight rye!" On the recording, Merman renders the lyrics with clear-eyed honesty, neither engaging in self-pity nor casting blame, but accepting a state of hopelessness by ordering a cocktail without the garnish that would have made it more attractive—straight rye. Stoicism served neat.

Panama Hattie enjoyed a run of 501 performances during the 1940–41 season. A one-hour version was telecast live on CBS-TV's *Best of Broadway*, November 16, 1954, with Merman as Hattie and Ray Middleton, her costar from *Annie Get Your Gun* (1946), as Nick Bullett. The score had been whittled down to three of the original songs: "Fresh as a Daisy," "Let's Be Buddies," and "Make It Another Old-Fashioned, Please." "Ridin' High," which was reprised at the end, and "I Love You" were interpolated from *Red, Hot and Blue* and *Mexican Hayride*, respectively. The telecast was the closest *Panama Hattie* ever came to a revival. Espionage in the Panama Canal Zone was no longer a relevant plot point.

ON SCREEN: *PANAMA HATTIE* (MGM, 1942)

It was an entirely different situation in the fall of 1942 when the film version of *Panama Hattie* was released. The canal was vulnerable, along with the West Coast. The United States officially entered World War II the day after the bombing of Pearl Harbor on December 7, 1941. *Panama Hattie* had been filmed between July 15 and October 3, 1941.

After a discouraging preview in November 1941, the studio deferred the film's release until certain scenes could be reshot and new ones added, one of which was Lena Horne singing "Just One of Those Things" from *Jubilee*, which added a touch of class to what turned out to be a pedestrian film. The attack on Pearl Harbor required further changes that were made between April 6 and May 25, 1942, including a finale with an oblique allusion to the war as the principals vowed revenge on "The Son of a Gun Who Picks on Uncle Sam," probably the most anemic song of retaliation ever written.

Jack Macgowan and Wilkie Mahonie reworked Fields and DeSylva's book aa a vehicle for Red Skelton, known as Red in the film, a totally new character, who, along with two other fine comics, "Rags" Ragland and Ben Blue—"Rags" and "Rowdy," respectively—are sailors stationed in the Panama Canal Zone. The three R's do not so much resemble the Three Stooges as the Keystone Cops, bumbling their way through the film and straight into the denouement where they expose a spy ring bent on sabotage. MGM hoped that their antics would deflect attention from the fact that *Panama Hattie* was a mediocre film that ran a mere eighty minutes, an indicator of the studio's lack of faith in it. Surprisingly, *Panama Hattie* turned a profit. Why not? It starred two popular stars, Red Skelton, billed first, and Ann Sothern as Hattie—quite a change from the original which had Ethel Merman's name above the title.

The *Panama Hattie* book was middling to begin with, but the screenplay makes Hattie a secondary character who gets to sing only two numbers, "I've Still Got My Health" and "Let's Be Buddies." Only three numbers from the score were used, the third being "Fresh as a Daisy" sung by Virginia O'Brien of the expressionless face, but here more animated than usual in keeping with the lyrics. O'Brien, who played Hattie's friend, Flo Foster, also had another solo, the supremely goofy "Did I Get Stinkin' at the Savoy" by "Yip" Harburg (lyrics) and Walter Donaldson (music), which added nothing to the film except another opportunity for O'Brien to display her knack for deadpan singing. Sothern's rendition of "Make It Another Old-Fashioned, Please" was filmed but discarded, perhaps because the studio thought it would send the wrong message to recovering alcoholics.

Since the writers made Hattie a singer at Phil's Paradise and no longer a cafe owner, she is just like the entertainer Maisie Revier, whom Sothern played in MGM's Maisie series (1939–47). In fact, *Panama Hattie* could have been retitled *Panama Maisie* with the same plot points, some taken from the Fields-DeSylva book and others created by the screenwriters. Hattie is still in love with a man in the military; he is no longer a captain in the navy but a soldier (Dan Dailey, then Dan Dailey Jr.), a divorced man from a socially prominent family with custody of his eight-year-old daughter, Geraldine (Jackie Horner).

As in the original, Geraldine laughs at Hattie's idea of ladylike attire, requiring Hattie to achieve some kind of rapport with her, which Sothern does tenderly in "Let's Be Buddies." The character of Leila Tree (Marsha Hunt) is also a carryover as Hattie's rival. The sabotage subplot was retained but with a significant change. The spies' names are vaguely Germanic: Lucas Kefler and two workers at Phil's Paradise, Bruno and Hans, who are planning to set off an explosion in a nearby house. The three R's learn of the plan and create mayhem in the house, which they believe is haunted. They collide with each other in the dark, knock over furniture, and manage to get out of the house before it goes up in flames. The spies are apprehended, the three R's are hailed as heroes, Maisie gets her soldier, and Leila Tree may get Red if she can put up with his antics. The closest *Panama Hattie* came to acknowledging the existence of a global war was Red's offering to show Leila where Japan once was. Watching *Panama Hattie* eight decades after the bombing of Hiroshima on August 6, 1945, makes Skelton's offer eerily prophetic.

ON STAGE: *LET'S FACE IT!* (1941)

It all begin when Vinton Freedley, who had produced *Red, Hot and Blue*, read a story in *Variety* about some middle-aged women showing their patriotism by inviting army privates to their homes for the weekend and seeing them off to their base on Monday morning. The subject matter was timely; the Selective Service Act was passed on September 16, 1940, and the military draft went into effect a month later. Hollywood found comic potential in the draft with such films as *You're in the Army Now* and *Caught in the Draft* (both 1941). Freedley then remembered Russell Medcraft and Norma Mitchell's hit comedy, *Cradle Snatchers* (1925), which ran for 478 performances and starred Mary Boland as a suspicious wife, who, along with two other women with philandering husbands, enlist the services of three collegians (one of whom was played by a young Humphrey Bogart) to behave as if they were their lovers at a party. Monogamy triumphs, the husbands swear off chasing flappers, and all is forgiven—for the moment. The play became a film two years later under the same title, directed by Howard Hawks with Louise Fazenda in the Mary Boland role.

Shortly after reading the *Variety* piece, Freedly was approached by Danny Kaye's agent. Kurt Weill and Moss Hart's *Lady in the Dark* (1941)—in which Kaye had a featured role, wowing audiences with "Tchaikovsky," a tongue-twister that required him to toss off the names of fifty Russian composers at break neck speed—was on summer hiatus. Kaye was interested in a starring vehicle, not one in which he would be billed under the title, as he was in *Lady in the Dark*, with Gertrude Lawrence's name above it. Did Freedley have anything?

Freedley immediately thought of a book for a musical in which the Jazz Age matrons of *Cradle Snatchers* would be transported to a 1941 Long Island health farm where they would not open their home to three recruits for a relaxing weekend but to three privates from the fictitious Camp Roosevelt whom they will pay to act as romantic escorts in retaliation for their husbands' escapades, which are allegedly fishing trips. The less-than-merry wives of South Hampton are Maggie Watson (Eve Arden, whose understudy was Carol Channing), Cornelia Abigail Pidgeon (Edith Meiser), and Nancy Collister (Vivian Vance, later Ethel Mertz in *I Love Lucy*); the privates, Jerry Walker (Danny Kaye), Frankie Burns (Benny Baker), and Eddie Hilliard (Jack Williams). Herbert and Dorothy Fields, who coauthored the book, changed the invitation to a financial arrangement, which Jerry accepts because he needs money to marry his fiancée, Winnie Potter (Mary Jane Walsh). When Winnie learns about the arrangement, she and the girlfriends of Frankie and Eddie show up at Maggie's summer house, creating complication no. 1: three wives, three privates, and their girlfriends, who plan to make their beaux jealous by feigning interest in older men, who (complication no. 2) turn up in Act 2 as the three husbands, this time having actually gone fishing. Recriminations (in song), explanations, apologies, amends. Finale. Curtain.

The plot was neatly triadic: three wives and their husbands, three soldiers, three girlfriends. The book was topical, not just with army privates as characters but also contemporary after the bombing of Pearl Harbor on December 7, 1941, which occurred a little more than a month after *Let's Face It!* premiered on October 29. Audiences were treated to a show that was set in the twilight of isolationism that they could relive for two-and-a-half hours before facing the reality of life in wartime. *Let's Face It!* was not a major musical, but it arrived at the right time and had the right star, which explains its phenomenal run of 547 performances—the longest of any Porter musical up to that point, soon to be topped by *Kiss Me, Kate* (1,077).

The score was another matter. None of the songs became popular, although "Let's Not Talk about Love" crops up occasionally in a cabaret act. There were two types of songs in *Let's Face It!*: those that either had a vague connection to the plot or to a character. Danny Kaye's specialty numbers with their bodily contortions and verbal pyrotechnics were in a class by themselves.

The women who live on the health farm appear to be avid readers of physical fitness guru Bernarr McFadden, who touted the curative powers of milk. Thus the opening number, "Milk, Milk, Milk," would have resonated with 1940s audiences, but would be meaningless today and even controversial. "Farming" is also tangential to the plot, mocking celebrities who have forsaken the city for the country like the three health farm matrons. Porter couldn't resist the urge to use "gay" in the vernacular: "Don't inquire of George Raft / Why his cow has never calfed / George's bull is beautiful but he's gay." Porter knew how far he would go with "gay," so he has Fred Astaire raising **a hare** who's **gray**. Porter had written wittier list songs, but "Farming" was suited to Kaye's ability to sing staccato without garbling the lyrics.

The love songs are as character-related as they can be in a musical in which characterization is subordinate to story and star. Winnie is smitten with Jerry ("Jerry, My Soldier Boy") and Jerry with her ("Ev'rything I Love"). Originally, the first verse and refrain of "Let's Not Talk about Love" were to have been sung by Arden; the second and third, by Kaye. Arden/Maggie wanted to talk about love ("My dear, let's talk about love"). In the second and third, Kaye suggests other topics, each refrain ending with "but let's not talk about love." Sylvia Fine, Kaye's composer-lyricist wife, decreed otherwise. The first verse-refrain would be dropped, and the number would be a solo. Porter conceded, but it never became a showstopper. The real showstopper appeared near the end of the show and was not written by Porter. It was "Melody in 4-F" by Fine and Max Liebman. Both numbers were intended to illustrate Kaye's versatility—"Let's Not Talk about Love," of his ability to sing a patter song with perfect enunciation; "Melody in 4-F," of his ability to tell a story combining pantomime, nonverbal sounds, and a scattering of words.

"Let's Not Talk about Love" begins casually with Jerry admitting that while women expect men to talk about love, he would prefer other topics. Kaye (forget the character) then went into double time, enumerating his preferences with a riveter's precision. In the second refrain, he brings up a subject that would have unnerved some members of the audience, but Kaye was delivering the lyrics at such a pace that the couplet whizzed by like all the others: "Let's heap some hot profanities on Hitler's inhumanities / Let's argue if insanity's the cause of his inanities." This is the old Porter, the master of internal rhyme, but so anxious to achieve it that he creates a weak balance between inhumanities and inanities. Inhumanity is not inane.

"Melody in 4-F" is a tour de force, with Kaye using his body as narrator and his voice as accompanist, with a largely wordless vocabulary of syllabified nonsense performed in the style of a skat singer carried away while improvising. "Melody in 4-F" traces the stages a draftee undergoes from the time he receives his Selective Service questionnaire in the mail to his physical, at which he implies he is unfit for service, calling attention to his flat feet and other bodily parts (Kaye even spread his legs and flapped his arms between them, suggesting genital impairment), only to hear the verdict: I-A. Kaye's performance of "Melody in 4-F" at an army base can be seen on YouTube. He repeated the number in his movie debut, *Up in Arms* (1944), where it was amped up to the point of slapstick in overdrive. When José Ferrer took over the role, with a substantial drop in attendance, the number disappeared from the score. Fine only intended it for her husband—and no one else.

"Melody in 4-F" reflected the attitude men were supposed to take toward the draft: a necessary interruption of plans that only the craven would try to avoid. On the home front, a 4-F classification was a stigma, and superpatriots would often confront a young man in civilian garb and ask why he is not in uniform. The YouTube clip of Kaye's performance was loudly applauded by the servicemen whose beaming faces made it clear that they were delighted that the draft dodger who hoped for a 4-F was classified 1-A

ON SCREEN: *LET'S FACE IT* (PARAMOUNT, 1943)

The *Let's Face It* credits are woefully misleading: "Based on the musical play by Dorothy and Herbert Fields" and "Songs by Cole Porter."

The singular "Song by" would have been more accurate, although Paramount was covering itself and protecting its investment by incorporating fragments of three other songs: "The Milk Song," "Let's Face It," and "Let's Not Talk About Love." Only the latter had any to claim authenticity; the others, with the exception of "Let's Face It," sung by army recruits, were the equivalent of incidental music. Paramount was more interested in

Jule Styne's song stylings, which came closer to what wartime audiences expected of a Bob Hope movie: just the basics, no frills.

When Betty Hutton launched into "Let's Not Talk About Love," the only song that survived Paramount's evisceration of a score that was never much to begin with, it may have seemed like an homage to the star, Bob Hope. Hutton is pleading with her companion to discuss any topic other than love, even "Paramount minus Bob Hope." Actually, the song came straight from the score, which Hutton delivered in a state of frenzied exasperation bordering on exhaustion. The sobering reference to "Hitler's inhumanities" was inserted between astrology and mythology as if madness and mythology were identical—which they were in Hitler's mind. What is the Master Race other than the Aryan myth of white supremacy? But Paramount was not interested in parsing Porter's lyrics. Hutton needed a number, and "Let's Not Talk About Love" served the purpose. What mattered was the self-referential homage to Bob Hope. That the studio seized the opportunity to celebrate Hope was more of an act of quiet desperation than attempt to capitalize on a persona that needed no amplification. It was not Hope's persona that needed burnishing; it was the picture.

Danny Kaye's dexterity made the score seem livelier than it actually was. Bob Hope was at a disadvantage. Hutton was given the only song that made the cut, leaving Hope with a string of one-liners until the plot reclaimed his attention. Sample: Hope, on his way to a farm for the calorically challenged (aka, "fat farm," where his fiancée works), says, "How come they have so much when butcher shops have so little?" The line might have gotten a laugh when food rationing was imposed during World War II, but is meaningless today. Army buddy to Hope: "For you, I'd kiss a cow." Hope to buddy, knowing they will be entertaining women with delinquent husbands: "You may have to."

Paramount was taking no chances with a plot that skirted adultery with husbands ogling nubile females and their wives attempting to beat them at their own game. Hope is only interested in getting extra money to pay for his wedding, and his buddies prefer their girlfriends to the matrons of South Hampton. Of the three, only Eve Arden, who costarred with Kaye in the original, might have attracted attention.

Let's Face It (no exclamation point) threatens to light up the sky, but the fireworks never arrive. Instead, Hope, seeing his commanding officer at a nightclub, feigns amnesia, announces the presence of saboteurs, and escapes in a boat that gets caught on the periscope of a Nazi submarine. It is impossible to imagine someone as inept as Hope steering the plot toward its climax after crashing through the wall of his barracks, yet he succeeds in directing the crew of the Nazi submarine to shore where they are apprehended. Hope and Hutton marry, and baby makes three.

Let's Face It is the weakest of any Porter musical. Audiences may have laughed their way through Hope's shtick and perhaps some wondered what was so amusing about foolish wives and their self-deluding husbands when a war was raging in the South Pacific.

ON STAGE: SOMETHING FOR THE BOYS (1943)

Something for the Boys was Merman's last Cole Porter musical. It also added the final touch to the Merman character that had been evolving since *Anything Goes*. Henceforth, the shows would be fitted to Merman the artist, not to the persona that had been created for her. In her Cole Porter musicals, Merman played a one-man woman who (a) has to come to the aid of someone she loves but who loves another (Reno in *Anything Goes*, "Nails" in *Red, Hot and Blue*); (b) is in love with a married man (*Du Barry Was a Lady*); or (c) must compete with a rival by performing an action that will attest to her worthiness (Hattie in *Panama Hattie*).

Since Merman was in love with naval officer in *Panama Hattie*, Herbert and Dorothy Fields switched the love interest to an army sergeant in *Something for the Boys*. And since her rival was an admiral's daughter in *Panama Hattie*, she now has to contend with a senator's daughter. What differentiates the Merman character in *Something for the Boys* from the other iterations is a sliver of carborundum embedded like a filling in her tooth that enables her to receive messages, making the denouement the oddest in musical comedy.

The writers cleverly provided the pre-curtain exposition in what was really a three-scene prologue, not designated as such, but only as "Announcement of Inheritance"—the heirs being three cousins with the surname of "Hart," whose Uncle Lou has left each of them a third of a 4,000-acre Texas ranch. In scene one, a lawyer informs Chicquita Hart (Paula Lawrence), an exotic dancer in a Kansas City club, of her share; in scene two, which takes place in New York at Sixth Avenue and Fiftieth Street, the lawyer informs Harry Hart (Allen Jenkins), a former carnival barker and now street vendor, of his; and finally at a Newark defense plant, he breaks the news to welder Blossom Hart (Ethel Merman), who makes her first appearance in overalls, which was certainly the most proletarian outfit Merman ever wore on stage.

The cousins meet for the first time at the ranch and discover that what was once a mansion is in a state of deferred maintenance. Blossom, who had been in show business before joining the sisterhood of Rosie the Riveter, wants to convert it into a boarding house for the wives of the soldiers stationed at a nearby base—her cue to break into the title song. The soldiers are delighted, especially an unmarried sergeant (Bill Johnson) who would prefer to change his status after meeting Blossom. Complication no. 1: he is unofficially engaged to a senator's daughter, who, when she senses competition in Blossom, spreads the rumor that the boarding house is really a brothel. Complication no. 2: Blossom discovers that she can pick up radio signals from the carborundum that got lodged in her tooth, presumably while welding. Where, one wonders, is the carborundum plot point headed? Answer: a disabled plane sends out a distress signal which Blossom's transmitter tooth picks up, making it possible for it to land safely. As in *Panama Hattie*, Blossom saves the day, gets her sergeant, and bests her rival, who has found herself another GI to beguile.

The Fields' book was either clever or hokey, depending on how plausible one finds a plot resolved by carborundum. None of the songs became hits, and yet the show ran for a year because, like *Let's Face It!*, it arrived at the right time, opening on January 4, 1943, a little more than a year after Pearl Harbor. There was some good news—victories at Midway and Guadalcanal—but there were also more defeats: Wake Island, the Battle of the Java Sea, Bataan, Corregidor. Like the movie musicals of the 1930s, which did not deny the existence of a depression but chose to depict a stratum of society unaffected by it, *Something for the Boys* assumed audiences knew there was a world war being waged, but not in Texas where men in uniform were ready to graduate from war games to combat; or on the stage of the Alvin (now Neil Simon) Theatre. In short, a wartime musical with a peacetime ambience, upbeat and unthreatening.

Near the end of the second act, Blossom and Chiquita perform "By the Mississinewah" at the Cadet Club for army personnel. Dressed as Native Americans with long braids and wearing moccasins, they pine for their wigwam on the banks of the Mississinewah and the "husband" they have in common. The antics of Merman and Paula Lawrence regaled the audience, but the broken French, a lame rhyme about life on the Mississine**wah** without a **bra**, and the implication that they are part of a daisy chain—not to mention the blatant racism—make one wonder why Porter ever wrote the number, except perhaps because he thought it would be a showstopper. By present standards, it is—but for the wrong reasons.

Merman clearly enjoyed appearing in *Something for the Boys*. Photographs from the performance in the Billy Rose Collection at the New York Public Library for the Performing Arts show an ebullient Ethel Merman in a typical 1940s tailored suit. In fact, she did not look like an actor, but rather like Ethel Zimmerman, stenographer. There was also nothing ostentatious about her dress in *Stage Door Canteen* (1943), in which she sang "Marching thru Berlin." She was just another Broadway personality in street clothes entertaining servicemen passing through New York to "destination unknown."

The Treasury Department, believing *Something for the Boys* to be a morale booster, authorized a transmission by short wave radio for servicemen and -women abroad. Merman, Johnson, and Jenkins reprised their original roles, but by the time of the broadcast, Paula Lawrence had left the show either to join the cast of *One Touch of Venus* (1943) or because she incurred Merman's wrath by engaging in scene-stealing in the Mississinewa number. Betty Garrett, Merman's understudy, and featured player Betty Bruce performed the duet. Why Merman demurred is unknown, particularly since she sang all of her other numbers. While it is always a pleasure to hear Merman in her prime, the score is minor Porter. *Something for the Boys* is rooted in a past when America was united as it had never been before and probably will never be again. It is a 1940s relic, like a ration book or an FDR button: a piece of memorabilia.

ON SCREEN: *SOMETHING FOR THE BOYS* (TWENTIETH CENTURY-FOX, 1944)

The credits read, "Based on the musical comedy, Book by Herbert and Dorothy Fields, Songs by Cole Porter." "Songs" is a misnomer; only one song, the title song, was used. Most of the others were written by Jimmy McHugh and Harold Adamson, and they are pleasant but unmemorable. The screenwriters—Robert Ellis, Helen Logan, and Frank Gabrielson—began with the news of the inheritance, as did the original, but reassigned the roles of the female heirs. Carmen Miranda, the "Brazilian Bombshell" known for her florid costumes, bulbous jewelry, and fruit-basket hats, was top billed as Chiquita Hart, no longer an exotic dancer but the welder with carborundum in her tooth. Twentieth Century-Fox newcomer Vivian Blaine played Blossom, now a singer hoping for her big break. With Miranda driving the plot and Phil Silvers as Harry Hart getting the laughs, all Blaine had to do was sing, which she did superbly, look disillusioned when she learns that Michael O'Shea, an army sergeant, is engaged to Sheila Ryan, and perk up when she hears it was never official.

Instead of a ranch, the cousins inherit a decrepit Southern plantation, which they renovate as a residence for army wives that is later mistaken for a brothel. The carborundum in Chiquita's tooth is still a transmitter, but instead of helping an imperiled plane land safely, as in the original, it enables O'Shea's team to beat its rival in a war games exercise. Unlike the finale of the stage musical, which was a reprise of "Something for the Boys," the film ends with a revue celebrating the reopening of the residence, with Miranda performing "Samba Boogie" in a green-and-white two-piece outfit and a hat festooned with imitation grapes, followed by Blaine and O'Shea providing a touch of normality with a reprise of "Wouldn't It Be Nice?" that allowed for a mellow fade-out.

If *Something for the Boys* has any significance, it is for the film debut of Perry Como, one of the finest vocalists of his generation, He made two more films at Twentieth Century-Fox, *Doll Face* and *If I'm Lucky* (both 1945), but achieved greater success on television with his own show, first on CBS (1950–55), then on NBC (1955–63). An Emmy Award-winner, Como was also the recipient of the Kennedy Center Honors for outstanding achievement in the performing arts. Audiences were indifferent to *Something for the Boys*, which cost $2 million and only grossed $1.2 million.

ON STAGE: MEXICAN HAYRIDE (1944)

Mexican Hayride reunited the *Something for the Boys* book writers Herbert and Dorothy Fields, director Hassard Short, and flamboyant producer Michael Todd in the most elaborate production of any Cole Porter musical thus far: a huge cast, lavish costumes, eye-filling sets, and an undistinguished score that was not so much composed as rushed into existence. Todd wanted another musical from Porter, who signed a contract for one on July 26, 1943. Six months after *Something for the Boys* opened in New York, *Mexican Hayride* began tryouts in Boston on December 29, 1943, opening in New York the following month, on January 28, 1944. Porter apparently did not believe in the Latin adage, *Festina lente* ("Make haste slowly"). While *Something for the Boys* could not be called a great musical, it at least had Ethel Merman, who was largely responsible for its 422 performances. The far inferior *Mexican Hayride* lasted a bit longer: 481 performances. It was the kind of musical that audiences wanted during a world war whose outcome and end point were still uncertain; while it did not feature a star of Merman's magnitude, it did have the popular Bobby Clark, a former vaudevillian who made an easy transition to Broadway with George and Ira Gershwin's *Strike Up the Band* (1930), *Ziegfeld Follies of 1936*, and especially *Star and Garter* (1942).

Todd was the kind of producer who believed that more is most—the most striking costumes, the most scene changes, and the largest number of cast members. His latest production was the revue *Star and Garter* featuring Bobby Clark with his trademark fake eye glasses and cigar, and the world's most famous ecdysiast, Gypsy Rose Lee. It is hard to know what made the show last for 609 performances: Clark's comedy routines or Gypsy's musical numbers such as "I Can't Strip to Brahms." Since burlesque had been banned in New York, Todd planned the equivalent in the form of a musical revue that would incorporate some of the same features of burlesque such as long-legged show girls and ribald sketches. This would be legitimate theater, not its bastard offspring. No one, however, was fooled, least of all *New York Times* critic John Anderson, who called *Star and Garter* "the season's most anatomical spectacle (June 25, 1942). It was burlesque, all right:

> Clark romped, ogled the girls, and regaled audiences as the judge at a murder trial. When the defendant, Gypsy Rose Lee, sat on the witness chair and crossed her legs, Clark slipped down from his chair and suddenly poked his head out of the curtains at the bottom of the judge's bench to get a better view of Miss Lee's shapely legs. . . . Miss Lee proved to be an expert comedienne as she spoofed her own act.

Although *Star and Garter* was a huge hit and exactly the kind of entertainment geared to World War II-era audiences, Todd realized he would fare better with critics if he produced a book musical. Encouraged by the success of *Something for the Boys*, he believed he had a winning team in Herbert and Dorothy Fields, Porter, Hassard Short, and Bobby Clark—but not Gypsy. He doubted that she could carry a book musical, but her sister, June Havoc, could. Havoc grew up in vaudeville, where she was Baby June, then Dainty June, singing and dancing her way into audiences' hearts. She had appeared on Broadway in a featured role in Rodgers and Hart's *Pal Joey* (1940), which brought her to the attention of Darryl F. Zanuck, production head at Twentieth Century-Fox. Cast in a secondary role in the Alice Faye musical *Hello, Frisco Hello* (1943), she was still the seasoned vaudevillian who could do shtick with Jack Oakie, execute a high kick, and go into an effortless split. While Havoc was doing personal appearances for *Hello,*

Frisco Hello in Chicago, Todd came backstage and offered her the female lead in what would become *Mexican Hayride*: "The idea of working with Bobby Clark was so fascinating I couldn't refuse."

How Herbert and Dorothy Fields came up with the plot of *Mexican Hayride* is a matter of speculation. RKO had limited success with the Mexican Spitfire films (1939–43) that starred Leon Errol and the fiery Lupe Valez as Carmelita Lindsay, a Mexican singer married to an American but bonding platonically with his uncle (Errol) in a series of adventures in which, at one point, Errol has to pass himself off as Lord Epping, causing much confusion when Epping himself (also played by Errol) is in the vicinity. Did Leon Errol, another great comic, inspire Bobby Clark's character, a racketeer using an alias in Mexico to avoid detection by the FBI? Did the "Mexican Spitfire" inspire June Havoc's character, Montana, a "lady bullfighter" working in Mexico? That would be a bit of a stretch for an American woman in 1944, although female bullfighters were common in Spain since the early nineteenth century. Call it an anachronism, like the clock that "hath striken thrice" in Shakespeare's *Julius Caesar* (Act 2, 1).

Or was *Mexican Hayride*, perhaps, a screwball contribution to the Good Neighbor Policy designed to ensure friendly relations between the United States and Latin America during the early days of World War II, when allegiances were in a state of uncertainty? The last, definitely.

President Roosevelt was so committed to implementing the Good Neighbor Policy that when the "Brazilian Bombshell," Carmen Miranda, was appearing on Broadway in the musical revue, *Streets of Paris* (1939), she was invited to the White House as a gesture of good will. After seeing her in the revue, Darryl F. Zanuck hired Miranda and featured her in Twentieth Century-Fox musicals with Latin American settings: *Down Argentine Way* (1940), *Week-end in Havana* (1941), and *That Night in Rio* (1941). The State Department sent Walt Disney on a tour of Latin America in 1941, with the intention of making a film that would combine animation and live action in a hybrid documentary with Donald Duck visiting Peru and Goofy visiting Argentina, intercut with shots of modern buildings and fashionably dressed Latin Americans to dispel the notion that the United States was the only nation with skyscrapers and haute couture. The result was *Saludos Amigos* (1942).

Significantly, *Mexican Hayride* takes place during *Amigo Americano* week in Mexico. Montana celebrates her victory in the ring by aiming the bull's ear in the direction of American diplomat David Winthrop (Wilbur Evans), to whom she is engaged. Instead, she becomes so distracted when she spots her shady brother-in law, Joe Bascomb, alias Humphrey Fisk (who else but Bobby Clark?), among the spectators, that she angrily tosses it at him, unwittingly making him *Amigo Americano*. Neither Bascom nor Montana wants publicity—Bascom, because of the attention it would draw; Montana, because having a brother-in-law in the rackets would jeopardize both her career and her engagement to Winthrop. When Bascom's wife, from whom he has been estranged, blows his cover, he and Montana's agent disguise themselves as tamale venders, with Clark in drag. Moralists might be satisfied with the ending in which Bascom is sent back to America to stand trial, which, one feels confident, will result in a sentence so insignificant that it would not have been worth the effort to extradite him. In a Bobby Clark musical, everything was played for laughs. Bobby Clark was the embodiment of the circus clown, the *zanni* of *commedia dell'arte*, and the top banana in burlesque who could get a laugh out of any situation, legitimate or otherwise. He kept the show running after June Havoc broke her leg and left on June 19, 1944.

Actually, the only touch of authenticity came from Corinna Mura, whose role was insignificant but who had two numbers, "Sing to Me, Guitar," which Porter claimed was his favorite, and "Carlotta." Mura had a great close-up in *Casablanca* (1942) as the entertainer passionately strumming her guitar as the patrons at Rick's Café drowned out the inebriated Nazis singing their anthem by countering with "La Marseillaise." *Mexican Hayride* was Mura's only Broadway credit.

The score was what critics often call "tuneful" when they cannot think of any other adjective. "Lesser Porter" would also apply. One song became popular, which Porter wrote as the result of a wager with Monty Woolley, who dared him to write a song entitled "I Love You." Porter did; it was sung by Wilbur Evans, a leading Broadway baritone, who later played opposite Mary Martin in the London premiere of *South Pacific*. In the verse, Evans's character admits that he cannot express his love for Montana as a poet might and calls on nature to do it for him: the April breeze, the hills, the dawn, the birds. Porter resorted to personification, the easiest way to write the lyric and win the bet. The matching simplicity of words and music made for easy listening; "I Love You" became a hit single, recorded by Bing Crosby, Jo Stafford, and Perry Como.

June Havoc had nothing comparable, although she claimed she stopped the show on opening night with "There Must Be Someone for Me," a list song with a verse and three refrains, in which Montana observes how the male and female of every species find each other—snails, hippos, lambs, clams, trout, scouts, and, hyperbolically, prunes: "So there must be someone for me." It was a novelty song, with no connection to the plot or character, since Montana is already engaged to David Winthrop. There may be lovelorn female bullfighters, but June Havoc did not fit the description. Unlike a similar lament, "Nobody's Chasing Me" in *Out of This World*, "There Must Be Someone for Me" is lacking in double entendre and, one might add, in wit.

Decca was supposed to issue the complete original cast recording of *Mexican Hayride*, but Bobby Clark bowed out because he did not like the sound of his recorded voice. Decca then released an album with eight numbers from the show sung by three of the original cast members: June Havoc, Wilbur Evans, and Corinna Mura. The CD is worth owning, since it includes Mura's two numbers, "Sing to Me, Guitar" and "Carlotta"; and "I Love You," which Evans makes into true show music, not a pop song. To compensate for the incomplete recording, Decca added *Cole Porter Songs Sung by Mary Martin* (1940). Since the songs were recorded a year after Martin made her sensational debut in *Leave It to Me*, hearing her sing "My Heart Belongs to Daddy" as she would have done it on Broadway the previous year is to hear innocence teased into experience.

ON SCREEN: *MEXICAN HAYRIDE* (UNIVERSAL-INTERNATIONAL, 1948)

When Universal merged with International in 1946 to become Universal-International (UI), the new studio sought to refurbish Universal's image as a maker of horror films and teenage musicals by releasing a spate of adaptations of two Broadway dramas and four musicals. In 1948, UI released the film versions of Arthur Miller's *All My Sons* and Lillian Hellman's *Another Part of the Forest*; and the musicals *One Touch of Venus* (1943), *Up in Central Park* (1945), and *Are You with It?* (1945). UI also paid $50,000 for *Mexican Hayride*—for the book, not the score, which it jettisoned. Although *All My Sons* and *Another Part of the Forest* were faithful to the originals, they failed at the box office. All that remained of Kurt Weill's score for *One Touch of Venus* were "Speak Low" and "That's Him." The same fate befell Sigmund Romberg's *Up in Central Park*. When preview audiences reacted negatively to the exquisite ballad "Close as Pages in a Book," it was cut, although it went on to become a favorite of cabaret performers. UI was so desperate for respectability that it even paid $100,000 for *Are You With It?*, a mediocre musical with a lusterless score by Harry Revel and Arnold B. Horwitt, which it replaced in its entirely with five songs by Sidney Miller and Inez James.

All that interested the executives at UI were Broadway shows with a pedigree reflected in the title. The *Mexican Hayride* credits indicate as much: "Produced on the Stage by Michael Todd. Based on the Musical Play by Dorothy Fields and Herbert Fields and Cole Porter." Perhaps as a matter of courtesy, Porter's name was added, although not a note of the score was used. Screenwriters John Grant and Oscar Brodney refashioned the book as a vehicle for (Bud) Abbott and (Lou) Costello, one of the most inventive teams in film comedy. Costello inherited Bobby Clark's role, Joe Bascomb (alias Humphrey Fish). A new character had to be created for Abbott: Harry Lambert, a con artist who scammed Bascomb and is now Montana's agent. Bascomb is no longer Montana's brother-in-law but her former boyfriend. Since tossing a bull's ear into the crowd would strike audiences as gross as well as inflame animal rights activists, Montana tosses her hat instead, which, to her annoyance, Bascomb catches, becoming *Amigo Americano* for a week. The musical's one hit song, "I Love You," was to have been a duet for Virginia Grey (Montana) and John Hubbard (David Winthrop), but Universal-International—or the producer, Robert Arthur—decided against it; it would have been out of place in a movie in which Montana and Winthrop have been reduced to secondary characters, although in the original their roles were played by June Havoc and Wilbur Evans, who had costar billing. The screenplay is more complicated than the Fields' book, perhaps to keep the audience from realizing that frenetic activity has been substituted for sense. Costello does a samba in the bull ring, appears in drag as a tamale vendor, and in the final shot dances a samba again while making his way along the road—a charming fade out to a charmless film.

It is gratifying to know that Abbott and Costello had been opposed to making *Mexican Hayride*, which ranks far below their classic *Abbott and Costello Meet Frankenstein* (1948), released the same year.

CHAPTER 12

Strange Interludes

Seven Lively Arts and Around the World

Gilbert Seldes, one of the most important cultural critics of the twentieth century, entitled his highly influential book about the so-called "minor arts," *The Seven Lively Arts* (1924)—"lively" being the key word to distinguish them from (1) other arbitrary septads (for example, architecture, sculpture, painting, poetry or literature in general, music, performing, film as a synthesis of other arts, or dance); and (2) from what elitists would call high culture (opera, ballet, classical theater, orchestral concerts). Seldes argued that what had been considered middlebrow at best (and lowbrow at worst) may be minor arts to the intelligentsia but that their universal appeal is undeniable. Seldes never enumerates the seven as such; in fact, there seem to be more than seven. For example, Seldes includes jazz and ragtime under the rubric of popular music rather than separately. But that is the point of his highly egalitarian book. Popular music is the people's music in which jazz and ragtime figure prominently. Other lively arts include silent comedy as epitomized by Chaplin; slapstick; news-writing on the order of Ring Lardner's sports columns; comic strips (Seldes was especially fond of *Krazy Kat*); and live entertainment (vaudeville, revues, musicals, one-person shows, the circus). If he had written *The Seven Lively Arts* a decade later, he would have added radio. One leaves *The Seven Lively Arts* convinced that their number is legion.

ON STAGE: SEVEN LIVELY ARTS (1946)

Twenty years after the publication of *The Seven Lively Arts*, another *Seven Lively Arts* appeared in the form of a musical revue, but without the definite article. It was the brainchild of the extraordinarily versatile Billy Rose (1899–1966), who graduated from stenographer to lyricist ("It's Only a Paper

Moon" and "Me and My Shadow" being among his best-known songs). In 1925, his songs began appearing in revues, but songwriting was only a stepping stone to producing. Rose was somewhat eclectic as a producer. An overheated melodrama like Clifford Odets's *Clash by Night* (1941) was followed by Oscar Hammerstein II's masterpiece, an all-Black version of Bizet's *Carmen, Carmen Jones* (1943); and a year later by *Seven Lively Arts*, into which, as *New York Times* critic Lewis Nichols wrote (December 8, 1944), "Billy Rose has piled a little bit of everything but the kitchen sink—and if that could dance or were pretty, it probably would be there, too."

Had Rose confined himself to Seldes's lively arts, making seven of them the basis of a musical revue, there would at least have been a common theme. At one point, Rose was considering centering the revue around seven art forms: "Music, ballet, theater, opera, movies, radio, and modern painting were arty and lively for a good show theme." "Arty and lively," the shotgun marriage of the high and the low. If Rose had read *The Seven Lively Arts*, he did not get the message: the lively arts have their own intrinsic merit and do not need validation from highbrows. Rose thought he could win over critics and audiences with world-class talent: sets by the renowned Norman Bel Geddes; an orchestra conducted by Maurice Abravanel, conductor of the Utah Symphony Orchestra who had also conducted at the Metropolitan Opera; singers under the direction of Robert Shaw, founder of the Robert Shaw Chorale; a book (in the loosest sense of the word) by George S. Kaufman and Ben Hecht; sketches by four writers, the best-known being Moss Hart; recognizable names like Bert Lahr, Beatrice Lillie, and Benny Goodman with his clarinet; performers at the beginning of their careers in musical theater (Helen Gallagher, Dolores Gray, Billie Worth, Bill [later William] Tabbert); internationally renowned stars from the world of ballet (Dame) Alicia Markova and her frequent partner (Sir) Anton Dolin, dancing to music composed by Igor Stravinsky; and, to top it off, a score by the equally celebrated Cole Porter.

Kaufman and Hecht's book was originally in the form of a framing device beginning with "Big Town"—in which seven young hopefuls (an artist, tap dancer, radio singer, ballerina, stage actor, playwright, and movie actor) come to the Big Town, wondering if they will "hit the heights" and see their "name in lights"—and possibly ending with "Yours for a Song," which suggested that if even if the aspirants did not achieve their dream, the journey was worth it if they found love, ideally through song. Enclosed within the frame would be the sketches, songs, dances, specialty numbers, and even classical ballet. It was a brilliant concept that, unfortunately, was never fully realized. One would assume from "Big Town" that the seven lively arts would be painting, dance (exclusive of ballet), music, ballet, theater (conceived as two arts, acting and playwriting), and film. The painter (Nan Wynn), who in "Big Town" vows to "paint the town red," is never shown doing it. The tap dancer never does tap, nor does the radio singer get on the air. The playwright never gets his play produced, and the would-be stage and screen stars never get a break.

Markova and Dolin may have epitomized ballet at its finest, but the music that Stravinsky composed for the *pas de deux* and *Scène de ballet* was second rate. Theater consisted of a sketch, "Heaven on Angel Street," a mash-up of three long-running plays: *Life with Father*, with Bert Lahr as Clarence Day, who resists his wife's appeal that he be baptized; *Angel Street*, in which Beatrice Lillie played Bella Manningham, whose husband (Anton Dolin) is slowly driving her mad; and *Tobacco Road*, with two actors impersonating Jeeter Lester, the head of a family of Georgia sharecroppers, and his sixteen-year-old son Dude, who agrees to marry a much older evangelist when she offers to buy him a car. The sketch seemed to have great potential as satire, but it failed to impress the critics. Theater was also to have been represented by "I Wrote a Play," which Porter composed for Bill Tabbert. For some reason, the song was cut, although it was Porter at his most sardonic, with a young playwright recounting his fruitless efforts to peddle his play, *Boy Loves Girl*, to various producers; in desperation he tries Hollywood, where Sam Goldwyn offers to buy the title, but not the play.

None of the newcomers aspired to a career in opera, yet the first act finale was "Billy Rose Buys the Metropolitan Opera House," with orchestral fragments from *Aida*, *Carmen*, *Das Rheingold*, *Die Walküre*, and *The Tales of Hoffman*, followed by a reprise of "Only Another Boy and Girl," which Bill Tabbert and Mary Roche sang in a sketch of the same name early in Act 1 with Bert Lahr and Beatrice Lillie posing as figures from a Fragonard painting. In the finale, Tabbert and Roche did not have to compete with two accomplished farceurs. The melding of operatic and show music may have been Rose's way of arguing for the coexistence of the two arts. If so, it would be ironic, since opera originated as a people's art. It is quite common to hear maids in Italian hotels singing operatic arias while cleaning tourists' rooms, even though most could not afford to see the operas themselves. It was only when opera became elitist that its "popularity" was limited to "popular" works in the repertory like *Carmen*, *Rigoletto*, and *La Traviata*.

Or perhaps the first-act finale was intended to subvert the distinction between the arty and the lively, rendering them meaningless. It would not have mattered to most theatergoers, for whom it was a thrilling way to bring down the curtain.

At one point, the second-act finale seems to have been a sequence of three songs, the first and last expressing the same theme: the malleable nature of popular music, which can be sung and orchestrated in myriad ways. First, Nan Wynn sang "The Band Started Swinging a Song," in which a young woman hears a swing arrangement of a song from a Broadway show that brings back memories of that show and the one with whom she saw it. The orchestration may have been different, but it did not affect the memory. Then came "The Big Parade," a tribute to the circus, which Seldes considered a lively art; the song may have been Rose's self-homage to Rodgers and Hart's circus musical *Jumbo* (1936), which he produced at the legendary 5,000-seat Hippodrome Theatre. And finally "Yours for a Song," in which the singer (perhaps Wynn) admits to having seen New York and the Fair (presumably the World's Fair of 1939, among whose attractions was Rose's *Aquacade*, starring Olympic swimmer Eleanor Holm, whom he married that year); neither New York nor a World's Fair can compare to true love, as expressed through music. If the message is that music is the food of love, as Orsino exclaims at the beginning of *Twelfth Night*, then *Seven Lively Arts* would have come full circle. The aspirants who expected to find their dream careers in Big Town may not have found them, but if they discovered love and music—or rather, love through music—the trip was worth it. That ending would have brought *Seven Lively Arts* full circle, from arrival to departure.

In musical theater, the original concept undergoes a form of tailoring, in which a show is shortened or lengthened, altered or accessorized, tightened or loosened. When *Seven Lively Arts* opened in New York on December 7, 1944, after a brief tryout in Philadelphia. Kaufman and Hecht's book had become a shadowy reflection of an initially exciting idea: a concept revue combining high culture and popular culture in a harmonious union. What audiences saw on December 7, according to *New York Times* critic Lewis Nichols, was a "big," "rambling," and "sometimes top heavy" revue.

Anyone attending *Seven Lively Arts* three weeks into the run would have received a playbill with the following act and scene divisions:

Overture

Act 1

Scene 1. Song . . . "Big Town"

MR. AUDIENCE　　　　　　　　"Doc" Rockwell

And The Young Hopefuls

PAINTER　　　　　　　　Nan Wynn
TAP DANCER　　　　　　Jere McMahon
RADIO SINGER　　　　　Paula Bane
BALLET DANCER　　　　Billie Worth
PLAYWRIGHT　　　　　Bill Tabbert
MOVIE ACTRESS　　　　Dolores Gray
STAGE ACTRESS　　　　Mary Roche

("Doc" Rockwell was a popular vaudevillian, who, according to Lewis Nichols, delivered "a cynical commentary in the style and from the pen of Ben Hecht," coauthor of the show's book, such as it was. The commentary may have been on the dreams of the Young Hopefuls, setting the tone for a revue that at times was wickedly satiric and irreverent. Except for the obligatory love song, nothing is sacred in *Seven Lively Arts*.)

Scene 2. Song "Is It the Girl?" ("Or Is It the Gown?")
Sung by Dolores Gray

(Does a gown attract a man or the woman wearing it? The number included a fashion show with the ladies of the chorus as models.)

Scene 3. "Local Boy Makes Good" by George S. Kaufman

(Bert Lahr, apparently the title character, played a stagehand in a theatrical office. Nothing else is known about the sketch.)

Scene 4. Song . . . "Evr'y Time We Say Goodbye"
Sung by Nan Wynn and Jere McMahon

(The only song from the show to become a standard).

Scene 5. "There'll Always Be an England" by Moss Hart

(Beatrice Lillie played Lady Agatha Pendleton, who is hosting a garden party for American soldiers stationed in Britain and uses a handbook of American expressions to converse with them. In his review, Nichols wrote that Lillie, who headed the cast, was a great favorite of American audiences and "stopped the show before she uttered a word.")

Scene 6. Song . . . "Only Another Boy and Girl"
Sung by Mary Roche and Bill Tabbert

"FRAGONARD IN PINK"   Lillie, Lahr, and Ensemble

(The juxtaposition of a "two kids in love duet" and a *tableau vivant* with Lillie and Lahr as figures in a Fragonard painting leads one to suspect that their antics left a greater impression on the audience than the duet.)

Scene 7. Song . . . "Wow-Ooh-Wolf!"
Sung by Nan Wynn, Dolores Gray, and Mary Roche

("Wolf" in the vernacular, meaning a randy male who ogles and whistles at women.)

Scene 8. "Ticket for the Ballet" by Moss Hart

(Beatrice Lillie tries to buy a ticket for the ballet, not knowing what she wants to see.)

Scene 9. Song . . . "Drink"
Sung by Bert Lahr and Male Ensemble

(A parody of the "Drinking Song," a staple of opera and operetta. "Drink" is repeated ad nauseam.)

Scene 10. Song . . . "When I Was a Little Cuckoo"
Sung by Beatrice Lillie

(In her current incarnation as a cuckoo, Lillie recounts her various metamorphoses: "As a royal snake charmer I made Egypt gasp / When I struck Cleopatra for kicking my asp.")

Scene 11. "When Billy Rose Buys the Metropolitan Opera House!"

(According to the playbill, the finale included a toreador dance by Jere McMahon.)

Intermission

Act 2

Scene 1. "Scène de Ballet" (Excerpts)
Music by Igor Stravinsky Choreography by Anton Dolin
Danced by Alicia Markova, Dolin, and Corps de Ballet

Scene 2. Song
Sung by Beatrice Lillie

(None specified. Perhaps it varied from performance to performance.)

Scene 3. "The Great Man Speaks" by Charles Sherman

(Bert Lahr as a patient in a doctor's office. The situation itself brings a smile.)

Scene 4. Clarinet Solo
Played by Benny Goodman

Scene 5. Song
A ... "Frahngee-Pahnee"
Sung by Bill Tabbert and Ensemble

(The title is the name of an alluring female islander with whom the singer had a tryst under a banyan tree, a diluted blend of "Night and Day" and "Begin the Beguine.")

B ... "Dancin' to a Jungle Drum"
Sung By Beatrice Lillie

(The number is a response to the faux "tropical splendor" of "Frahngee-Pahnee." Porter was willing to risk self-parody by having Lillie complain about getting numb from "the beat, beat, beat, the tick, tick, tock, and the drip, drip, drop," all coming from a common source, a jungle drum. "Goddam drums," she exclaims. Even a masterpiece like "Night and Day" is not sacred; Porter must have believed that satire is flattery in disguise, which is especially true when the composer is the satirist.)

Scene 6. Song . . . "Hence It Don't Make Sense"
Sung by Nan Wynn, Mary Roche, Dolores Gray, and Billie Worth
Danced by Jere McMahon and Billie Worth

(Porter, the word spinner, sends heads spinning as he runs through the changing vernacular: a girl is a babe; a babe, a chick; a chick, a bird; a bird, a fowl; a fowl, a ball; a ball, a dance. "But a girl ain't a great big dance. / Hence, it don't make sense.")

(There is no Scene 7 in the playbill. Perhaps what had been Scene 7 was removed after the second week.)

Scene 8. "Heaven in Angel Street" by Moss Hart

(The setting is a living room in London's Angel Street, where characters from *Angel Street*, *Life with Father*, and *Tobacco Road* converse with the [then] dean of drama critics, George Jean Nathan.)

Scene 8. Song . . . "The Band Started Swinging a Song"
Sung by Nan Wynn

Scene 9. Pas de deux
Danced by Markova and Dolin

Scene 10. Finale
Mr. Audience and Entire Company

While the playbill specified the nature of the first-act finale, it only implied that *Seven Lively Arts* ended with "Doc" Rockwell returning as Mr. Audience to offer concluding remarks and bring the revue full circle. Perhaps the closing number was still tentative and varied from performance to performance. "Yours for a Song" would have been the perfect ending, with the cast singing about New York and the World's Fair, neither of which could compare with the blending of love and music. Perhaps Porter was thinking of Conrad Aiken's poem "Music I Heard," which begins: "Music I heard with you was more than music." Music and love are two separate entities, each capable of arousing different emotions. When experienced together, they unite in a single emotion, rich in associations that remain even when love may be no more. If "Yours for a Song" was the company's envoi, it would have been a fitting ending to a revue that was far better in conception than it was in execution. But one will never know.

Although some numbers may have been changed or even dropped during the 183-performance run, there was one constant: the poignant "Ev'ry Time We Say Goodbye," the only number to become a standard, recorded by such diverse artists as Ella Fitzgerald, Sarah Vaughan, John Coltrane, Carly Simon, Ray Charles and Betty Carter, and Lady Gaga. The gender-neutral song is a lament by one party in a relationship marked by frequent separations, as indicated by the title which is repeated four times in the eighteen-line refrain. The text itself has an unpretentious candor, turning metaphorical only at the end. In the verse, the one who is always left behind wonders why two people who are presumably in love find themselves quarreling and periodically separating. There is something quaint and even archaic about the verse, with its two inversions ("quarrel ever," "be enough clever"). The end and internal rhymes have a graceful simplicity; "-bye" admits of easy rhyming. Lines one and three of the refrain end in "good**bye**," which finds its mate in line four ("I wonder **why** a little"). Porter even uses repetitive internal rhyme in lines ten and twelve ("spring about it," "sing about it"). Then the song turns elegiac at line thirteen, textually and musically, ending on a note of bittersweet resignation: "There's no love song finer / But how strange / The change / From major to minor." "Major" and "minor" are meant literally. The song, which began in A-flat major, ends in A-flat minor, as hope resolves itself, in words and music, into an acceptance of a relationship of extremes.

Seven Lively Arts was not a happy experience for Porter. His name in the playbill appeared way down under the title, after that of the director, Hassard Short, and even "featuring Doc Rockwell." Lillie and Lahr carried the show, not Porter's score, which was reduced to nine numbers. This was a Billy Rose Production with everything coming up *Rose*.

Porter's next encounter was with a far greater talent and an ego to match.

ON STAGE: *AROUND THE WORLD* (1946)

Seven Lively Arts at least had one standout song. *Around the World* had none. Produced, directed, and adapted from Jules Verne's *Around the World in Eighty Days* (1873) by Orson Welles, who also played detective Dick Fix,

Around the World had a cast of seventy; film sequences, now lost; a circus as the first act finale with Welles doing a magic act, a skill that he mastered at an early age and "learned in part from Harry Houdini himself"; and nine unmemorable songs by Cole Porter. Welles was a magician in another sense. John Housman, who produced Welles's still-unparalleled film debut in *Citizen Kane* (1941), characterized him as "a magician whose particular talent lies not so much in his creative imagination . . . as in his proven ability to stretch the familiar elements of theatrical effect far beyond their normal point of tension." Welles proved his mastery of stagecraft in his Mercury Theatre productions; his imaginative use of sound in Mercury Theatre of the Air, notably in his 1938 adaptation of H. G. Wells's *War of the Worlds*, in which he combined ambient sound and unnervingly realistic on-site reporting of a Martian invasion, ending in the absence of sound; and his integration of the visual and the aural in film, an outstanding example of which occurs near the end of *Citizen Kane* when Kane and his wife Susan Alexander Kane (Dorothy Commigore) are arguing in a tent during an elaborate picnic while outside, unseen by the viewer, a man is committing an act of violence against a woman. Both actions are occurring simultaneously; one inside, the other outside. The one inside is visual and verbal; the other is in silhouette and uncomfortably audible. Then there is the climax of *The Lady from Shanghai* (1948), one of the most shattering (literally) in film: Rita Hayworth and Everett Sloane firing at each other in a funhouse hall of mirrors, their images reflected in the bullet-shattered glass. Welles indeed extended the line of tension until it reached the breaking point.

In *Around the World*, there was nothing to extend except the running time, which usually reached—or on some occasions exceeded—three hours. It was stage surfeit with twenty scenes in Act 1, scenes one and seventeen on celluloid; the same with scenes one and four in Act 2, which was a bit shorter: fourteen scenes. Welles followed the trajectory of Verne's plot, omitting some episodes and inventing a few of his own. Phineas Fogg (Arthur Margetson) accepts a wager of 20,000 pounds from members of the Reform Club (renamed Whist Club in the musical) that he can travel around the world in eighty days. He and his French valet Pat Passepartout (Larry Laurence) leave London by train and, for the rest of their journey, alternate between rail and streamer. On one occasion in India, Fogg has to travel by elephant and later on a wind-powered sledge. Following Fogg and Passepartout is Detective Dick Fix of Scotland Yard (Welles), who has noticed Fogg's resemblance to a bank robber. Determined to bring the "robber" to justice, Fix pursues the pair as they navigate the globe with an itinerary that includes stopovers in Egypt, India, Hong King, Japan, and San Francisco until they reach London in time for Fogg to win the bet. In terms of plot, the India sequence is the most important. Fogg and Passepartout stumble upon a ritual in which a recent widow, Aouda (Mary Healy), is about to take her place on her husband's funeral pyre. Fogg and Passepartout interrupt the ceremony and rescue Aouda, sparking a romance between Fogg and Aouda which leads to marriage.

Welles could not afford a stellar cast; that did not matter because he was the star of his own mammoth production which dwarfed everyone except himself. The closest to a recognizable name was Arthur Margetson, who had made a number of British and American films and appeared on Broadway in several productions, including *Charley's Aunt* (1940) with José Ferrer and as a replacement as Father in *Life with Father* at the end of the run. Two other cast members went on to successful careers. Larry Laurence became the popular recording artist and actor Enzo Stuarti, who appeared on Broadway in *Two on the Aisle* (1951), *Me and Juliet* (1953), and *By the Beautiful Sea* (1954). Mary Healy had a long and varied career in film (*Second Fiddle, Star Dust*, both 1939; the cult classic *The 5,000 Fingers of Dr. T.* [1953]); radio, television, nightclubs, and Broadway, costarring with her husband, Peter Lind Hayes, in the hit comedy *Who Was That Lady I Saw You With?* (1958).

Although *Around the World* only lasted for seventy-five performances, Welles intended to make it part of his legacy by producing a half-hour version as the initial offering on his short-lived radio show, *Mercury Summer Theatre of the Air* (June 7, 1946–September 13, 1946). Sponsored by Pabst Blue Ribbon beer, the program aired on CBS on Friday evenings at 10 o'clock and introduced by "your obedient servant, Orson Welles," who signed off with "obediently yours." It was a humble gesture from a man to whom humility was alien. Yet one must marvel at Welles's ability to fit commentary, dramatization, and narration into a thirty-minute, two-act format, with a commercial break between the acts. He had accomplished on radio what he did not on the stage: he paired a literary work down to its essentials, leaving the audience satisfied with the redaction and in no need of anything further

Listening to the truncated version, one can see more clearly how Welles adapted the novel for the stage. He added a new character, Molly Muggins, as a romantic interest for Passepartout so there would be a double pairing off at the end, like that of Olivia and Sebastian and Viola and Orsino in *Twelfth Night*. Since Welles was a master of accents, he decided to make Dick Fix both the bank robber and Fogg's nemesis as he pursues him and Passepartout, intending to arrest him in Hong Kong, then a British colony.

Making a Scotland Yard detective a bank robber is a bit of a stretch, but Welles, of the many voices, became the Evil Genius, capable of assuming various identities.

Welles made it evident that the radio audience was getting an abbreviated version of the show currently running in New York by having four cast members repeat their roles and perform three numbers. Larry Laurence (Passepartout) and Julie Warren (Molly Muggins) sing a love-at-first-sight duet, "Look What I Found," bringing ardor and, in Laurence's case, a strong tenor, to Porter's forgettable music and banal lyrics ("I wake to see / How sweet life could be / That great big moment when I found you"). Far better is "There He Goes, Mr. Phineas Fogg," in which Fogg instructs Passepartout in his duties as valet. Margetson issues his orders in the form of a patter song, turning what might have been a duet into a dialogue. He delivers the lyrics in a combination of pitched speech and speak-song, in contrast to the more musical Lawrence. The number did not afford many opportunities for clever rhymes, but Porter did get some mileage out of "under**wear**/**where**/**there**." The third number was Aouda's admission of her love for Fogg, "Should I Tell You I Love You?" Mary Healy had an operetta-type voice that would have served her well in the days of Victor Herbert and Sigmund Romberg. Hers was a delicate soprano, silvery at the top, ideal for a romantic ballad that did not require a plush sound.

It was evident from the score that Porter had little interest in the material. This was an Orson Welles production *with* songs by Cole Porter, not "Cole Porter's *Around the World*, produced, directed, and adapted from Jules Verne's novel by Orson Welles." He was through with showmen with gargantuan egos. He had gone through the brimstone and fire with Billy Rose and Orson Welles. He did not know on August 3, 1946, when *Around the World* closed, that within two years he would have the greatest triumph of his career.

CHAPTER 13

Journey's End

Kiss Me, Kate

The genesis of *Kiss Me, Kate* is fairly well documented. Arnold Saint Subber was a stagehand and stage manager before becoming a Broadway producer of such shows as *Kiss Me, Kate,* William Inge's *The Dark at the Top of the Stairs*, and the early plays of Neil Simon. During the 1935–36 season, Saint Subber was working backstage at the Guild Theatre in a production of *The Taming of the Shrew* starring the legendary team of Alfred Lunt and Lynn Fontanne as Petruchio and Katherine. He observed that the Lunts' offstage bickering mirrored the onstage sparring between their characters. He recalled the incident a decade later, envisioning a play with a double plot: an onstage production of *Shrew* with a backstage subplot involving the principals. He and scenic designer Lemuel Ayres (*Oklahoma!*, *Bloomer Girl*) decided to produce a musical version of *Shrew* that would take place both on- and offstage. Their ideal team was Pulitzer Prize-winner Thornton Wilder (book) and Burton Lane (score). At this stage, Porter, who had two unsuccessful shows in a row (*Seven Lively Arts*, *Around the World*), was not even a remote possibility. When Wilder declined and Lane was unavailable, they approached Bella and Sam Spewack, who had coauthored the book of *Leave It to Me*. The Spewacks were having marital difficulties and living separately. Bella believed the project would be perfect for Porter. The result was *Kiss Me, Kate*, with a book by the Spewacks (largely by Bella) and Porter's most ambitious score.

It was not an easy conversion of one of Shakespeare's less endearing plays into a musical. The text had to be judiciously pruned to accommodate the unusually large number of songs. Furthermore, Shakespeare's comedies contain elements of cruelty, and *Shrew* is no exception. Characters abuse each other physically and verbally. Katherine mistreats her younger sister Bianca, tying her hands and even striking her (Act 2, 1); according to the stage directions, Petruchio "wrings [his servant Grumio] by the ears" (Act

1, 2). Then there is the play's misogyny, which Elizabethans would have accepted far more readily than twentieth—and certainly twenty-first—century audiences. To the Elizabethans, there was a hierarchical order, originating with the deity, below whom was the monarch, followed by man (and beneath him, woman), animals, plants, and minerals: a chain of being from highest to lowest. It was a tall order, but Bella was ready for it.

THE TAMING OF THE SHREW (C. 1589)

The Taming of the Shrew is Shakespeare's only play with an induction, an introduction designed to set the tone of the play and nothing more (as contrasted with a prologue, which provides information necessary for an understanding of the play, often by recounting what had occurred before the main action). The induction, which might be titled "The Gulling of Sly," is set in an inn, where a tinker, Christopher Sly, is in a drunken stupor. A Lord and his hunting party arrive. Seeing the sleeping Sly, the Lord decides to play a trick on him. He has Sly brought to his chamber and dressed in finery, with the page Bartholomew posing as his wife. When Sly awakens, he is told that he is a Lord who has been asleep for fifteen years. To add to the deception, a troupe of players asks if they can perform a play for the "Lord," who agrees. And the play, of course, is the one the audience will be seeing as well: *The Taming of the Shrew*. To make certain the audience knows it is watching a play-within-a-play, a servant, observing that Sly is dozing off, reminds him that the play has just begun. "Would 'twere done" (Act 1, 1) is his response. Sly makes no further appearance—at least not in *The Shrew*, although Sly returns in the epilogue of one of Shakespeare's sources, *The Taming of a Shrew*, in which he awakens, believing that what he had experienced was a dream and is now ready to go home and tame his shrewish wife. An earlier version of *The Shrew* might have also contained such an epilogue, thus bringing the play full circle. If the epilogue had been retained, it would have provided an interesting contrast between Sly's intention to tame his wife and Petruchio's belief that he has "tamed" Katherine. At the end of *The Shrew*, as Petruchio and Katherine are about to retire, Hortensio says, "Now go thy ways, thou hast tamed a curst shrew." If that were the curtain line, there would have been no doubt that Petruchio has succeeded. But Lucentio has the final—and frustratingly ambiguous—line "'Tis a wonder, by your leave, she will be tamed so." Lucentio uses the future "will," not the present "is." As will be noted, much depends on the director's vision of this highly ambivalent comedy and the actors' line readings to come to any conclusion about the taming of Katherine. For example, if a director chooses to end the play with the epilogue, *The Shrew* becomes Sly's dream in which Petruchio and Katherine are dream figures, with Petruchio as the dreamer and Katherine as the dream object. Understandably, productions of *The Shrew* do not include the epilogue since it is not part of the authorized text. Most even omit the induction, which is important in terms of the play's structure but not necessarily in terms of performance.

The induction introduces *The Shrew*'s two main themes: deception and transformation. In fact, the comedy could have been called "The Transforming of the Shrew," since Katherine changes from a "wildcat," as Gremio calls her (Act 1, 1), to a (supposedly) obedient wife, depending on how the final scene is played, in which Katherine lectures women on their duties to their husbands.

Deception

In the course of five acts:

Lucentio and his servant Tranio exchange clothes and identities so that Lucentio can pass himself off as a tutor to woo Bianca, Katherine's younger sister;

Hortensio passes himself off as a music master for the same purpose;

a Pedant pretends to be Lucentio's father, Vincentio;

as is common in Shakespeare's comedies, there is one central plot and concentrically arranged subplots.

Transformation

Main Plot

Baptista Minola of Padua has two daughters: Katherine and Bianca, the latter unable to marry until "curst Katherine" does. Petruchio offers to marry Katherine, and once the financial details are agreed upon (a wife is chattel, and the language indicates as much), they wed. In repartee, Katherine is every bit Petruchio's equal. Whatever phrase he throws at her, she can turn it. When Petruchio says he is "mov'd" by her, Katharine replies, "Let him that mov'd you hither / Remove you hence. I knew you at the first / You were a removable" (Act 2, 1). Katherine is a complex character and a challenge to any actor playing her. She does not question her father's decision that she marry Petruchio, although if she were really a "wildcat," she would. Is she perhaps attracted to Petruchio? Even when he tries to starve her into submission, she does not throw a tantrum. When Petruchio insists that the moon is out when it's daylight, she corrects him. When he persists, she humors him. But she still surpasses him in verbal jousting. When Petruchio claims his eloquence derives "from my mother's wit," Katherine is ready with a rejoinder: "A witty mother, witless else her son" (Act 2, 1). Petruchio asks her for a kiss several times in the play. In Act 5, 1, he asks again. Katherine is taken aback or pretends to be: "In the midst of the street?" Petruchio suggests then that they go home. But Kate the clever acquiesces: "Nay, I will give thee a kiss." If acted properly, the scene offers ample proof that while Katherine will occupy a lower rung than her husband on the hierarchical ladder, in matters of affection, they are equals.

Subplots:

The Courting of Bianca

The middle-aged Gremio and the younger Lucentio and Hortensio woo Bianca.

Lucentio has the financial edge (money talks in sixteenth-century Padua) and can claim Bianca for himself if his father, Vincentio, attests to his wealth.

Odd Man In

If Lucentio marries Bianca, Hortensio will be left without a potential mate. (Shakespeare has apparently forgotten about Gremio.) To have three sets of couples, a favorite Shakespearean arrangement, Hortensio has to be paired off with someone. Enter a rich Widow, who becomes his wife.

The False Father

A Pedant in financial need agrees to impersonate Lucentio's father, Vincentio. Meanwhile, the real Vincentio arrives in Padua, seeking his son, which results in a confrontation between the faux and the true father, who vouches for his son's wealth, thus making Lucentio a suitable husband for Bianca.

Coda

Since Petruchio, Hortensio, and Lucentio are now wiv'd, Petruchio proposes a wager of one hundred crowns. Each wife is ordered to leave her room and come into their midst, the winner being the one whose wife appears first. Both the Widow and Bianca decline. Only Katherine emerges. Delighted, Petruchio orders her to fetch Bianca and the Widow. Katherine obliges and returns, followed by the two women. Did they perhaps discuss among themselves who would be first and whose husband would win the wager? Lucentio and Hortensio are much better off financially than Petruchio. Did Katherine persuade them to let her come out first? And if the Widow and Bianca originally refused to leave their rooms, why did they obey when Katherine summoned them? And when they appear, neither is what she had seemed. The Widow finds the order foolish, and Bianca reveals an independent spirit, quite the opposite of the demure maiden she was purported to be. When Lucentio blames Bianca for causing him to lose the wager, she replies that he was foolish to have assumed she would obey such a command: "The more fool you for laying on my duty" (Act 5, 2). Is Bianca a potential shrew? Shakespeare's characters are more complex than one would think.

When Petruchio charges Katherine with the task of telling the Widow and Bianca what they "owe their lords and husbands," Katherine replies with the longest speech in the play (Act 5, 2, 137–80), a model of classical oratory with an exordium, proposition, confirmation, and peroration:

Exordium
The purpose of the exordium is to gain the audience's attention— or, if necessary, jolt it into attention. Katherine does the latter, specifically addressing the Widow: "Fie, fie! Unknit that threatening unkind brow."

Proposition
The proposition is what is to be proved: "Thy husband is thy lord, thy life, thy keeper, / Thy head, thy sovereign."

Confirmation
The confirmation offers proof of the proposition.

1. The husband toils for his wife, enduring "painful labors both by sea and land," while his wife is "warm at home, secure and safe."
2. Within the great chain of being, a woman owes her husband the same "duty as a subject owes the prince."
3. Nature has made the sexes distinct from each other. Since women's bodies are "soft, and weak, and smooth," women should be similarly soft of heart.

Peroration
The peroration is the summary. Women should "place [their] hands beneath [their] husband's foot" as Katherine does by setting an example: "My hand is ready, may it do him ease."

Whatever one thinks of Katherine's arguments, there is no doubt that Shakespeare has shown her to be as proficient at flyting as Petruchio and his superior in speech-making. Whether Katherine is simply telling Elizabethan men what they want to hear or giving a bravura performance depends on the director's concept of the play and interpretation of her climactic speech, which can be delivered sincerely, ironically, or even comically with the Widow and Bianca giggling at Katherine's examples of masculine superiority and feminine inferiority. *Kiss Me, Kate* ends with an abbreviated version of the speech "I Am Ashamed That Women Are So Simple." In the 1999 Broadway revival, Brian Stokes Mitchell (Petruchio) bowed to Marin Mazzie (Katherine) after she sang, "My hand is ready, may it do him ease." One suspects Shakespeare would have approved. After such a display of eloquence, Katherine deserves a bow from Petruchio, who, chauvinist that he is, can only respond: "Why, there's a wench! Come on, and kiss me. Kate."

And so, a musical was born.

ON STAGE: *KISS ME, KATE* (1948)

The Book

The prominent actor-manager David Garrick (1717–79) created a three-act redaction of *The Taming of the Shrew*, titled *Catherine and Petruchio*, eliminating the subplots, including the courting of Bianca, by having Bianca married to Hortensio, not Lucentio, at the start of the play. Bella Spewack took a similar approach to the book for *Kiss Me, Kate*. She, too, eliminated the subplots, except for the courting of Bianca, to which she gave short shrift, as did Shakespeare, who only thought it was worthy of one scene (Act 3, 1). Bianca is mainly a plot point; she can only marry after Katherine does. Thus Hortensio and Gremio encourage Petruchio to wed Katherine so they might have an opportunity to woo Bianca (Act 1, 2).

In *Kiss Me, Kate*, the courting consists of the number, "Tom, Dick or Harry," in which Gremio (much younger than Shakespeare's pantaloon) offers her wealth; Lucentio, love; and Hortensio, social status. Bianca does not care about any of their offers; she "will take double quick" any Tom, Dick, or Harry just to get married. As in *The Shrew*, Lucentio prevails over the others, although Spewack's Lucentio does not have the wealth of his Shakespearean counterpart. In keeping with her streamlining of the play, Spewack wisely eliminated the scene in which Lucentio wins Bianca's hand because he is richer than his competitors (Act 2, 1), since it would only have added another unnecessary complication. Lucentio must produce his father as a witness to his wealth. Like Garrick's redaction, Spewack's centers around Katherine and Petruchio.

Just as Garrick was faithful to the spirit of the original, Spewack was equally scrupulous in adhering to the play's structure, including retaining the play-within-a-play concept, resulting in a double-plotted musical. Just as Sly is watching a performance of *The Shrew* (when he isn't nodding off), the *Kiss Me, Kate* audience is watching a musical *version* of the comedy on stage and witnessing the melodrama taking place offstage, which even spills over into the performance, making it impossible to think of them not as two distinct plots but of one plot with another neatly folded into it. *Kiss Me, Kate* is a special kind of play within a play. Shakespeare's induction, in which a company of actors is performing *The Shrew* for "Lord" Sly, gave Spewack the idea of having the four principals of the offstage story (Fred Graham, Lilli Vanessi, Lois Lane, and Bill Calhoun) play Petruchio, Katherine, Bianca, and Lucentio as members of a sixteenth century "troupe of strolling players," thus uniting the onstage performance with the offstage imbroglio involving a forged signature on an IOU, flowers delivered to the wrong party, gangsters demanding payment, and the leading lady walking out before the show is over.

The Doubled Plot

Fred Graham, an actor-director-producer like David Garrick, is starring as Petruchio in a musical version of *The Taming of the Shrew*, with his recently divorced wife, Lilli Vanessi, as Katherine. The setting is Baltimore's Ford's Theatre, suggesting an out-of-town tryout. Perhaps out of revenge, Graham has become so dictatorial toward Lilli that she calls him a "bastard," which also happens to be her first line. To spite him, Lilli reminds him that it is the first anniversary of their divorce and that she is now engaged to Harrison Howell, a prominent Washingtonian, flashing her engagement ring as proof. Like Hildy Johnson (played by Rosalind Russell in *His Girl Friday*, 1940), she may be hoping that Graham will extricate her from the engagement and realize that, for all their self-dramatizing, they are still a team—preferably a married one.

Graham has discovered a nightclub singer, Lois Lane, whom he is trying to groom into a serious actor and whom he has cast as Bianca. Lois, however, is in love with Bill Calhoun (Lucentio), a compulsive gambler who signed Graham's name to a $10,000 voucher. Graham and Lilli still feel some affection for each other as they reminisce about their days in operetta. To bolster Lois's spirits, Graham has flowers sent to her which are accidentally delivered to Lilli. Since they are identical to her wedding bouquet, Lilli believes Graham still loves her. When she discovers the truth, she threatens to leave the show just as two low-level gangsters arrive to collect the $10,000. Lilli is forced to stay on when Fred reminds them that if she leaves, the production will shut down, and there would be no payment. The show continues until the gangsters get word that their boss has been murdered, which makes the voucher a moot point. Lilli, still feeling betrayed, leaves before the final scene. Graham is forced to improvise, but then Lilli, having had a change of heart, comes on stage to sing her declaration of dependence, "I Am Ashamed That Women Are So Simple," leading into the finale as Lilli/Katherine calls Fred/Petruchio "caro" and "carissimo," and each pledges to be "thine" to the other. Happy ending, nice and tidy, with the onstage and offstage actions becoming one.

As late as October 30, 1948, two months before the New York opening, Spewack had the curtain rising on Lilli's dressing room where she and Lois were rehearsing their first scene (Act 1, 1), in which Gremio and Hortensio seek Baptista's permission to court his daughter. Baptista assumes they mean Katherine, but it is really Bianca. Katherine, annoyed, responds in her usual acerbic manner, causing Bianca to ask if she is satisfied with the friction she has caused ("Sister, content you in my discontent"). Spewack apparently thought that opening with Lilli and Lois working on their lines would indicate that the action will take place both offstage and onstage. In the second scene, Graham is going over the order of the curtain call and is especially critical of Lilli, who retaliates with "Bastard!" Still no musical number, just two scenes; the first says nothing except that two women are running over their lines, whose source only a Shakespeare scholar might recognize; the second suggests an offstage battle of the sexes parallel to the one on stage between Petruchio and Katherine. Finally, in the third scene, we get the first number: "Another Op'nin', Another Show."

Kiss Me, Kate as Integrated Musical

By the time of the New York premiere, December 30, 1948, the dressing room scene with Lilli and Lois had been dropped, and the curtain went up on the stage of Baltimore's Ford Theatre with Fred rehearsing the curtain call. "How about a little smile, Miss Vanessi?" Lilli has a one-word rejoinder: "Bastard!" The rehearsal ends with Fred thanking the company. Then Hattie, the "wardrobe mistress" and probably Lilli's dresser, comes on singing "Another Op'nin', Another Show," joined later by the company (minus the four principals). In some productions—for example, the 1989 revival—the rehearsal *followed* "Another Op'nin.'"

Unlike Irving Berlin's "There's No Business Like Show Business" in *Annie Get Your Gun* (1946), in which "show business" is Buffalo Bill's Wild West Show (although the sentiments expressed are applicable to any of the performing arts), "Op'nin'" recounts the preparatory stages of a Broadway-bound musical: the expectations, the doubts, the grueling four weeks of rehearsal, the physical pain—all leading up to "that big first night" when the curtain rises after the overture, and what had been a book and a score coalesce into what Julian Marsh (Warner Baxter) in *42nd Street* (1933) called "the most glorious words in the English language": musical comedy.

In seventeen lines—three sections of four lines each and a five-line coda that brings "Op'nin'" to a triumphant finish—Porter has traced the genesis of a musical from the rehearsals to opening night, depicting mounting intensity through accent displacement, so that dissyllabic words like "hello" (unstressed/stressed) and "future" (stressed/unstressed) become two stressed syllables, slowing down the lines by augmenting the anxiety that comes with uncertainty. The rhyme scheme is fairly simple: the first section is A/A/A/A (show/**moe**, as in Balti**moe**/ hello/show); the second, A/A/B/B (last/past/grow/show); the third, really the middle part, A/A/B/B again (re**hearse**/worse/right/night). Just when you think Porter is deviating from the four-line format, he begins the last section as he did the second and third: A/A/B/ (start/heart/go). You expect "show" next, but Porter wanted to end the number with an operatic high note, so the fourth line is "another op'nin'"; and the fifth, "just another op'nin' of another show," with "show" at the apex as a resounding E-flat.

The revised opening was a vast improvement over the original that had Lilli and Lois rehearsing their lines, which would only make sense to someone familiar with the play and knew the source of the line, "Sister, content you in my discontent." "Another Op'nin'" makes it clear, without any spoken dialogue (much less Shakespeare's), that the stage is being set up for a musical ("The overture is about to start"). The curtain call rehearsal suggests that whatever this musical may be, it will have something to do with the director and his leading lady. Regardless of the order of the first two scenes, "Another Op'nin'" is atypical of Porter. One writer has wisely observed that Porter chose not to imitate the innovative opening of Rodgers and Hammerstein's *Oklahoma!* (1943), in which the curtain rose on a woman churning butter as offstage a baritone, later identified as Curley, begins singing "Oh, What a Beautiful Mornin'" as he enters. "Beautiful Mornin'" is a solo; "Op'nin'" is a production number. Some of Porter's musicals—for example, *Anything Goes*—open with spoken dialogue followed by a musical number; others, with a plot- or mood-setting chorus. *Du Barry Was a Lady* opens with the ensemble singing "Where's Louie?" The audience does not know who Louis is yet, only that he's a sweepstakes winner, an important plot point; *Panama Hattie*, with "A Stroll on the Plaza Sant'Ana," with vendors peddling their wares, singing of Panama's diverse culture ("the white meat and the dark") and unhurried lifestyle. But none of his shows had ever opened like *Kiss Me, Kate*. Porter wanted to top everything he had ever done. And he succeeded.

Structurally, each of the two acts consists of eight scenes. In Act 1, Scenes 1–3 and 6–7 take places back stage (offstage plot); 4, 5, and 8 onstage (*The Shrew*). Act 2 opens in the alley behind the theatre with the crew performing "Too Darn Hot" in foxtrot tempo, which parallels the first musical number of Act 1, but with highly suggestive lyrics, implying that sex is impossible when it's "too darn hot." Scenes 3 and 8 are part of *The Shrew*, while Scenes 4, 5, 6, and 7 belong to the offstage plot. For a musical version of *The Shrew*, the audience sees more of what is happening offstage than what is being enacted onstage. Spewack was more interested in the Fred-Lilli/Lois-Bill/voucher/gangsters/Lilli's fiancé/her precipitous departure plot threads than she was in winnowed-down Shakespeare. Spewack was temporarily separated from her husband Sam, who, like Fred Graham, had been having an affair with a younger woman; theirs was a stormy marriage but it never led to divorce. Perhaps Bella felt that the fractious relationship between Fred and Lilli was similar to hers with Sam and had greater dramatic potential than the Petruchio-Katherine plot.

The songs in the offstage plot—"Why Can't You Behave?" "Wunderbar," "So in Love," "Always True to You in My Fashion," and "Brush Up Your Shakespeare"—achieved greater popularity than those in *The Shrew* plot, which are primarily character songs: Katherine's "I Hate Men," which is totally uncharacteristic of Shakespeare's Katherine; Petruchio's haunting "Were Thine That Special Face"; and the rollicking "Where Is the Life That Late I Led?" The last two—"Were Thine That Special Face" and "Where Is the Life That Late I Led?"—derive from the text; the former, inspired by Bianca's admission that she has yet to see "that special face / Which I could fancy more than any other" (Act 2, 1); the latter, from a ballad that Petruchio begins singing in Act 5, 1.

"So in Love" became an instant hit, recorded by both popular vocalists (Bing Crosby, Frank Sinatra with Keely Smith, Tony Bennett, Ella Fitzgerald, Peggy Lee, Patti Page, Dinah Shore, Eddie Fisher) and opera singers (Mario Lanza, Placido Domingo, Cesare Siepi, Robert Merrill with Roberta Peters, Lily Pons, Mimi Benzell, Renée Fleming with Bryn Terfel), who treated it as an aria.

In Act 1, 2, the offstage plot begins. Bill, who was absent from the curtain call rehearsal because he was gambling, admits to Lois that he lost $10,000 and signed Graham's name to a voucher. Lois is disheartened and expresses her disappointment in him ("Why Can't You Behave?"). Porter composed the song in 4/4 time like a pavane—slow and measured with ascending and descending vocal lines reflecting Lois's frustration at her attempts to get Bill to "turn that new leaf over." Porter specified "slow blues," indicating that "Why Can't You Behave?" is not a rueful torch song but a lament. Lisa Kirk, who created the role of Lois, had a smoky contralto that was perfect for the number and comes through clearly on the original cast recording. The problem, however, is that the song has greater depth than the character. In the middle part, Lois sings about a farm she knows where they "could settle down." It's pure fantasy; show business is their world, and Lois is not a one-man woman. In Act 2, 4, she encounters Harrison Howell backstage and reminds him of the last time they were together. Bill overhears her, which is her cue for "Always True to You in My fashion," a list song in which she enumerates the various men who have lavished her with gifts, adding that she is always true to Bill—in her fashion. "Always True to You in My Fashion" is more in character than "Why Can't You Behave?," which is a bluesy reaction to an admission of forgery.

Fred and Lilli's adjoining dressing rooms is the setting for Act 1, 3. The tension generated during the curtain call rehearsal has dissipated, and Lilli and Fred reminisce about the past. Lilli recalls a duet they sang in an operetta, which was "something about a bar." Fred remembers it: "Wunderbar," a Viennese confection like Sacher torte, which Porter composed in waltz time, specifying "*Tempo di Valse Viennese*." Musically, it's a glorious duet in swirling ¾ time, evoking a ballroom with waltzing couples. The verse begins: "Gazing down on the Jungfrau/From our secret chalet for two." Since the Jungfrau is an extremely high mountain in the Bernese Alps, the chalet would have had to be in the empyrean. But if Shakespeare could set *The Winter's Tale* "on the seacoast of Bohemia," Porter should be allowed his geographical gaffe.

The duet has rekindled the affection Lilli still feels for Fred. When the flowers intended for Lois are mistakenly delivered to her with a note, which Lilli ignores for the moment, she is thrilled that they are the same as her wedding bouquet ("Snowdrops and pansies and rosemary. My wedding bouquet"). Lilli assumes that since Fred remembered the floral arrangement (which was probably accidental), the love they shared has not died. She begins one of the best loved songs in American musical theater, "So in Love." The text consists of eighteen lines—three four-line segments, and a fourth cum coda. Segment one is A/A/B/B (**dear/dear/sky/I**); the second, C/C/B/B (**you/you/why/I**); the third or middle part, D/D/E/E (**mysterious/delirious/there/care**). The surprise comes in the fourth: F/F/B (**me/me/die**). You expect "**I**," but Porter extends the lyric—and the music—for three more lines until the song ends with the complementary rhyme: "So in love / . . . am **I**." Porter used remote rhyme before but here the extension of the lyric and the vocal line has a dramatic function: it reflects the change that Lilli undergoes as love, the emotion, becomes her love, the person.

Like "Always True to You in My Fashion," "So in Love" is both motivated and in character. When Lilli sings, "So taunt me, and hurt me / Deceive me, desert me," she is not playing masochist or martyr. She is playing Lilli Vanessi, diva, and a tempestuous one at that, which becomes evident when she finally reads the note that came with the flowers. She is the type of actor who is always "on," reacting to situations as if she were starring in a melodrama in which she has to say, "Do with me what you will. I'm yours forever." One can imagine Lilli expressing such sentiments onstage and in real life. For her there is no difference. One can also imagine her calling Fred a bastard in front of the company, storming onstage and interrupting a scene, and then walking out of the show. Life for her is theater without a set; ordinary emotions are elevated to whatever level they can reach, and should calm prevail, they drop to ground level. "So in Love" requires warmth *and* passion, best sung by an artist who can make oversized emotions seem like natural states of mind.

The Shrew plot begins in Act 1, Scene 4. The four principals—Fred, Lilli, Lois, and Bill—come onstage dressed in multicolored *commedia dell'arte* costumes as traveling players making the rounds of Italy ("We Open in Venice"), unlike Act 1 of Shakespeare's *Shrew*, which begins with the arrival of Lucentio and his servant Tranio in Padua, where Lucentio intends to study at the famed university. Spewack was apparently dissatisfied with this opening and found a line that could better set the plot in motion. In Act 1, 1, Gremio, frustrated by Baptista's refusal to allow his younger daughter to marry before the elder, wishes that someone "would thoroughly woo [Katherine], wed her, and bed her." Spewack transferred Gremio's sentiments to Baptista, becoming his first line and very much in character, since he wishes the same. What Baptista and the other men do not realize is that Katherine's "scolding tongue" is a weapon of wit, enabling her to hold her own in any verbal volley.

Spewack's Katherine is indifferent to marriage and goes so far as to express her contempt for men in general, which Shakespeare's Katherine never does. But Katherine as created by Spewack and given voice by Porter is truly a wildcat, which was the simplest way of portraying her for audiences who have not read the original—which would include most of them, since *Shrew* is not commonly read in schools or even in a typical undergraduate Shakespeare class. Porter composed "I Hate Men" in 4/4 time, specifying "solemnly" at the beginning as Katherine bangs a tankard on a table, declaiming the first line of each of the four refrains which begins with the title. Then the vocal line is marked *cantabile* and "gaily" as she runs through various types of males, the most loathsome being the vain athlete who may have hair on his chest but "so has Lassie." That was a metaphor worthy of Shakespeare's heroine. In fact, the entire song would have been in keeping with Shakespeare's Katherine if it were entitled "I Know Men," which she clearly does.

Baptista finds an ideal match in the recently arrived Petruchio, who states his sole reason for coming to Padua, and it is not to study at the university: "I've come to wive it wealthily in Padua; / If wealthily, then happily in Padua" (Act 1, 2: 74–75). These became the opening lines of Petruchio's first number, "I've Come to Wive It Wealthily in Padua," which begins in a march-like tempo with a succession of B-flats and E-flats suggesting unrelenting determination. Spewack's Petruchio is far more mercenary than Shakespeare's, admitting that if his wife has a bag of gold, it makes no difference "if the bag is old"—wordplay that is not especially witty but revelatory. It is best not to take these lyrics too seriously since they reveal a cynicism that is more Porter's than Petruchio's.

Porter took the title of Petruchio's next number, "Were Thine That Special Face," from Bianca's admission to her sister that she has yet to see "that special face / Which I could fancy more than any other" (Act 2, 1). The song, composed in 4/4 time, begins with a ten-line verse to be delivered "quasi recitativo and tenderly," in which Petruchio recalls a poem that he had originally written tongue-in cheek, but on seeing Katherine realizes that everything in it applies to her. Rhythmically, the verse is irregular with lines of varying length as one might expect in recitative. The ten-line refrain that follows is in "slow foxtrot tempo." Whether the refrain is Petruchio's poem is unclear, although the verse implies that it is. The poem was written in the subjunctive mood with "were thine" repeated six times. Petruchio's ideal woman must have "rhythm'd grace," a form "so lithe and slender," arms "so warm and tender," and "the kiss divine." The poem suits Spewack's Petruchio, who, in addition to being mercenary, is also vain, thinking nothing of writing a poem, however tongue-in-cheek, exercising his masculine superiority by listing his requirements for a wife. Shakespeare's Katherine would have realized he was playing the ardent suitor, eager to wive it wealthily. Spewack's Katherine has no other choice but to believe she possesses "all these charms," until she makes her exit and finally reads the note that came with the flowers. Furious, she goes into wounded diva mode, rushes onstage, and interrupts the performance, which Fred, more professional than she, continues as if her behavior were part of the script, even spanking her while staying in character, with Lilli unwittingly living up to Katherine's reputation as a "wildcat."

In the penultimate scene of Act 1, Lilli, still in diva mode, informs Fred she is leaving the show. Just then the gangsters arrive for the $10,000, only to have Fred inform them that the leading lady is quitting, and if she does, the show will close. Lilli is forced to remain; the gangsters, to make certain she does, don *dell arte* costumes and mingle with the crowd for the first act finale, which takes place outside a church after the wedding of Petruchio and Katherine. Fred sticks to the script ("So kiss me, Kate"). Lilli goes off script and says, "No!" When he sings "Mine," she replies, "Swine," even rhyming "Dastard" with "Bastard." In the play, the marriage ceremony takes place offstage, which Gremio describes as a raucous affair (Act 3, 2), with Petruchio and his "mates" drinking heavily and creating mayhem. What should have been one of the seven sacraments became, in Gremio's words, "such a mad marriage never was before."

In the musical, Act 1 ends with the Chorus pleading, "Kiss him, Kate." When Lilli refuses, Fred, who has had enough, throws her over his shoulder as the curtain falls. Act 2 is the reverse of Act 1. Just as the first act opened on the stage of the Ford Theatre with "Another Op'nin," the second act begins in the alley behind the theatre with "Too Darn Hot," which is not a musical map of the arduous journey to opening night but a list song, jazzy and syncopated in 4/4 time, about the waning of the libido when "the thermometer goes way up," In Act 2, Scene 2, the musicalized *Shrew* continues with Petruchio trying to starve Katherine into submission. Spewack included some of the original dialogue from *Shrew* Act 4, 1, in which perfectly cooked meat is brought in, which Petruchio rejects as "burnt and dried away," leaving Katherine desperately hungry. Spewack, however, omits his other deprivations, including a cap that Katherine fancies but that Petruchio dismisses as "paltry" and her gown of choice, which he calls "a skein of thread." The denial of food is sufficient. Shakespeare's Katherine stands up very well to Petruchio's tyranny, nor does she behave like a suppliant, suggesting perhaps that she can beat him at his own game, which in a sense she does. It is evident that they have come to an understanding when she agrees to give him a kiss in public at the end of Act 5, 1.

In the musicalized *Shrew*, Fred/Petruchio takes great delight in tormenting Lilli/Katherine, with Lilli behaving more like her betrayed self than her character. They are not so much playing Petruchio and Katherine as they are a divorced couple, still drawn to each other but too self-absorbed—and in Lilli's case, too self-dramatizing—to admit it. Shakespeare's Petruchio pines for his old life (Act 4, 1), and one suspects that at this point Fred does, too, after having had to play two scenes, including the first act finale, with a costar who refused to stick to the text. In *Kiss Me, Kate*, all of Petruchio's songs were inspired by lines from the play, including his last, "Where Is the Life That Late I Led?" In Act 4, 2, Petruchio begins singing a popular ballad now considered lost: "Where is the life that late I led? / Where are those—" In the first performances of *Shrew*, Petruchio may have sung the entire ballad, which Porter completed in typically high style. Shakespeare's Petruchio has led a life filled with adventure: "Have I not in my time heard lions roar? / Have I not heard the sea puff'd up with winds"

(Act 1, 2: 199–200). Apparently Petruchio's adventures did not include romance. Porter's Petruchio is kin to the Don that Leporello describes in his catalogue aria in *Don Giovanni*, who seduced one thousand three women in Spain alone. In "Where Is the Life That Late I Led?," Petruchio's adventures were solely with women. In the verse, he admits that ever since puberty, he "always had a multitude of girls." And in the refrain, he cites them by name and city, as opposed to Leporello, who cites the Don's by country and number.

The best example is Lisa from Pisa: "And lovely **Lisa**, where are you **Li-i-i-sa** [four syllables]? / You gave a new **meaning** to the **leaning** tower of **Pi-i-i-sa** [four syllables]." Porter fashioned "Where Is the Life That Late I Led?" as an operatic aria, ending with the last line of the title. With "**led**," the tempo changes, and the song ends with a flourish like an operatic cadenza with "led" embellished and held for six measures—the kind of a bravura finish that generates lusty applause.

After Fred/Petruchio finishes "Where Is the Life That Late I Led?," the offstage plot resumes. Lois spots Harrison Howell, who has come backstage to see Lilli. Lois reminds him of their onetime fling, and he begs her not to tell Lilli. Bill overhears their conversation, and questions Lois's fidelity. Lois responds with the opening lines of "Why Can't You Behave?," which function as the verse to her big number, "Always True to You in My Fashion." The tempo of the verse marked "*moderato*" slowly begins to change as Lois insists that she loves Bill, and then adds—"but naturally." Suddenly, there is a switch from *moderato* to "medium bounce" as Lois launches into the refrain, a list song in which she enumerates the various men in her life, insisting that she is always true to Bill—in her fashion, implying that he is at the head of the line. Porter specified "bright and in strict rhythm" for the four refrains, in which Lois describes each of her suitors/lovers/gentleman callers/whatever in three lines, with the fourth and fifth being, "But I'm always true to you, darlin', in my fashion / Yes, I'm always true to you, darlin', in my way."

Harold Lang, a classically trained dancer with a decent, if not great, voice, complained to Porter that, of the four principals, he was the only one without a solo. Porter obliged by writing "Bianca" for him realizing that, if monogamous Bill and tarnished Lois would get together, as they must for the Act 2 finale, Bill needs to respond in song to Lois's declaration of flexible fidelity. Originally Porter envisioned a modest production number with Bill trying out a song and dance routine with some ladies of the chorus, in which five messengers arrive, one after the other, singing "Package for Miss Lois Lane," to which the ladies add, "For your Bianca," and, for some reason, laugh. "Bianca" is a standard verse–refrain number. In the verse, Bill admits that, although his Bianca has "been around," "I still love her more and more." Apparently, her checkered past is an asset. Bill hopes she will accept his song, even though he is an amateur when it comes to verse. Porter makes certain that Bill lives up to his word. "Bianca" is a heartfelt, if sappy, response to "Always True to You in My Fashion." The sentiments are puerile, and the rhymes are typical of a neophyte: "Bianca"/"spanka": "You better answer yes or papa spanka," which mellow-voiced Lang sings playfully, making it sound ingenuous rather than sexist. Someone must have realized that, as conceived, "Bianca" would require a full stage. Since Lois sang "Always True to You in My Fashion" in the corridor back stage, that is finally where Lang performed "Bianca," sans messengers and chorus, singing the song wistfully and doing a soft shoe. Lois is touched, and all's well.

Meanwhile, Lilli has to explain to an incredulous Howell that two gangsters in *commedia dell arte* costumes are forcing her to continue the performance. But once they learn that their boss has been murdered, Lilli is free to leave. Fred, in an effort to dissuade her from quitting, takes a page from Cary Grant's playbook in *His Girl Friday*, when he succeeded in preventing ace reporter Rosalind Russell from leaving the newspaper world to marry insurance representative Ralph Bellamy, which would require their living in Albany with his mother. Fred tries the same approach, reminding Lilli of how boring life will be in Washington with Howell, when the only world she has ever known is the theater.

But it doesn't work. "Your cab's waiting, Miss Vanessi," the doorman announces—Fred's cue for a reprise of "So in Love," this time scored for a lyric baritone and sounding more personal, as if he were reliving the "night mysterious." From the way Alfred Drake, the original Fred/Petruchio, sings it on the recording, one can hear the deep yearning welling up in his voice. as he brings the song slowly to an end with "am I." The meditative "So in Love" is followed by the best remembered number in the show. In trying to leave the theatre, the two gangsters get caught onstage during a scene change and morph into vaudevillians with "Brush Up Your Shakespeare" as their routine. The gangsters are only identified in the playbill as First Man and Second Man and have no counterparts in Shakespeare's play, nor were they intended as comic relief. The show needs a scene-changer, and the two men provide it.

In the score, Porter called "Brush Up Your Shakespeare" a "Bowery Waltz," referring to a popular vaudeville act in which two Bowery types, slightly inebriated, perform a crudely executed waltz. The number was set to boozy ¾ time, calling for a delivery with little concern for cadence. The men do not so much sing the lyrics as play hopscotch with them. Take the opening line: "The girls today in society." The rhythm is askew; like the waltzing couple, it also seems under the influence. "The girls" are unstressed/stressed (x ′); "to-day" is two stressed syllables (′ ′), not one unstressed and the other stressed; "in" is unstressed (x); and "so-ci-e-ty," unstressed/stressed unstressed/stressed (x ′ x ′). It's a deliberately syncopated, jerky nine-syllable line.

The genius of "Brush Up Your Shakespeare" does not lie in the rhythm, which is reminiscent of a folksy singalong in a nickelodeon, but in the lyrics, in which Porter makes reference to thirteen plays and *Venus and Adonis*. The men claim that to attract a woman, do not quote Keats or Shelley, but rather "the bard of Stratford-upon-Avon." Porter knew it would be a showstopper and wrote five twelve-line refrains, each beginning with "brush up your Shakespeare," with a list of recommendations in perfect iambic pentameter. The recommendations show Porter at his wittiest. The references to the plays do not require any knowledge of them but only the ability to see the connection between the situation and the title. Porter, who could lay on innuendo with a heavy hand, wears a velvet glove in this wonderfully risqué couplet: "When your baby is pleading for pleasure / Let her sample your 'Measure for Measure.'"

After the last encore, the stage is ready for the final scene: the wedding of Bianca and Lucentio. In the play, Katherine and Petruchio are married offstage (Act 3, 2), as are Bianca and Lucentio (Act 5, 1). Spewack and Porter wanted parallel endings for Acts 1 and 2. Just as the first act ended with the festivities following the marriage of Katherine and Petruchio, with Lilli out of character railing against Fred trying to stay in character, the second—and last—act was to end with Katherine singing of a wife's duties before Bianca's wedding. When Lilli does not enter on cue, Fred keeps improvising. Just when it seems that he will have to make an announcement, Lilli walks onstage, fully costumed. Fred gently asks her to tell women "what duty they do owe to their lords and husbands" (Act 5, 2: 132). "I am ashamed that women are so simple" is her response, taken, for the most part, from the last eighteen lines of Katherine's climactic speech, but, as Porter notes in the score, "slightly altered by Cole Porter, with apologies."

Porter discarded the first twenty-four lines of the speech (Act 5, 2: 137–61), whose pentameters are weighted down with consonants, impeding the flow of the verse. When Katherine becomes dogmatic, she speaks in iambic prose: "Thy husband is thy lord, thy life, thy keeper" (Act 5, 2: 147). When she gets to "I am ashamed that women are so simple," the rhythm changes; it becomes unfettered and limpid, continuing in that vein until she starts reprimanding Bianca and the Widow (Act 5, 2: 170). Then it becomes leaden again: "Come, come, you froward and unable worms," which Porter cut both because of the gross metaphor and Spewack's elimination of Shakespeare's ending, in which the Widow and Bianca are onstage during the speech. Porter also cut the next six lines and, needing a bridge between "Should well agree with our external parts?" and "And place your hands below your husband's foot," added a line of his own and revised one of Shakespeare's. The new line is "So wife, hold your temper"; the revised, "And meekly put your hand 'neath the sole of your husband's foot," returning to Shakespeare for the concluding couplet: "In token of which duty, if he please. / My hand is ready, may it do him ease." By a change from plural to singular ("hands" to "hand"), the substitution of one preposition for another ("'neath" for "below"), and the addition of "sole," Porter has muted the patriarchal echoes of the original.

"I Am Ashamed That Women Are So Simple" is one of Porter's most perfectly constructed compositions, whose grace and rhythm derive in large part from Shakespeare. The first line (there is no verse) is the song title, to be delivered, as Porter wrote, "with calm diction, almost solemnly," with the music played underneath it; then *sempre legato* (literally, "always connected"), meaning that transitions should be smoothly executed and unobtrusive. But at "So wife, hold your temper," Porter has written "broader, with great emphasis," and *poco ritardo* at "may it do him ease." Porter wanted the music to linger a bit at the end, marking the last bars *tempo morendo* ("dying away"). Ideally, there should be a moment of silence at the end, followed by applause. Elated, Petruchio exclaims, "Come on and kiss me, Kate," and what follows is one of the most joyous endings in musical theater. A chastened Lilli/Katherine calls Fred/Petruchio "caro," carissimo," "bello," and "bellissimo," and each promises fidelity to the other. As Lilli and Fred (forget the characters) sing "Darling, mine" and "I am thine," the chorus take up their sentiments, changing the pronouns from first person to third ("And she is thine"). The curtain comes down with an explosion of joy: *crescendo molto*.

Porter included a "Grand Finale–Last Curtain," in which, after the curtain calls, the company sang a chorus of "Brush Up Your Shakespeare" but with new lyrics: "So tonight just recite to your matie. / Kiss me, Kate, Kiss me, Kate, Kiss me, Katie."

Kiss Me, Kate was Cole Porter's crowning achievement: 10,077 performances in New York, first at the long-gone New Century Theatre at Columbus Circle in New York and then at the Shubert Theatre on

W. Forty-fourth Street. It has been performed worldwide and even at opera houses in Europe, where it is treated as operetta. There would be three more Broadway musicals, two of which were hits. But none was a *Kiss Me, Kate*.

ON SCREEN: *KISS ME KATE* (MGM, 1953)

Finally, a studio showed some respect for a Cole Porter musical. Screenwriter Dorothy Kingsley—who had worked on a number of MGM musicals and had written the screenplays for *Bathing Beauty* (1944), *Broadway Rhythm* (1944), and *Two Weeks with Love* (1950)—stayed reasonably close to the book, which she modified to make *Kiss Me Kate* (no comma) into the kind of musical with which moviegoers were familiar. Rather than open in a Baltimore theater, which would betray its stage origins, the film begins with Cole Porter (Ron Randell) at the piano playing the *Kiss Me, Kate* score in his apartment (obviously not the Waldorf Towers) for Fred Graham (Howard Keel), who will play Petruchio as well as direct. At first, his ex-wife, Lilli Vanessi (Kathryn Grayson), is indifferent to the project until she is offered the role of Katherine. Lois Lane (Ann Miller) arrives to audition for Bianca. It just so happens that she is wearing red tights and sporting a black fan; she then proceeds to tap her way around the room while singing "Too Darn Hot," apparently having been given the song in advance. But in a movie musical, plausibility does not matter. Audiences had become used to seeing an actor look at a piece of sheet music and then sing the song without even giving it another glance. Kingsley was bringing Broadway to a mass audience that had grown accustomed to the film musical's codes and conventions. By 1953, movie audiences would have been familiar with the name of Cole Porter, but with a mobile Ron Randell playing the composer, one would never have thought that he was disabled. Lilli's fiancé is no longer a politician but a wealthy Texas rancher, renamed Tex Calloway (Willard Parker); the gangsters are no longer Man 1 and Man 2, but Lippy (Keenan Wynn) and Slug (James Whitmore). These were minor changes that did not affect the storylines.

Except for "Another Op'nin', Another Show" and "Bianca," which is heard but not sung, Porter's score remained intact. There was one interpolation, "From This Moment On," which was originally written for William Eythe's character in *Out of This World*. Although Eythe had achieved some success in Hollywood (*The Song of Bernadette*, *The Eve of St. Mark*, *The House on 92nd Street*), he was not a singer. The song went unused but was added to *Kiss Me Kate* as a showpiece for Ann Miller and three outstanding dancers, Bobby Van, Tommy Rall, and Bob Fosse. It was turned into a duet for Lilli (Marin Mazzie) and Harrison Howell (Ron Holgate) in the 1999 Broadway revival. Both Mazzie and Holgate could do the song justice. Each had a background in musical theater; Mazzie had major roles in Stephen Sondheim's *Passion* (1994) and *Ragtime* (1998); Holgate, in addition to appearing in the musicals *1776* (1968) and the revival of *Annie Get Your Gun* with Bernadette Peters, had also been an opera singer.

In the film, choreographer Hermes Pan made "From This Moment On" a continuation of the courting of Bianca, the complement to the earlier "Tom, Dick or Harry." Bianca is again in the company of her suitors, Gremio (Bobby Van), Lucentio (Tommy Rall), and Hortensio (Bob Fosse). It is also a song and dance number with the couples—Rall and Miller, Van and Jeanne Coyne, and Fosse and Carol Haney—dancing out of the entrances of a façade on stage left (the audience's right). While Miller, Rall, Van, and Coyne were superlative dancers, there was nothing distinctive about the choreography that Pan had devised for them. Suddenly a leg emerged from an entrance, and Carol Haney danced on to the stage. Then Bob Fosse came sliding in on his knees, striking an ardent pose. Fosse choreographed his and Haney's segment, uncredited. One could see the Fosse signature in its early stage: the puppet-like pose, arms dangling, head to the side, knees turned in. It was as if all tensions had been resolved, leaving him loose-limbed and free to respond to the rhythms oscillating within. In his *dell'arte* costume, Fosse was a cool harlequin, less of a clown and more of an acrobat of God, as Martha Graham might have said.

The casting was perfect: Howard Keel and Kathryn Grayson as Fred/Petruchio and Lilli/Katherine, Ann Miller as Lois Lane/Bianca, and Bobby Van as Bill Calhoun/Lucentio. Keel's virile baritone may have lacked the suavity of Alfred Drake's, but it worked to the film's advantage, as did Kathryn Grayson's lyric soprano with a higher range than Patricia Morison's mezzo. Since both Keel and Grayson had voices that were ideal for operetta, *Kiss Me Kate* inadvertently became one. On stage, *Kiss Me, Kate* was a Broadway musical; on the screen, it became an operetta, sung by two actors at the height of their vocal powers. If some of their songs, particularly "So in Love" and "Were Thine That Special Face," sounded like arias, it was because both had sung opera. Keel, then Harold, had done Rossini's *The Barber of Seville* in Los Angeles; Grayson generally performed arias in her musicals—"Sempre libera" from Verdi's *La Traviata* in *Thousands Cheer* (MGM, 1943); "Caro nome" from Verdi's *Rigoletto* in *That Midnight Kiss* (MGM, 1949); the first act love duet from Puccini's *Madame Butterfly* with Mario Lanza in *The Toast of New Orleans* (MGM, 1950). Grayson even played an opera singer in *Grounds for Marriage* (MGM, 1951), in which she sang Mimi's first act aria from Puccini's *La Bohème*.

Since the Production Code was still in full force, the dialogue and lyrics were far less racy than they were on stage. Lilli no longer calls Fred "Bastard!" but "Louse!" In "I Hate Men, "mother had to marry father" became "mother deigned to marry father." Katherine originally advised against marrying a businessman because "the business is the business that he gives his secretary." The advice still holds, but the line was changed to read: "his business is the business with his pretty secretary," which is still suggestive but in a different way. When she warned against traveling salesmen, she predicted, "'Tis he who'll have the fun, and thee the baby," which was replaced with: "When he's away in Mandalay, it's thee who'll have the baby." Only those who knew the original lyrics would have noticed their dilution.

Director George Sidney, whose specialty was the MGM musical (*Thousands Cheer, Bathing Beauty, Anchors Aweigh, The Harvey Girls, Holiday in Mexico, Annie Get Your Gun*), conveyed the impression of a show-in-progress with long shots of the First Nighters in their orchestra seats. Sidney also opened up the backstage area so Fred and Lilli could sing "Wunderbar" while waltzing in and out of their dressing rooms. He extended backstage to the alley by the stage door where Lois sings "Always True to You in My Fashion," and where Lippy and Slug perform "Brush Up Your Shakespeare" to cheer up a despondent Fred, who has just lost his leading lady. Sidney made *Kiss Me Kate* into a movie that looked like a stage play.

Kiss Me Kate was filmed between May and early July 1953 during the short-lived 3D craze, when Hollywood was resorting to any gimmick to keep audiences from defecting to television. Not knowing how long the fad would last, MGM filmed *Kiss Me Kate* in both 3D and the standard 1.33:1 aspect ratio for a rectangular screen that was about 1⅓ times wider than high. Anyone seeing *Kiss Me Kate* in 3D might have ducked when Grayson sang "I Hate Men" and threw a tankard that looked as if it were coming straight at you. And at the end, Grayson and Keel seemed to be coming right off the screen and on to your lap.

MGM also produced the film version of Porter's last Broadway musical, *Silk Stockings*. It was also faithful to its source, but was not another *Kiss Me, Kate*.

Cole Porter (1891–1964). Private Collection.

Irene Bordoni (1885–1953), star of Porter's first hit musical, *Paris* (1928). Photograph Research.

Fred Astaire and Eleanor Powell in *Broadway Melody of 1940* (1939). Private Collection.

Eleanor Powell in *Born to Dance* (MGM, 1936). Private Collection.

Red Skelton and Ann Sothern in *Panama Hattie* (MGM, 1942). Private Collection.

Patricia Morison and Alfred Drake in the live telecast of *Kiss Me, Kate*, NBC-TV, November 20, 1958. Private Collection.

Three Broadway legends: Ethel Merman, Richard Rodgers, and Mary Martin in 1978. United Press International, Inc.

Frank Sinatra and Bing Crosby singing "Well, Did You Evah!" in *High Society* (MGM, 1956). Private Collection.

Fred Astaire and Cyd Charisse in *Silk Stockings* (MGM, 1957). Silver Banks Pictures.

Janet Blair in *Something to Shout About* (Columbia, 1943). Private Collection.

Judy Garland and infant daughter Liza Minnelli on the set of *The Pirate* (MGM, 1948). Private Collection.

Ethel Merman, Victor Moore, and William Gaxton (with a fake beard) in *Anything Goes* (1934). Wisconsin Center for Film and Theater Research.

Ethel Merman in *Something for the Boys* (1943). Wisconsin Center for Film and Theater Research.

Mary Martin singing "My Heart Belongs to Daddy" in *Leave It to Me* (1938). Wisconsin Center for Film and Theater Research.

Don Ameche and Hildegarde Neff in *Silk Stockings* (1955). Wisconsin Center for Film and Theater Research.

Bert Lahr as Louis XV of France in *Du Barry Was a Lady* (1939). Wisconsin Center for Film and Theater Research.

Ethel Merman as May Dally in *Du Barry Was a Lady* (1939). Wisconsin Center for Film and Theater Research.

Fred Astaire and Rita Hayworth rehearsing in *You'll Never Get Rich* (Columbia, 1941). Wisconsin Center for Film and Theater Research.

Gwen Verdon in *Can-Can* (1953). Wisconsin Center for Film and Theater Research.

Charlotte Greenwood as Juno in *Out of this World* (1959). Wisconsin Center for Film and Theater Research.

CHAPTER 14

Regards to Broadway

Out of this World, Can-Can, and *Silk Stockings*

Greek mythology has always fired the imaginations of dramatists. The stories are timeless, and even more important—at least from a commercial standpoint—they are in the public domain, ready for updating, reworking, and rethinking. The Greeks themselves did not consider their myths sacrosanct. In the *Oresteia*, Aeschylus adhered to the traditional account of Agamemnon's sacrificing his daughter Iphigenia so that the weather would improve and his army could continue on to Troy where the Trojan prince Paris has carried off Helen, his brother's wife. In Euripides's *Helen*, however, the woman that Paris abducted was a phantom; the real Helen spent the duration of the war in Egypt. Euripides also offered two different versions of the fate of Iphigenia. In *Iphigenia at Aulis*, even though Achilles vows to save her, Iphigenia agrees to be sacrificed, believing that her death will bring glory to Greece. In *Iphigenia at Tauris*, a later play, the goddess Artemis substitutes a deer in Iphigeneia's place and brings her to Tauris where she becomes a priestess,

Some twentieth-century playwrights retained a myth's ancient setting (e.g., Andre Gide's *Oedipus*, Jean Cocteau's *The Infernal Machine*), but most changed time and place, following the same plot trajectory with a mix of new characters and others who evoked their mythical counterparts. In *Mourning Becomes Electra*, Eugene O'Neill's retelling of the *Oresteia*, the setting is New England at the end of the Civil War; Agamemnon has become Ezra Mannon; his wife, Clytemnestra, Christine Mannon; their children, Orestes and Electra, Orin and Lavinia. He added a gardener and townspeople who function as a Greek chorus; and a brother and sister, Peter and Hazel Niles—the former in love with Lavinia; the latter, with Orin. O'Neill could evoke the same mood of inexorability that broods over Greek tragedy without setting the action in ancient Greece, as evidenced in *Desire under the Elms*, with its overtones of the Hippolytus myth; and

Strange Interlude, with its oedipal conflict between a son and his biological father of whom he has no knowledge.

The French playwright Jean Giraudoux preferred to retain the classical settings of *Amphitryon 38* (1929), *The Trojan War Will Not Take Place* (1935, better known as *Tiger at the Gates*), and *Electra* (1937). One of the gems of the 1937–38 Broadway season was *Amphitryon 38*, a Theatre Guild production adapted by S. N. Behrman, with Alfred Lunt and Lynn Fontanne, that ran for 153 performances. The Amphitryon myth reads like a bedroom farce. Jupiter, who had assumed other forms in the past to seduce women (as a bull to carry off Europa, a swan to impregnate Leda, a shower of gold to penetrate Danäe), has now taken the form of Alcumena's husband, Amphitryon, while he is away at war. When Amphitryon returns, he is surprised that Alcumena has not welcomed him, unaware that she believes she spent the night with him. Only Jupiter can set matters right. Alcumena, who was pregnant when Amphitryon went off to war, gives birth to two sons; Iphicles, by Amphitryon; and Hercules, by Jupiter. And so, a god gets a son, who will be a demigod; and Amphitryon, one who will be mortal like himself and Alcumena.

Arnold Saint Subber, who came up with the idea of an onstage-backstage musical that evolved into *Kiss Me, Kate*, was still working as a stage manager for the Theatre Guild in 1937 when *Amphitryon 38* opened. It may have been he who convinced Porter that another musical based on a play could be the successor to *Kiss Me, Kate*. The Amphitryon myth would have appealed to Porter's sense of the bawdy, which had not been on display since *Du Barry Was a Lady*. However, Giraudoux's was supposedly the thirty-eighth retelling of the myth. In the booklet included in the *Out of this World* CD, Didier C. Deutsch wrote that the musical was "based on Titus Maccius' Plautus' comedy." Porter's biographer cites *Amphitryon 38* as the source. Both are correct.

Plautus, *Amphitryon* (c 188 BCE)

In the expository prologue, Mercury, Zeus's son disguised as Amphitryon's servant, Sosia, provides the background information and announces that the play to be performed is a tragicomedy, where it seems to be heading when Amphitryon accuses Alcumena of infidelity, causing a sudden switch from farce to melodrama, as Alcumena professes her fidelity to her husband. Perhaps Sophocles, who wrote an *Amphitryon* that is lost, brought out the story's tragic potential, but Alcumena is not a wronged wife like Shakespeare's Desdemona in *Othello* or Hermione in *The Winter's Tale*. Nor is she the stock *matrona* of Roman comedy. Alcumena is unique; a faithful and devoted wife whom Jupiter has chosen to bear his son—a privilege she would have refused if she had not been deceived. Plautus has refashioned the myth into a comedy of double mistaken identity. Not only does Jupiter take on Amphitryon's form, but Mercury also assumes Sosia's. When Sosia sees his lookalike, he is thoroughly confused. As a god, Mercury has the upper hand and bars Sosia from entering the house. When Sosia informs Amphitryon, who has just returned from the war, about the second Sosia, Amphitryon thinks he is mad. He thinks the same about Alcumena when she reminds him that they had spent the previous night together—a night that Jupiter deliberately prolonged to gratify his desires. Amphitryon is on the verge of becoming unhinged himself, when a roll of thunder signals that Alcumena has given birth to two boys. Jupiter absolves Alcumena of wrongdoing, explaining to Amphitryon that his son by Alcumena is Hercules; and that the other, Iphicles, is his. The breezily amoral comedy ends with Amphitryon giving thanks to Jupiter for the clarification. Few wives have had the privilege of a visit from a god, much less the supreme Olympian. Amphitryon has every reason to rejoice. His wife has given birth to a demigod who will generate a mythology of his own—a demigod who, technically, is Amphitryon's stepson

Jean Giraudoux, *Amphitryon 38* (1929)

Giraudoux retained five characters from Plautus's *Amphitryon*—Jupiter, Mercury, Amphitryon, Alcumena (now Alcmena), and Sosie (Sosia)—and added a few of his own, notably Leda, whom Zeus impregnated in the form of a swan. Since *Amphitryon 38* is neither travesty nor farce, Sosie and Mercury remain separate characters, who never meet even though at times Mercury assumes Sosie's form. But Giraudoux's most radical change in the myth is the absence of any physical contact between Jupiter and Alcmena, whose virtue remains intact. He dispenses with the Plautine prologue, choosing to begin with a conversation between Mercury and Jupiter, who is a sensualist like Mozart's Don, rhapsodizing about Alcmena's beauty and describing it in discreet but vivid detail. Mercury sounds more like his father's valet rather than his son, complaining that while Jupiter has access to the lady of the house, he winds up with the lady-in-waiting. Jupiter may be the supreme seducer, but he is unable to create a seduction scenario. All he can do is take on Amphitryon's appearance as if it were a costume, which is one of Giraudoux's distinctions between mortals and deities. Humans can mimic but not inhabit another's bodily form. The deities are actors whose idea of impersonation is not to pretend to be another but actually to *be* the other. They can intervene in human affairs but can experience only the most basic human emotions—passion, not love; acquaintanceship, not friendship.

Jupiter is so besotted with desire that Mercury has to provide him with a reason for Amphitryon's absence from Thebes: He must start a war. Giraudoux was especially adept at treating dialogue as *raisonnement*, as if it were a form of debate with one character stating a proposition and another rebutting it. Sosie has just finished extolling the virtues of peace when war is declared. The Warrior than enumerates the advantages of war: national unity and the birth of more male children, Giraudoux's Alcmena is not only the embodiment of the valiant woman in Proverbs 31: 10–31 but also one of subtle wit and keen intellect. Jupiter as Amphitryon tries to find out what Alcmena thinks about the gods. He asks if she would want to be immortal like them, adding that she would be admired and venerated. She scoffs at the idea: "Don't speak to me about immortality until there is an immortal vegetable. It's treason for a human to become immortal, Besides, when I think of the rest death will afford, from all of our petty fatigues and cheap annoyances, I'm grateful for its abundance, its plenitude."

When Mercury announces that Jupiter will visit Alcmena in the evening and make her the bearer of his child, the Thebans are delighted that the king of the gods has honored them with his presence. Alcmena and Leda resort to the bed trick with Leda substituting for her just as Mariana did for Isabella in Shakespeare's *Measure for Measure*. Jupiter is aware of the deception but is so impressed by Alcmena's unswerving fidelity to her husband that he offers her immortality, which she again rejects: "I detest adventures, and immortality is an adventure." Oddly, in James M. Barrie's *Peter Pan*, Peter says the reverse about death at the end of Act 3: "To die will be an awfully big adventure." Either way, death or life everlasting is an adventure. To Alcmena, the former is inevitable; the latter, unfathomable. But Alcmena can offer Jupiter something that only a mortal can: friendship, a word that he has never heard before. As the play comes to a close, one can see how Giraudoux transformed the myth of a lecherous god's deception of a mortal into a defense of conjugal love threatened by one who has never known it. Love conquers all, even a god's lust for a mortal. At the end, Jupiter addresses the audience, asking them to leave as he brings down the curtain of night which falls like the one at the end of a play. An ancient myth has been ennobled by the transformative power of theater.

ON STAGE: *OUT OF THIS WORLD* (1950)

Amphitryon 38 is a dazzling work, a blend of the artifice of theater and the *gravitas* of debate. As written, it is too dialectical for a Broadway musical. Richard Strauss might have made it work as a chamber opera along the lines of *Capriccio*, which attempted to answer the question—but cannot—as to what is more important in opera, the words or the music. Yet there were elements in both Plautus and Giraudoux that could be incorporated into a musical version of the Amphitryon story. The musical was originally entitled *Amphitryon* (which would have meant nothing to most theatergoers). Then it was changed to *Heaven on Earth*, and finally *Out of this World*, with book by Dwight Taylor, as revised by Reginald Lawrence. Taylor kept Plautus's prologue delivered by Mercury, which would signal that the musical is an updating of a Greek myth. Mercury appears in disguise as he does in both Plautus and Giraudoux. Night, which Jupiter invokes at the end of *Amphitryon 38*, is played by a dancer in a nonspeaking role who prolongs the *nuit d'amour* as Jupiter did in Plautus's *Amphitryon*. Taylor borrowed two other details from Giraudoux: Jupiter's offer of immortality to Alcmena (now called Helen), which she rejects; and a deity's parting words to the audience—the deity being neither Jupiter nor Mercury. In *Out of this World*, Jupiter's desire for Helen is sheer lust; he has no intention of fathering a child. There is no climactic birth, bed trick, or celebration of conjugal love, only a night in a Greek mountain inn where a woman believes she had slept with her journalist husband, only to discover that he was off tracking down a lead.

Neither Plautus nor Giraudoux alludes to Jupiter's wife, Juno, whose overbeating nature has led him to satisfy his desires with mortal women. For the Amphitryon story to work as a musical comedy, the plot could not revolve around a libidinous god, a virtuous wife, and her warrior husband—material for a one-acter about a god seducing a woman in the form of her husband. It might work if Juno, upon learning that Jupiter is infatuated with the wife of an American journalist, leaves Mount Olympus in search of her womanizing mate. As an added complication, the gangster, whose whereabouts the journalist is trying to discover, is the owner of the Arcadia Inn where the couple is staying and where Juno arrives in disguise.

Juno, then, would be the starring role. But who would play her? It would have to be a well-known comedienne with a passable voice for a score that made fewer demands on her than on the two sopranos, Priscilla Gillette as Helen and Barbara Ashley as Chloe, a worker at the inn courted by a shepherd but wanting a millionaire as a lover. Porter originally wanted

Carol Channing, who preferred to remain in *Gentleman Prefer Blondes*, which made her a star; then Judy Holliday, who declined. Finally, Charlotte Greenwood, who had not been on the stage since 1927, accepted the role.

Taylor's book had undergone so many changes that the musical numbers were inserted wherever they seemed appropriate. Mercury (the delightful William Redfield) delivers the prologue, which is not expository like Plautus's but a summary: "'Tis the tale of my sire / And his sudden desire / For a fair American mortal." A thunder roll signals the appearance of Jupiter (George Jongeyans, more famous as George Gaynes), who celebrates his libido in "I, Jupiter, I, Rex ("am positively teeming with sex"), with the male chorus chiming in with the onomatopoeic sound of the frogs in Aristophanes's *The Frogs*: "Brek-ek, co-ack, co-ack," adding "sex" to rhyme with "rex.," as if "rex" and "sex" were synonymous, which in Jupiter's case, they are. "I, Jupiter" can at least be considered a character song, but "Use Your Imagination" is awkwardly introduced. Jupiter instructs Mercury to find a way to bring the newly wed Helen and her newspaper reporter husband Art to Greece. In a New York bar, Helen (Priscilla Gilette) hears a strange melody sung by the invisible Mercury. She then sings "Use Your Imagination" to Art (non-singer William Eythe), promising that if he does, "ev'ry day will be a dream." Greece is their destination so that Art can track down small-time gangster and fugitive from justice Niki Skolianos (David Burns). When they arrive, Mercury in disguise offers to be their guide and sings the second refrain, adding that if Helen uses her imagination, Jupiter "will make your honeymoon a dream." "Use Your Imagination" is an excuse for Gillette to spin our Porter's music in 4/4 time and for Redfield to remind the audience that Helen has a surprise in store for her. It also happens to be the only song from the show to become popular, recorded by Frank Sinatra, Gordon MacRae, Mabel Mercer, and best of all by Jo Stafford, who observed Porter's markings—"moderato" at the beginning, then "freely." Stafford sang with such effortless conviction that you could believe that every day will be a dream.

In Act 1, 5, Juno (Charlotte Greenwood of the swinging legs) makes her entrance. "I Got Beauty" is not a great entrance number, but Greenwood is such a trouper that she turns it into one. The song is more clever than witty; the verse combines the music of "I, Jupiter" with lyrics more suited to Juno: "Me and he / Jupiter," in which she explains to the Olympians, who repeat "Brek-ek, co-ak, co-ak" (but not adding "sex"), that she is aware that her husband has designs on an American woman and wonders about her own appeal, listing all the qualities that she possesses. Disguised as a tourist, Juno ends up at the Arcadia Inn, where Chloe (Barbara Ashley) sings the most exuberant song in the musical, "Where, Oh Where?," dreaming of a lover "who'd still be a millionaire." Like "Wunderbar," the song is in ¾ time, so waltz-like that you can imagine Chloe dancing to it. It starts "moderato" and then accelerates, its swirling rhythms producing a heady effect. Although Ashley won a *Theatre World* award as a performer of promise, *Out of This World* was her third, and last, show in a stage career that only spanned a few years, from 1948 to 1951.

Du Barry Was a Lady had "Do I Love You?"; *Mexican Hayride*, "I Love You." One interrogative title, one declarative title, and now a title in the passive voice, "I Am Loved," which Helen, still in honeymoon mode, sings about Art. The music, composed in 4/4 time in a slow foxtrot tempo, as Porter indicated, is superior to the lyrics that are intended to be rapturous ("I'm adored / Absolutely adored") but only succeed in being banal, which was not the case with "Where, Oh Where?" That is the problem with the score. There are too few jewels and too many baubles. One of the jewels is Porter's list song, "They Couldn't Compare to You," which Mercury sings to the servers at the Arcadia Inn, boasting of being the lover of women both mythical (Circe, Calypso, Medea) and historical (Queen Isabella, Nell Gwynn, Anne Boleyn). "They Couldn't Compare to You" has the same rollicking rhythm of Petruchio's list song, "Where Is the Life That Late I Led?" but is far more suggestive, ending with a word, which, if uttered, would have infuriated the Boston censors, who had enough issues with the musical during the pre-Broadway tryout. Mercury ends his catalog recalling Melisande's "**locks**" and Pandora "who let me open her," and just as he is about to say "**box**," the servers break in with: "They couldn't compare to us." It may have taken a moment or two to register, but most theatergoers would have gotten the point.

As Act 1 comes to an end, Jupiter is ready for his rendezvous with Helen, summoning Night to prolong their *nuit d'amour*, which Jupiter did by himself in Plautus's *Amphitryon*. Juno, not knowing that Jupiter is already in Helen's room in the form of Art, guards the door, which gives Greenwood an opportunity for another number, "I Sleep Easier Now," grateful that the heyday in the blood is over.

Act 2 opens with the Olympians and Juno singing "Climb Up the Mountain," which sounds like a gospel-inflected "Blow, Gabriel, Blow" as Juno tries to persuade Skolianos, whom she believes is Jupiter in disguise, to return to Olympus, but to no avail. "Climb Up the Mountain" at least is motivated, with Greenwood singing with the fervor of an evangelist urging repentance. "No Lover for Me" is more of an ironic commentary on Helen's night with Jupiter than a reflection on it. In *Amphitryon 38*, Jupiter as Amphitryon pries into Alcmena's personal life to test her fidelity. When he asks if she wants a lover, she replies in the negative, citing several reasons and ending with "because I like to keep my windows opened and my bed nicely aired."

Porter seems to have been familiar with the play (Taylor definitely was), which may explain why Helen sings, "No lover for me, / My husband / Suits me to a 'T'"), unaware that she did not spend the night with her husband. The context may have appealed to Porter's sense of the perverse, since Helen had a lover in Jupiter. By trying to remain as faithful to Giraudoux as a musical comedy librettist can, Taylor kept losing the giddiness that the book needed, especially with Greenwood in the lead. Despite Taylor's objections, Reginald Lawrence was brought in to revise the book so that it would be the "crazy tale / We're about to unveil" that Mercury promised in the prologue. Yet Lawrence kept the denouement which is essentially Giraudoux's. Jupiter finally appears to Helen as himself, eager to take her to Olympus. Helen now knows the truth about that blissful night; when Jupiter offers her immortality, she rejects it, preferring a mortal with all of his imperfections. The rejection of immortality is straight out of *Amphitryon 38*, but with a difference: Alcmena rejects immortality not because she prefers a mortal, warts and all (her Amphitryon is perfect) but because it is an adventure, and she is not the adventuresome type.

The last number is the show's standout, Greenwood 's spectacular delivery of "Nobody's Chasing Me," throwing one of her legs out at a right angle and then swinging both of them as if they were on springs. She even went into a split, which was remarkable for a woman of sixty. "Nobody's Chasing Me" is similar to Montana's lament, "There Must Be Someone for Me," in *Mexican Hayride*. In four refrains (there is no verse), Juno goes through the natural, animal, and human world, lamenting that while the breeze chases the zephyr; the bull, the heifer; Isis, Osiris; Ravel, Debussy—nobody's chasing her. Greenwood gave audiences a double treat: you could marvel at the physicality of her performance and also at the way Porter sneaked in a bit of the bawdy, which he did not do in "There Must be Someone for Me," since it would not have suited the character. But Greenwood could make innuendo seem like denotation, even when singing, "The gander's chasing the goosey / But nobody's goosing me"; and "the fox is chasing the vixen / But nobody's vixin' me." It was a triumphant but short-lived (157 performances) return to Broadway. Greenwood never came back to the stage and made a few more films—*Oklahoma!* (1955) being the best known—before retiring. She died in 1977 at age eighty-seven.

Just as Jupiter delivered an envoi to the audience at the end of *Amphitryon 38*, Juno has some parting words, too:

> Ladies, a word. Patience above all and silence. What men don't know won't hurt them. It will only hurt you. And take a tip from a goddess. A kiss in the dark can't compare to a head on a shoulder on the way home.

Juno is drawing a moral from a morally ambiguous story in addition to resolving the plot. Art doesn't know about Helen's night with Jupiter. When she tries to tell him, he dismisses it as a dream. Juno is arguing that an indiscretion, intentional or otherwise, is a private affair. Besides, who would believe that a god donned a husband's form as if were apparel and slept with his wife? The entire company then reprises "Use Your Imagination," excellent advice to an audience that has spent two and a half hours with Greek deities intermingling with mortals until it was time for both to go their separate ways.

ON STAGE: CAN-CAN (1953)

After *Kiss Me, Kate*, Porter composed the scores of three more musicals—*Out of This World*, *Can-Can* (1953), and *Silk Stockings* (1955)—working as if time's wingèd chariot were at his back. Perhaps he felt that his Broadway days were drawing to a close, as indeed they were. Seven years after *Kiss Me, Kate* opened in New York, his last musical, *Silk Stockings*, arrived at the Imperial Theatre. There would be an abortive revival of *Can-Can* in 1981 and highly successful ones of *Anything Goes* and *Kiss Me, Kate*, but nothing new for Broadway.

The following time line shows how rapidly he worked, even though he was plagued by ill health and suffered from excruciating pain in his damaged legs:

> *Kiss Me, Kate* opened on December 30, 1948.
> *Out of This* World opened on December 21, 1950, and closed on May 5, 1951.
> *Can-Can* opened on May 7, 1953, and closed on June 5, 1955.
> Rehearsals for *Silk Stockings* began on October 18, 1954.
> *Silk Stockings* opened on February 24, 1955, and closed on April 14, 1956.

Since Linda had pulmonary problems throughout her life, eventually requiring an oxygen tent in the Waldorf Towers apartment, her death on May 20, 1954, did not come as a surprise. But it did not stop Porter from composing. *Silk Stockings* may have been his last musical for Broadway, but Hollywood was another matter. There, he only wrote the songs but was not involved in production. He wrote eight new songs for *High Society* (MGM, 1956) and resurrected "Well, Did You Evah" from *Du Barry Was a Lady*; he wrote five for *Les Girls* (MGM, 1957). What really disillusioned him about Broadway was his experiences with the producers of his last two shows, particularly *Silk Stockings*—the team of (Cy) Feuer and (Ernest) Martin, "Mr. Jekyll and Mr. Hyde," in the words of George S. Kaufman.

After Seymour "Cy" Feuer graduated from Julliard with a specialty in trombone, he relocated in Los Angeles, first becoming musical director of Columbia Records, then owned by CBS, and later a member of the CBS Orchestra, which filled in the time slots with musical interludes when there was no programming There was a restlessness about Feuer; he sensed that music in some form would be his life's work, but probably not on the West Coast. After serving as musical director of a few CBS dramatic shows and scoring films for Republic Pictures, Feuer joined the army shortly after Pearl Harbor.

In 1942, the same year Feuer enlisted in the army, Ernest Martin graduated from UCLA with a major in political science. He, too, had a CBS connection: during his undergraduate days, he worked as a CBS tour guide. After graduation he became program director at CBS, producing or supervising such popular shows as *My Friend Irma*, *Suspense*, and *Life with Luigi*. In 1946, Martin was invited to a party celebrating Feuer's return to civilian life. Each wanted something other than working in radio, which Martin believed would soon give way to television, or scoring B westerns at a studio like Republic that would be extinct by the end of the next decade. Feuer had the talent; Martin, the business acumen, or as Feuer put it: "Ernie was the sparkplug, and I was the engineer."

Their first production was *Where's Charley?* (1948), a musical romp with a score by Frank Loesser; it was a triumph for Ray Bolger, who turned his big number, "Once in Love with Amy," into an audience singalong. Two years later, they produced another—and far greater—Frank Loesser musical, *Guys and Dolls* (1950), one of the most perfectly integrated musicals in Broadway history, with the songs being extensions of the story. Around 1952, Feuer and Martin envisioned a musical set in Belle Époque Montmartre, which would require a highly sophisticated score of the sort that only Cole Porter could write. Porter signed on, and Abe Burrows, who had written the book for *Guys and Dolls*, would do the same for *Can-Can*, which he would also direct. The show had a built-in appeal: a colorful period made familiar by John Huston's meticulous recreation of Toulouse-Lautrec's Montmartre in *Moulin Rouge* (1951); spectacular choreography by Michael Kidd, whose work had thrilled moviegoers with the barn-raising sequence in *Seven Brides for Seven Brothers* (1952), which featured, as one of the brothers, one of the world's greatest dancers, Jacques d'Amboise; Porter's atmospheric score, which found favor among vocal artists (Frank Sinatra, Bing Crosby, Ella Fitzgerald, Dean Martin, Doris Day et al.); and evocative posters with the title and cast in blue-green lettering against a purple background and a black-stockinged leg on the right. Unlike *Around the World*, Cole Porter's name appeared in the possessive case above the title in the ads and the playbill. The production values compensated for the absence of recognizable names. Some audience members may have been familiar with the male lead, Peter Cookson in his first musical, from television and the stage; Hans Conreid, from radio (Schultz in *Life with Luigi*, Professor Kropotkin in *My Friend Irma*, which he repeated in the 1949 film of the same name) and as a character actor in such films as *Nightmare* (1942), *Hitler's Children* (1942), and *Mrs. Parkington* (1944). Parisians may have known the star, Lilo, from the *Folies Bergère*, but she was a newcomer to Broadway. In a supporting role was a performer who would go on to become one the best loved artists of the musical stage, Gwen Verdon.

Burrows's book was at odds with both the score and the production. The premise was the scandal that the can-can caused when it was introduced in the mid nineteenth century. *Can-Can*, however, is set in 1893 when the dance had become a staple in cabarets, some of which, like the one in the musical, were known as can-can cabarets. What was scandalous initially was not so much the dance as the crotchless pantalettes, which, by 1893, were no longer worn. The can-can was physically demanding. The dancers did high kicks and cartwheels; at the end, they would turn their backs to the audience, throw their ruffled skirts over their backside, and, one by one, go into a split. There may have been arrests, but the can-can was never banned.

Burrows selected a few historical facts—the furor over the can-can (which by 1893 had subsided), the performers' arrests, and its alleged obscenity (which by 1893 was no longer an issue), and imposed the *Guys and Dolls* template on them. Just as Loesser's musical centers around two couples (big-time gambler Sky Masterson and Salvation Army sergeant Sarah Brown; small-time gambler Nathan Detroit and nightclub entertainer Miss Adelaide), so does *Can-Can*: La Mome Pistache (Lilo), owner of Bal du Paradis, known for its can-can dancers; and Aristide Forestier (Peter

Cookson), a straight-laced magistrate determined to find enough evidence to close it down; Claudine, a can-can dancer (Gwen Verdon) and her lover, Boris, a sculptor (Hans Conreid), who receives unfavorable reviews from an art critic with designs on Claudine.

In *Guys and Dolls*, each couple encounters an obstacle to their relationship. Sky and Sarah return from a trip to Havana to discover that, in their absence, gamblers used the mission house for a crap game, for which Sarah holds Sky responsible; Nathan's ongoing floating crap games has deferred his marriage to Adelaide for fourteen years. In *Can-Can*, Aristide's scruples get the better of him and, despite his growing attraction to Pistache, he sends her and her dancers off to jail. (What future can there be, you wonder, for the jailer and the jailed?) Although Claudine is in love with Boris, she has to feign affection for Hilaire, an art critic, so he would review Boris's exhibit favorably. The Claudine-Boris subplot is easily resolved: Boris gets a laudatory review. The Pistache-Aristide main plot gets a few more twists. A picture of Aristide kissing Pistache at Bal du Paradis circulates and results in his being disbarred. Pistache suggests they go into business together and open a new cabaret. Aristide agrees, arguing that if they are business partners, he can mount a defense to clear their names, which he does in the courtroom finale where Lilo sings all five tricky refrains of "Can-Can," with a demonstration by the dancers that wins over the judge and jury.

The book was a variation on the familiar "two people from different worlds" plot, common to both theater (middle-class male/Main Line female in *The Philadelphia Story*, efficiency expert and reference librarian in *The Desk Set*) and film, especially screwball comedy (reporter and heiress in *It Happened One Night*, rich male/female office worker in *Easy Living*). In musical theater, the cultural disparity theme is better suited to serious musicals like *South Pacific* and *The King and I*. Burrows's book might have succeeded as a nonmusical, a battle of the sexes comedy like *Twentieth Century*. In *Can-Can*, Peter Cookson, a stage and film actor, was trying to create a character that existed only in outline, which was like trying to flesh out a shadow. Aristide was a type, an inhibited man who gradually succumbs to an uninhibited woman, like lexicographer Gary Cooper in *Ball of Fire* (1941) or herpetologist Henry Fonda in *The Lady Eve* (1941), spellbound by Barbara Stanwyck as a nightclub entertainer and card sharp, respectively. Cookson had to act his role; Lilo had to sing hers as well as give Pistache the toughness of the only woman in Montmartre who operated a cabaret. If Montmartre could sing, it would sound like Lilo, wise in the ways of the world and wiser in those of love.

Even if a musical theater veteran like Alfred Drake or Ray Middleton had costarred with Lilo, it wouldn't have mattered. Norwood Smith, who succeeded Robert Alda as Sky Masterson in *Guys and Dolls*, took over the role of Aristide for the last year of the run (June 6, 1954–June 4, 1955) and probably gave a much different performance, which only a critic would have noticed. If *Can-Can* managed to rack up 892 performances, it was not because of the stars or the book—which *New York Times* critic Brooks Atkinson, in a later appraisal of the musical, dismissed as "old fashioned and pedestrian" (May 17, 1953)—but because it lived up to the audience's expectations of an elaborate production, discreetly rowdy, set in a colorful era with performers in period costumes and dancers shaking their ruffled skirts and kicking their legs high into the air. All of that plus a score by Cole Porter that included a song, "I Love Paris," recorded by, among other vocalists, Bing Crosby, Frank Sinatra, Ella Fitzgerald, Andy Williams, Doris Day, Etta James, Tony Martin, and Jack Jones.

On opening night, a star was born, Gwen Verdon, but the author, then seventeen, who saw *Can-Can* in June 1953, had no idea who she was. By that time, he had seen Ethel Merman in *Call Me Madam*, Mary Martin *in South Pacific*, and Carol Channing in *Gentlemen Prefer Blondes* and knew what a Broadway voice sounded like. But he had never heard anyone like Lilo singing in seductively accented English, neither clarion clear like Merman or playfully ingenuous like Channing, but like someone who has seen it all and is keeping it to herself. Even at seventeen, he knew the plot was just an excuse for spectacular dancing, especially by a redheaded performer, who stood out from the rest. He could not have described what made her unique, but theater historian Abe Laufe could:

> [Verdon's] sparkling personality, her exuberance as a comedienne, and above all, her superb dancing made her the top performer in the cast. Playing Eve in a humorous ballet set in the Garden of Eden, she enchanted the audience from the time she took a bite of the apple and discovered sex. By the time she appeared in her next routine, the apache dance, the audience anticipated something spectacular, but Miss Verdon exceeded their expectations as she danced with abandon, kicking chairs and sending men spinning with a flick of her ankle. In one sequence, she did a slow motion routine that was even more spectacular than her whirlwind dancing. . . . [She] of course, excelled in the finale as she led the dancers in the frenzied can-can.

Lilo was devastated when the newspaper critics devoted more space to Verdon than to her. Although *Can-Can* was not a dance musical like *A Chorus Line*, the title itself implied the preeminence of dance. Lilo must have seen Verdon's numbers during rehearsal and should have realized that not only she but also the non-dancers in the cast were secondary, the equivalent of support staff. Neither Lilo nor Verdon remained in the show for the entire run. By the time *Can-Can* closed on June 4, 1955, Verdon was starring in *Damn Yankees* (1955) two blocks away at the Forty-sixth Street Theatre (now the Richard Rodgers), stopping the show with "Whatever Lola Wants, Lola Gets."

The two best-known songs from *Can-Can* are "I Love Paris" and "It's All Right with Me," which Burrows, in at an attempt at integration, managed to fit into the plot. In Act 2, Pistache is on the roof of the new venue, gazing down at the city of light. The six-line verse is more evocative than the nine-line refrain, in which each of the first five lines as well as the seventh begins with "I." The rhymes are elementary. Pistache loves Paris year round. At least the verse offers a sketch of the "timeless town" that inspires such deep devotion, regardless of the color of the sky or the sounds from the streets. "I Love Paris" ends with Pistache's explanation of her love for the city: "because my love is near"—meaning, one assumes, Aristide. The last lines contradict her unconditional love of the city, which has nothing to do with Aristide's proximity but with the city itself. Porter tries to balance "every season of the **year**" with "because my love is **near**," perhaps hoping that no one would parse the song and wonder why someone who loves Paris for what it is and what it represents now loves it because it is her lover's city.

Or are city and lover identical in some symbiotic way? The refrain is the heart of the song; the verse is generally omitted in recordings, since it only makes sense in terms of the plot. "I Love Paris" is a song of reflection, deepened by the sound of the accordion. The refrain is in C-minor and 4/4 time ("slow foxtrot tempo," as prescribed by Porter), but at the fifth line, "I love Paris every moment," the melody soars, and the key changes from minor to major, allowing the song to end gracefully as both a love song to a city and to a lover.

"It's All Right with Me," also in C minor but without the sonic leap to major, is more problematic. Burrows had made owners of establishments with can-can dancers subject to prosecution, although the can-can was never officially banned. But the "illegality" of the dance is an important plot point; if Aristide can convince a jury that the can-can is not obscene, Pistache will be vindicated, and their future will be secure. As it stands,

Pistache will have to stand trial if she continues to feature can-can dancers. Burrows altered the facts of history to make for a plot-heavy second act that includes Aristide's disbarment, a business partnership with Pistache, the breakup of the partnership, his own arrest, and his successful defense of the can-can. But Burrows could not do much with the character of Aristide, a conflicted conservative, torn between his moral code and his love for Pistache, which he acknowledged near the end of Act 1 ("I Am in Love"); nor could Porter, even though he provided the character with a love-on-the-rebound song, "It's All Right with Me."

At this point, Aristide does not know that the incriminating photograph is circulating and will result in his disbarment. When a young woman indicates her availability, Aristide is intrigued but too principled to yield to his impulses. Such was the motivation for "It's All Right with Me." The lady may have the wrong face, the wrong smile, and the wrong lips. She's not Pistache, but if some night she's free, "it's all right with me." Porter seems to have written the song because Cookson needed one in the second act to complement "I Am in Love" in the first. Although Cookson was the male lead, he only had two solos compared to Lilo's eight.

"It's All Right with Me" has been recorded by such artists as Ella Fitzgerald, Bing Crosby, Frank Sinatra, Steve Lawrence, Peggy Lee, Mel Tormé, and Harry Connick Jr. Sinatra was especially fond of the song and included it in many of his concerts.

Despite mixed reviews, *Can-Can* enjoyed the second longest run of any Cole Porter musical. His next—and final—musical was moderately successful, but soured Porter on Broadway.

ON SCREEN: CAN-CAN (TWENTIETH CENTURY-FOX, 1960)

All that the Dorothy Kingsley-Charles Lederer screenplay owes to Abe Burrows's book is the controversy over the can-can, which has been branded as "lewd and lascivious." The creation of new characters—a lawyer, François Durnais (Frank Sinatra), and a magistrate, Paul Barrière (Maurice Chevalier)—the elimination of the sculptor-art critic-Claudine storyline, and the demotion of Claudine from supporting cast to dancer with a few lines (the awesome Juliet Prowse) resulted in a plot so overburdened with characters deceiving and double-crossing each other that the only way to keep audiences in their seats for 131 minutes of machinations was to insert a song or dance routine at various intervals to remind them that they were watching a musical.

Except for Claudine, the main characters have been renamed: La Mome Pistache is now Simone Pistache (Shirley MacLaine), still the owner of Bal du Paradis, where she also performs; the young magistrate, whose first name was originally Aristide, has become Philippe Forrestier (Louis Jourdan). Perhaps the writers thought "Simone" and "Philippe" seemed more French, but it would not have mattered. This is Montmartre as recreated on Twentieth Century-Fox's back lot that would later become the famous New York Street in *Hello, Dolly!* (1968). It is also a Montmartre where Sinatra and MacLaine sound like American transplants in Paris 1896 (the year has been changed), in contrast to Chevalier and Jourdan who seem, and sound, very much at home. What matters is that Sinatra can still entice with his voice and that MacLaine can still dazzle in dance even if neither is believable as a French lawyer and a club owner in turn-of-the-century Paris. Chevalier and Jourdan provide the authenticity; Sinatra and MacLaine, the razzle dazzle. Whenever the plot began to bifurcate, the script went its way; the performers, theirs. Sometimes they converged, but mostly it was a case of separate but equal.

Much of the score survived the transition from stage to screen. Chevalier and Sinatra had been filmed singing the musical's only hit, "I Love Paris," but it was cut when the studio felt it slowed down the action. A choral arrangement is heard during the main title and again at the end. The company dances to an orchestral arrangement in the Garden of Eden ballet. Some of the songs were transferred to different settings or given to other characters. The stage musical opened with the can-can dancers in court, insisting that they are convent-educated and churchgoers ("Maidens Typical of France"). In the film, the servers at Bal du Paradis led by Juliet Prowse perform "Maidens Typical of France" as they rush down a staircase with white aprons over their skirts, shaking them to reveal their shapely legs in tight-fitting black stockings. Prouse added a few anachronistic bumps at the end as the dancers took off their aprons, shaking them back and forth, burlesque style. "Live and Let Live," originally entrusted to Lilo, became a duet for Chevalier and Jourdan, the former urging the latter to give up his crusade against the can-can. It is reprised when Chevalier tries to dissuade the younger magistrate from marrying Simone, prompting him to tell his colleague to practice what he preached. "C'est magnifique" is sung twice; first by Sinatra to Jourdan as a defense of his pursuit of romance; and again by MacLaine to Jourdan, with whom she is falling in love even though she knows he could send her to jail.

Then there were the interpolations: "You Do Something to Me" (*Fifty Million Frenchmen*), Philippe's reaction to feelings that had previously been dormant; "Let's Do It" (*Paris*) as a clumsily staged duet for Sinatra and MacLaine, in which they suggest how kangaroos and giraffes "do it." Barrière sings "Just One of Those Things" (*The New Yorkers*) to Philippe as one way of accepting the end of an affair. While "Let's Do It" reduced Porter's witty lyrics to witless banter, Jourdan's rendition of "You Do Something to Me" as a monologue, as well as Chevalier's of "Just One of Those Things" as advice to the lovelorn, show how successfully songs from two totally dissimilar musicals can be interpolated into a third with their meaning intact and the only change being one of context.

The song that approximates the way it was performed in the original is "It's All Right with Me." François, believing he has lost Simone to Philippe, comes into the Bal du Paradis in the afternoon and goes behind the bar to pour himself a drink. Claudine comes in and joins him. He sings it to her, or, to be more accurate, Sinatra sings it to Prowse, since at this point François Durnais is in the wings, and Frank Sinatra is center stage. His voice still had the mellow clarity with a hint of yearning that raised him above the level of crooner. At this point in his career, he was treating the lyrics as words with meaning, no just words with notes. No longer a heartthrob, the mature Sinatra invests "It's All Right with Me" with a poignant honesty that is lacking in other renditions. At the end, he kisses Prowse tenderly on the lips—either director Walter Lang's idea or the screenwriters'—to leave audiences wondering if Simone will end up with Phillippe, and François with Claudine.

Although MacLaine was second billed, *Can-Can* was clearly her movie. The Apache Dance and the Garden of Eden ballet, which Michael Kidd had originally choreographed for Gwen Verdon, became showpieces for MacLaine. If the film were faithful to its source, they should have been performed by Juliet Prowse, who could certainly have done them justice. Claudine has little to do in the film, while Verdon had a large enough role to win a Tony for Best Supporting Actress in a Musical.

The Apache Dance was considerably more violent in the film than it had been on the stage. It is a dance of menace, in which a man and a woman enact a tale of *amour fou*, with MacLaine dragged around the floor by her putative lover, who is then joined by two other men—one taking her by the feet, the other by the arms, as if they are going to toss her into a bin. Apparently, roughhouse appeals to her; to prevent her lover from leaving, she holds onto his leg, only to be dragged along the floor again. This is sadomasochism in dance, ending with the woman stabbing her lover, which appears to be the only way she can return to an upright position. One had to admire MacLaine's professionalism. If this is choreographer

CHAPTER 14

Hermes Pan's idea of an Apache Dance for moviegoers, she must go along with it—and she did.

The Garden of Eden ballet is the complete opposite. Eden is a wonderland with dancing butterflies and frolicsome rabbits. Eve (MacLaine) arrives on a glider and promptly awakens Adam asleep under a tree, which turns out to be the Tree of the Knowledge of Good and Evil in Genesis. Eve is wearing a flesh-colored body stocking sprinkled with white sequins and a wig with hair streaming down her back. Adam (unbilled), who comes off as something of a dolt, looks like a body builder in gold trunks and tights. You would have to do a search to learn that the Serpent that slithers down the tree is Juliet Prowse in a faux snakeskin unitard. Prowse cannot upstage MacLaine, but she makes every bit of screen time count. The Serpent tempts Eve with the apple, but the butterflies warn her against taking a bite. Still, the apple, even if pressed to the mouth, has a demonic effect. The music suddenly changes from a waltz-like orchestration of "I Love Paris" that made for graceful dancing to a jazzed-up version that sends everyone into a frenzy. Eve, Adam, and the Serpent go into jive mode, as if they were under a Dionysian spell and no longer in control of their movements. Partners change, and even the Serpent boogies with Adam, causing Eve to push her away. When the spell is lifted, an eerie calm descends upon Eden. Adam lies exhausted, and Eve contemptuously steps on his abdomen like a conqueror and then drags him off by the leg as she tosses the apple in the air. So much for original sin.

The writers tailored the characterizations to the actors' screen image as reflected in their recent films. Chevalier and Jourdan played uncle and nephew in *Gigi* (1958). In *Can-Can*, they are senior and junior magistrates. In *Guys and Dolls* (1955), Sinatra was Nathan Detroit, engaged to Miss Adelaide (Vivian Blaine) for fourteen years. In *Can-Can*, he is playing another marriage-averse character, while MacLaine, like Miss Adelaide, is eager to marry. By creating a couple with opposing views on marriage, and a marriage enthusiast (Jourdan), the writers have fashioned a triangular plot to keep audiences guessing which man will MacLaine choose. At first it seems to be Jourdan. At their engagement party, Simone is visibly nervous at the prospect of mingling in high society. François recommends champagne as a relaxant and then encourages her to perform for the guests. More than slightly tipsy, Simona does a spectacular "Come Along with Me," originally sung by the art critic, as she works the room, sitting on laps, rubbing bald heads, and scandalizing the bluebloods, who sit in stony silence until she finishes. Only Philippe applauds. So it seems it will be François and Simone.

Not yet. It's payback time. Simone approaches François for a loan, with Bal du Paradis as collateral, making him the temporary owner. She then alerts the police, who raid the club just as the can-can begins. It is trial time again, with Barrière asking permission for the entertainers to perform the dance for the president of the League Against Filthy Dancing. It is an exuberant finale; the can-can is danced to the music of the title song, which is heard but not sung. Burrows's book made it possible for Lilo to sing the entire number. But in revising the ending, the screenwriters made it impossible for Simone, now a witness, to do so. The president of the league withdraws her objections, but the plot is still unresolved.

Two gendarmes inform Simone that she is under arrest and escort her from the courtroom into a police van, where she finds François, who had staged the false arrest and is now ready for marriage. It is an irritatingly rushed resolution as well as implausible. But with Sinatra and MacLaine in the leads, and Jourdan fourth-billed, it was never a question of who ends up with whom, but how long will it take to happen.

If Darryl F. Zanuck had his way in 1955, Sinatra, MacLaine, Chevalier, and Jourdan would never have appeared in the film, which, with the right screenplay and cast, could have been released earlier than 1960. While still production head at Twentieth Century-Fox, Zanuck was planning a screen version of *Can-Can* shortly after the musical closed in June 1955. He envisioned a companion piece to *Gentlemen Prefer Blondes* (Twentieth Century-Fox, 1953), which, like *Can-Can*, had a double love story: Marilyn Monroe and Tommy Noonan, Jane Russell and Elliott Reid. Nunnally Johnson was entrusted with the adaptation, which Zanuck, writing to screenwriter Henry Ephron, felt was "not a good script" but "has some good things, particularly the development of the second love story [Claudine and the Boris, the sculptor]."

Since Johnson was involved in several projects, Zanuck offered Ephron the opportunity to serve as screenwriter and producer. Ephron was not interested in either role, perhaps because he agreed with Zanuck that the musical is "very weak in story" but has "the possibility of good characterizations." From the beginning, Toulouse-Lautrec was to have been a character. Zanuck may have been thinking of offering the role to José Ferrer, who gave a stunning performance of the painter in John Huston's *Moulin Rouge* (1951).

Zanuck was determined to get a successor to *Gentlemen Prefer Blondes*, which had a "vague and thinner storyline but was a hit because it had sex and comedy and several magical numbers." Zanuck was considering an international cast with Jean-Pierre Aumont as Aristide, Jeanmarie as

Pistache (a role she actually got to play in the short-lived 1981 Broadway revival), Martine Carol as Claudine, and Victor Borge as Boris. Apparently, it did not bother him that the four would never draw the same crowds that Jane Russell and Marilyn Monroe did with *Gentlemen Prefer Blondes*. But his instincts were correct; the movie must have a continental air. Zanuck could be myopic when it came to casting. His idea of the ideal Billy Bigelow and Julie Jordan in *Carousel* (1957) were Frank Sinatra and Judy Garland. What interested him primarily was the performers' present status. Since Sinatra had won an Oscar for *From Here to Eternity* (Columbia, 1953), he was, to use the industry's honorific, bankable; Garland, less so, although she had been nominated for *A Star Is Born* (Warner Bros., 1954). For Pistache and Aristide, Zanuck also considered the unlikely combination of Anna Magnani, who was rumored to win the Oscar for Best Actress in *The Rose Tattoo* (Paramount, 1955)—and did; and Bing Crosby, who was nominated for *The Country Girl* (Paramount, 1954). They would be "out of this world," Zanuck gushed They certainly would be, eerily so.

By February 1956, Zanuck had no further interest in *Can-Can* or Twentieth Century-Fox. Disillusioned with a Hollywood in which agents wield more power than producers, he announced that he would be leaving for Paris where he would set up his own production company. When he was lured back to the studio in 1962 to take over as president, *Can-Can* had come and gone.

Twentieth Century-Fox had great hopes for *Can-Can*. It was filmed in 70mm Todd-AO for two-a-day roadshow engagements and distributed in CinemaScope for general release in theatres unequipped for Todd A-O. Initially, the film seemed to be a financial success, but the final audit proved otherwise: the $5 million production only brought in $4.2 million in rentals.

ON STAGE: *SILK STOCKINGS* (1955)

When Feuer and Martin proposed the idea of a musical based on Ernst Lubitch's *Ninotchka* (1939), Porter was delighted. The film, graced by the immaculate Lubitsch touch, was a seamless blend of satire and romance, in which three Soviet agents are sent to Paris to sell a jewelry collection that had been confiscated after the Bolshevik Revolution. When the owner, a Grand Duchess, learns of the plan and threatens litigation, special envoy Nina Yakushova (Ninotchka), played by Greta Garbo with a sphinx-like air, is dispatched to facilitate the sale. There, she encounters Count Leon (Melvyn Douglas); just as the three agents succumbed to the lure of capitalism, Paris-style, so does Ninotchka—to the Count, *haute couture*, and champagne. Previously, Ninotchka had criticized the Count for being too talkative. When he kisses her without resistance, he asks, "Was that talkative?" She replies, "No, that was restful. Again." It seems all that is necessary to convert a Communist to capitalism is a city known for romance, fashion, and fine wine. Lubitsch kept the plot points afloat like champagne bubbles. That was the essence of the Lubitsch touch: it was like champagne that keeps fizzing and never goes flat. But champagne was not what Feuer and Martin wanted. Vodka was more to their taste.

Silk Stockings had a troubled history. George S. Kaufman and his wife, Leueen Macgrath, were entrusted with the book, which initially augured well. Kaufman's sense of satire was double-edged; he could prick or sear; he could be genial or mordant. But there was always wit in abundance. Since the ads for *Silk Stockings* read "Based on Ninotchka by Melchior Lengyel," but not on the screenplay by Billy Wilder, Charles Brackett, and Walter Reisch, the Kaufmans drew only on the salient plot points: three Soviet agents sent on a mission to Paris; a female envoy dispatched to check on them; her romance with a capitalist and subsequent conversion to the ways of the West; and an ending in which none of the former Communists return to Mother Russia.

Ninotchka was released on the eve of World War II and a year before the fall of France to the Nazis. The opening title expressed the disparity between the Paris of the film and the Paris of the present. The audience is asked to remember a time when "a siren was a brunette, and not an alarm—and when a Frenchman turned off the light, it was not because of an air raid." The Kaufmans realized that a musical set in pre-World War II Paris would have little appeal in 1955. That war had ended a decade earlier; the Korean War, in a 1953 armistice. The present conflict was the Cold War, then in its early stages. And so the setting became Cold War Paris. Ninotchka could still be a Soviet envoy, and three agents could still be sent to Paris, not to sell jewelry but to bring back Peter Ilyich Boroff, a famous composer who has discovered Paris and has been discovered by Steve Canfield, a Hollywood agent, who wants his proletarian tone poem, *Ode to a Tractor*, for a musical version of Leo Tolstoy's *War and Peace*.

The character of Ninotchka appealed to Kaufman: a woman who started out with one ideology and ended up with another, just as his protagonists embark on an enterprise with one goal in mind which they either achieve indirectly or abandon in favor of another. In *The Butter and Egg Man* (1925), Kaufman's sole play without a collaborator, a young Midwesterner, eager to invest $20,000 in a play in order to make enough money to buy a hotel, is conned by two producers into backing one that flops out of town. When the producers bow out, the young backer, who initially seemed a naif, reworks it into a hit and sells it back to the producers at a considerable profit once he learns it had been plagiarized. Kaufman took particular delight in skewering Hollywood. The title character of *Merton of the Movies* (1922), written with Marc Connelly, is a would-be serious actor who is so laughably bad that his movies become hugely successful comedies. Three vaudevillians in *Once in a Lifetime* (1930), his first collaboration with Moss Hart, pass themselves off as diction coaches in early sound era Hollywood.

Another feature of Kaufman's plays is the *à clef* character. Helen Hobart, the gossip columnist in *Once in a Lifetime*, is a stand-in for the gossip columnist Hedda Hopper. *The Man Who Came to Dinner* (1939), written with Moss Hart, abounds in such characters. Sheridan Whiteside, the acerbic critic, was modeled after the equally acerbic Alexander Woollcott; Banjo, a popular movie comedian, after Harpo Marx; British actor and playwright Beverly Carlton, after Noël Coward; and the self-dramatizing stage star, Lorraine Sheldon, after Gertrude Lawrence

Boroff bears a resemblance to the young idealist in Kaufman and Connelly's *Beggar on Horseback* (1924) who fancies himself a serious composer, not a hack songwriter. Kaufman was able to get in some digs at Hollywood in the *Silk Stockings* subplot, in which Janice Dayton (Gretchen Wyler), a movie star whose specialty is the aquacade movie (think Esther Williams in MGM musicals), is planning to go dramatic and star in the musical version of Tolstoy's *War and Peace* (think Marilyn Monroe, who allegedly yearned to play Grushenka in Dostoevsky's *The Brothers Karamazov*).

By replacing the Soviet agents' attempt to sell a jewelry collection with Canfield's attempt to acquire Boroff's composition, the Kaufmans had a skeletal plot that only needed to be fleshed out. Canfield believes *Ode to a Tractor* will add authenticity to the *War and Peace* musical that will star his client, Janice Dayton. Ninotchka, on the other hand, wants Boroff to return to Moscow. Canfield and Ninotchka meet, clash, and fall in love. Janice has *Ode to a Tractor* re-orchestrated for a flashy production number with dancers in tights and herself as Josephine, Napoleon's consort, in a two-piece costume more suited to a house of burlesque than the Tuileries Palace. When Boroff sees what has been done to his score, he and the others head back to Moscow. In a rushed ending, Canfield arrives as deus ex machina and convinces the Commissar of Art that he will represent him in America where he can make millions from his memoirs, which is enough of an incentive for him, the three former agents, and Ninotchka to defect to the land of the free where the agents can become Wall Street plutocrats, Canfield can get his twenty percent for the memoirs, and he and Ninotchka can enjoy the fruits of capitalism.

The *Ninotchka* denouement was better plotted. The Grand Duchess, who does not appear in *Silk Stockings* but who is an important character in the film, agrees to authorize the sale of the jewelry if Ninotchka returns to Moscow. Knowing how desperately the money is needed, Ninotchka consents, even though it means giving up Leon. The cramped apartment in Moscow that Ninotchka shares with two other women is in stark contrast to her hotel suite in Paris. When one of her roommates notices a piece of elegant lingerie on the clothesline, she informs Ninotchka that some of the women are envious while others find it a mockery of Soviet ideals. Ninotchka's reply may have inspired the musical's title: "All you have to do is wear a pair of silk stockings and they suspect you of counterrevolution." To negotiate a sale of Russian furs to Turkey, the same three agents that had been sent to Paris are ordered to (then) Constantinople. After reports are received about their reckless behavior, Ninotchka is sent to make certain the sale goes through. There she finds Leon, who has masterminded the entire affair, ensuring that the Paris scenario will be replayed in Constantinople. When Leon convinces Ninotchka that she can do more for her country by staying in Constantinople, she yields: "No one can say Ninotchka was a bad Russian." Constantinople may not be Paris, but it will do for the time being.

Feuer and Martin's demands for rewrites was especially irksome to Porter, which meant new songs or substitutions. It was bad enough that the ad for the musical was a stack of five gift-wrapped packages with all the names in lowercase and Porter's *under* the title:

feuer & martin
present
hildegarde neff   don ameche
in
"silk stockings"
music and lyrics by [very small font] cole porter [same size font as the stars' names]
book by [very small font] george s. kaufman
leueen macgrath
and abe burrows.

Under "burrows" was "suggested by Ninotchka by Melchior Lengyel." This was obviously not Cole Porter's *Silk Stockings*.

In her autobiography, Neff traced the long journey toward opening night, beginning with her introduction to Feuer and Martin, the latter telling her that she is Ninotchka, if she can sing, which Porter insists she can. The casting of Neff and Don Ameche in the leads was the easy part; then came the rehearsals, the cuts, the rewrites, the replacements, the frayed nerves, the outbursts, the song switching, the out-of-town tryouts (Philadelphia, Boston, Detroit), Neff's bout with measles, onstage mishaps, and, worst of all, the gradual erosion of the book's sophistication until "Kaufman's soufflé had become hash, liberally salted." As for the composer and lyricist: "Cole Porter observes each disfiguration of his work with the reserve of an English butler."

Feuer and Martin were dissatisfied with Kaufman's direction. The pace, they felt, was too slow; at one point in Philadelphia, *Silk Stockings* was running over three hours. The book also needed revisions. When Kaufman refused, Martin fired him, but later denied it. Feuer took over the direction, and Abe Burrows was brought in for the rewrites. Burrows may have punched up the dialogue, making it more suited to a musical than to a Kaufman and Hart comedy. Whatever alterations Burrows made in the book, the basic plot that the Kaufmans created remained the same. Anyone familiar with Kaufman's stage work would see his imprint. Steve Canfield is kin to Sheridan Whiteside in Kaufman and Hart's *The Man Who Came to Dinner* (1939). Just as Whiteside was determined to keep his loyal secretary in his employ even if it meant interfering with her marital plans, Canfield will do anything to keep Boroff in Paris, even if it means lying about his citizenship.

When Marlene Dietrich saw *Silk Stockings* during the Philadelphia tryout, she was effusive: "It's a play with music, not a musical, and that's exactly its charm." That was the problem. Feuer and Martin wanted a musical, not a play with music. Not a soufflé, but not hash, either. Just a hearty cassoulet.

The rewrites affected the score; at least four songs were eliminated, and six others replaced. The result was fourteen musical numbers, including two reprises. Their allocation was odd. Hildegarde Neff and Don Ameche each had two solos, but Gretchen Wyler as Janice Dayton had three. Hildegarde Neff (née Hildegard Knef)) had been a film star in her native Germany before making her American debut in *Decision before Dawn* (Fox, 1951), followed by, among others, *The Snows of Kilimanjaro* and *Diplomatic Courier* (both Fox, 1952), She was not a singer then (but would later become one); however, her speaking voice was pleasantly cadenced and able to impart a songlike quality to a lyric without having to resort to *Sprechstimme* ("speak-song"), which is more like recitation than singing. Her two solos are character songs, the first, reflecting her view of sex when she arrives in Paris ("It's a Chemical Reaction, That's All"); the second, "Without Love," reflecting her view of it after falling in love with Canfield. Her character evolves from a Stalinist arguing that what the "uninstructed faction" calls "mutual attraction" is merely a "chemical reaction," to a romantic who feels that without love a woman is "a zero in the void," one of the most precise metaphors for emotional emptiness ever penned. "Without Love," composed in 4/4 time to be sung in a "slow foxtrot tempo," lay within Neff's vocal range. Neff's voice had a soft huskiness that suited the song's meditative tone. In fact, *Daily News* critic John Chapman called Neff "a fascinating actress with a slinky, smoky voice, and her singing of 'Without Love' is the high point of the show." Neff's experience in *Silk Stockings* resulted in a second career; as Hildegard Knef, she became a vocalist and recording artist who released a number of albums that included some of her own compositions.

Although both Ella Fitzgerald and Rosemary Clooney recorded "Without Love," it never became popular. The show's hit song, "All of You," was introduced by Don Ameche early in Act 1. Canfield scoffs at Ninotchka's theory of sexual chemistry. What attracts him is the total person—"the east, west, north, and the south of you." Ameche's suave delivery kept the number from sounding like a cartographer's sexual fantasy. "All of You" admits of easy rhyme; if "I'd like to make a tour of you" is too explicit, change "a tour" to "quite sure." "All of You" became one of Porter's most widely recorded songs; it appealed to vocalists as diverse as Frank Sinatra, Billie Holiday, Ella Fitzgerald, Nancy Wilson, Robert Goulet, Sammy Davis Jr., and Tony Bennett.

Ameche's other solo, the title song, is the reverse of Ninotchka's "Without Love." While hers is a song of discovery, his is one of loss. Ninotchka has returned to Moscow with the three agents, and Canfield is left with 365 pairs of silk stockings that he had bought for her. Porter specified that "Silk Stockings" be sung "dreamily without dragging." Ameche sang it pensively, meditating on the last vestige of femininity that Ninotchka required for her transformation into a desirable modern woman. She had previously slipped out of her military attire that made her look like a cadet and into a glamorous red evening gown that matched her hair color; the stockings, one pair for each day of the year, were to be the final touch.

Yvonne Adair, who played Carol Channing's sidekick in *Gentleman Prefer Blondes* (1949), had been cast as Janice Dayton. During rehearsals, she experienced a number of health issues, including shingles, which caused Feuer and Martin to consider replacing her. But the main health issue, as Neff disclosed in her autobiography, was that Adair was pregnant. Even when she miscarried, it was too late. She had been replaced by Gretchen Wyler, who understudied Vivian Blaine in the role of Miss Adelaide during the run of *Guys and Dolls* (1950–53).

Janice's first number, "Stereophonic Sound," is one of Porter's wittiest. It is a spoof of the widescreen revolution in the early 1950s when Twentieth Century-Fox introduced CinemaScope, a wide screen process in which the film is projected on a curved screen two and one-half times wider than high. CinemaScope was not enough; the audience had to be enveloped in three-dimensional sound: "If Zanuck's latest picture were the good old-fashioned kind, / There'd be no one in front to look at Marilyn's behind"—unless it had "glorious Technicolor, breathtaking CinemaScope, and Stereophonic Sound." In her second number, "Satin and Silk," Janice does a strip for Boroff to entice him into allowing *Ode to a Tractor* to be used for her big production number. She celebrates the appeal of fancy underwear by demonstrating how it can alter a woman's personality and attract men at the same time: "You cannot expect a lady to exert that certain pull, / If she's wearing cotton stockings and her bloomers are made of wool." And how could a burlesque queen develop a following "if her bra is made of buckram and her G-string is made of rope?" This was Porter in high risqué mode. Boroff is so overwhelmed by the gyrations and display of flesh that he concedes.

Janice's third song, "Josephine," is all we see of the musicalized *War and Peace*. It is a typical Cole Porter list song in which the Empress enumerates the physical attributes that made her attractive to Napoleon: "Agitating eyes / Titillating thighs / Lubricating lips / Undulating hips." The problem is that Josephine does not appear as a character in Tolstoy's novel, although Napoleon does. Porter and the Kaufmans are satirizing Hollywood's tendency to buy the title of a work—or, with un-copyrighted material, appropriate it—and tack it on to a totally different plot. James Whale's *Frankenstein* (Universal, 1931) is a classic horror film that owes nothing to Mary Shelley's 1818 novel of the same name except the title. Twentieth Century-Fox bought the rights to the popular stage revue *Call Me Mister* (1946), which was virtually plotless, and used only the title for a 1951 Betty Grable and Dan Dailey musical about a divorced couple who meet up in post-World War II Japan. MGM did the same with the Gershwins' Broadway musical *Strike Up the Band* (1927), which bore no resemblance to the 1940 film of the same name with Mickey Rooney and Judy Garland. But what did it matter? *Strike Up the Band* made a profit of $1.229 million

Although *Silk Stockings* was Porter's last stage musical, he at least had the satisfaction of knowing that it received a glowing notice from the (then) dean of drama critics, Brooks Atkinson of the *New York Times*, who wrote in his opening-night review (February 24, 1955): "Everything about *Silk Stockings* represents the best goods in the American musical comedy emporium. This is one of Gotham's most memorable shows on a level with *Guys and Dolls.*"

Guys and Dolls has had several Broadway revivals; *Silk Stockings* has had none.

SILK STOCKINGS (MGM, 1957)

Although *Silk Stockings* was a success on Broadway, the movie version registered a $1.4 million loss. The stars, Fred Astaire as Steve Canfield and Cyd Charisse as Ninotchka, did not have the drawing power they once did. Neither would make another musical, unless one wishes to include *Finian's Rainbow* (1968), in which Astaire played Petula Clark's father and was quite agile for a man approaching seventy. Charisse would leave MGM a year after the release of *Silk Stockings*. Ironically, her last film for the studio was a nonmusical, *Party Girl* (1958). Yet one has to marvel at Astaire, still nimble in his late fifties; and Charisse, a marvel of balletic grace, paired with him for the last time.

The screenwriters, Leonard Gershe and Leonard Spiegelglass, streamlined the Kaufmans-Burrow's book but remained faithful to its contours. Steve Canfield is now a movie producer eager to acquire Boroff's services for a musical version of *War and Peace* to be filmed in Paris. When the three agents arrive to return the composer to Moscow, Canfield fabricates a story about Boroff's French parentage to delay his return, as he had done in the original. When the Soviet authorities hear nothing from the agents, Ninotchka is charged with bringing everyone back to Moscow. From then on, the plot points fall into place. Ninotchka's disdain for Western decadence gives way to the irresistible appeal of lingerie and champagne. The screenwriters have Ninotchka admit that she had formerly been a dancer, as if any explanation were needed for Charisse's consummate artistry.

The *War and Peace* subplot remained the same. Peggy (formerly Janice) Dayton, played by Janis Paige, nearly took the film away from the leads. None of her numbers were cut, but "Stereophonic Sound" was no longer a solo. Since Astaire felt the film gave him too few opportunities to demonstrate his art, "Stereophonic Sound" became a song-and-dance number for himself and Paige, which had them dancing on a conference table, swinging from a chandelier, and landing on their knees with outstretched arms like vaudevillians begging for applause. Neither dominated the number, and Paige proved to be a superb dancer whose musical gifts were seen more often on Broadway (*The Pajama Game, Here's Love*, Angela Lansbury's replacement in *Mame*) and in summer stock (*Annie Get Your Gun, Guys and Dolls, Applause, Gypsy*) than in Hollywood.

Paige performed "Satin and Silk" in a fitting room before a dazed Boroff. The space was more constricted that it had been on the stage, but Paige, in a form-fitting teddy, made it work to her character's advantage by personalizing every gyration, as if she were giving Boroff a private performance. Suggestive lyrics were either sanitized or omitted (there is no reference to a burlesque queen's bra and G-string), but "Josephine" looked as if it had been staged at one of the burlesque houses on the Minsky circuit. Curiously, "All of You," with its reduction of the female form to a map, encountered no opposition from the Breen Office. Ameche sang it seductively, but Astaire took a different approach; he was playful and debonair as he sang to Charisse, who was aloof but intrigued.

Unlike the steamy "Girl Hunt" ballet that Charisse and Astaire performed in *The Band Wagon* (MGM, 1953), their dancing in *Silk Stockings* is coolly sensual, the equivalent of choreographed courting. He makes the first move; she at first is evasive; he persists; she succumbs; they dance as if buoyed up by passion so rarefied that they seem to be afloat. Their dancing is in character. Astaire is not aggressive, nor is Charisse impassive. They are two civilized people who also are discreetly amorous, valuing taste and decorum above all else.

Ninotchka's two songs, "It's a Chemical Reaction, That's All" and "Without Love," were retained, with Carol Richards as Charisse's voice double. Although Don Ameche sang "Silk Stockings" when he was left with 365 pairs of them after Ninotchka departed for Moscow, Astaire does not sing it in the film. Nobody does. Charisse dances to it. She already has the stockings, along with elegant lingerie, a bit of which we see as she dances around her hotel room after discovering how soft they are to the touch. Looking transfixed as she feels the silk against her legs, Charisse exuded a childlike amazement as poignant as it was sensuous.

Knowing that his days in musicals were coming to an end (and realizing that, despite the billing, Charisse was the star and Paige, the scene-stealer), Astaire needed a dance number to show he was still at the top of his game and could appeal to a younger generation of moviegoers. Porter wrote a parody of rock 'n' roll called "The Ritz Roll and Rock," which took a backward look at the song that Astaire introduced a decade earlier in *Blue Skies* (Paramount, 1946), Irving Berlin's "Puttin' on the Ritz." Dressed in his signature attire (top hat and tails, cravat, boutonniere, and white spats, and handling his cane as if it were his partner), Astaire was "then at his peak, even dancing with mirrored reflections of himself. "The Ritz Roll and Rock" is a pale reflection of "Puttin' on the Ritz," one of the most dazzling displays of dance in film. In "The Ritz Roll and Rock," Astaire wore the same evening clothes, but there were no emanations of himself—only similarly dressed male dancers who were younger, moved faster, and kicked higher. Rock 'n' roll was as alien to Porter as it was to Astaire. It was not an embarrassment, but it was a sign that Astaire's glory days were behind him.

CHAPTER 15

Porter in Hollywood

In addition to film adaptations of his stage musicals, Porter also contributed to movie musicals produced by MGM and Columbia Pictures: At MGM, Porter was involved in the productions *Born to Dance*, *Rosalie* (1937), *Broadway Melody of 1940* (1939), *The Pirate* (1948), *High Society* (1956), and *Les Girls* (1957).

Porter's initial exposure to Hollywood was mixed. Warner Bros., then First National, released *Paris* (1927) as a Vitaphone Picture, celebrating its new sound-on-disk system, promising audiences that they would "hear Irene Bordoni sing." They did, but nothing by Porter. E. Ray Goetz, Bordoni's husband at the time, replaced Porter's songs with those of other composers, including himself. "Times Have Changed," as Reno Sweeney announced in *Anything Goes*. After the success of *Anything Goes*, Porter was wooed by MGM executives who gushed over his proposal for a film about John Barrymore starring Clark Gable as Barrymore. Nothing came of the proposal, which was typical of an industry in which more scripts remain unproduced than ever reach the screen.

MGM had hired Porter to compose the scores for three Eleanor Powell musicals starring the "Queen O' Taps" herself: *Born to Dance*, *Rosalie*, and *Broadway Melody of 1940*. The experience taught Porter a valuable lesson: in Hollywood, the composer is only a songwriter, not the star. That was evident when director Roy Del Ruth made it clear that he did not like Porter's finale in *Born to Dance*: "This is not personal, but I definitely do not like your finale. It seems to me that the lyric is entirely wrong and reminds me of everything I had ever heard since I was a boy." Powell, on the other hand, liked it, demonstrating how she would perform it and causing Porter to call it "one of the most exciting dances I had seen in my life." But it was Powell who proved to Del Ruth that she could perform the number as written, and it was her word that mattered. She was the star, and if it was good enough for her, it was, quite simply, good enough for the film.

BORN TO DANCE (1936)

If sequels were in vogue in the 1930s, *Born to Dance* would have been entitled "Broadway Melody of 1936, Part Two." Released seven months after *Broadway Melody of 1936*, *Born to Dance* offered some surprises, not the least of which was a surprisingly agile James Stewart in a role that called for him to sing "Easy to Love" to Eleanor Powell, which he did in an attenuated falsetto that fell softly on the ear without the slightest hint if strain. Otherwise, the film was the familiar boy-girl-complication-resolution-grand-finale-finish, with Stewart as a sailor who has been at sea for four months; and Powell as the first woman he meets at the Lonely Hearts Club. He makes the first move; she resists; he beckons with "Hey, Babe, Hey"; she responds. Porter fashioned "Hey, Babe, Hey" as a courtship ritual, but with a difference. Powell is a virtuoso; Stewart is a novice. He keeps up with her as best he can. Powell, sensing that Stewart was on unfamiliar terrain, generously allowed him to display his modest talent in his way as she displayed her far greater talent in hers.

"Hey, Babe, Hey" consisted of three refrains, the first of which is sung by Stewart and Powell; second by Sid Silvers and Una Merkel, who turn it into jazz; and finally by the remarkable Buddy Ebsen, who treats it as tap.

Romance blooms *until* Stewart rescues the Pekinese of diva Virginia Bruce, whose agent plants a story in the columns that Stewart and Bruce are romantically involved. *Plot twist*: Stewart makes amends by getting Powell hired as Bruce's understudy, signaling that she will go on in her place *when* Bruce throws a tantrum and leaves the show, allowing Powell to have the finale all to herself. Outfitted in a feathered hat, sheer stockings, and a black jacket with sequined cuffs, she balanced herself on one foot, extending the other in a perfect arabesque, and doing a cartwheel at the finish. This was the number "Swingin' the Jinx Away," a remedy for alleviating the Great Depression blues by swinging them away, to which Roy Del Ruth objected and that Powell championed, knowing that it was exactly the kind of climax audiences expected of the "Queen o' Taps."

Compared to Stewart's deeply personal version of "Easy to Love," Virginia Bruce's "I've Got You Under My Skin" was an art song. One could not fault her delivery. She caught the mood of the piece, but only at the surface. Her version was too refined for lyrics that described a passion that permeated the singer's entire being. When she came to the lines, "Don't you know, little fool, you never can win," she rose from their table on the veranda and, turning her back to Stewart, confessed her frustration as if she were delivering a soliloquy, too personal for another to hear.

Shortly thereafter it was as if Stewart never existed. Bruce went into diva mode, criticizing everything about her new show from the costumes to the musical numbers. Exit Virginia Bruce, enter Eleanor Powell. A star was born, and a show was saved.

ROSALIE (1937)

Porter followed *Born to Dance* with *Rosalie*, in which Powell played a Vassar-educated princess from a mythical country who performs a native dance that required her to leap over rows of hassocks and on to the floor. Powell's costar was Nelson Eddy, best remembered as Jeanette MacDonald's costar in MGM's attempt elevate the taste of moviegoers by bringing back the palmy days of operetta with two stars who captured the artifice of the genre. Eddy expressed some discomfort with "In the Still of the Night," one of Porter's most exquisitely crafted and soul-baring lyrics. Eddy had difficulty with the line, "Are you my life-to-be, my dream come true?"—not realizing that the rapid succession of monosyllables was the speaker's way of seeking assurance that theirs is more than a short-term relationship. Porter, knowing that this was one of his best ballads, asked Louis Mayer to arbitrate. Mayer was moved by the song's candor and Porter's decision to leave unanswered the possibility that the dream conceived in the still of the night also "fade out of sight."

Eddy sang the ballad as written.

BROADWAY MELODY OF 1940 (1939)

The best of the Broadway melody series was *Broadway Melody of 1940*, the only pairing of Powell and Fred Astaire. Powell is the star of a musical revue for which George Murphy has been mistakenly hired instead of Astaire. Regardless, Astaire goes on for an intoxicated Murphy on opening night to great acclaim. The same scenario recurs, but this time Murphy knowingly becomes incapacitated to allow Astaire to get the recognition he deserves. It is an inspiring tale of brotherly love, except that it bears little resemblance to the world of show business.

In "Juke Box Dance," Astaire asks Powell to demonstrate a dance step that intrigues him. Powell obliges, and the years fall away as they become two teenagers on their first date at the local ice cream parlor. In

"I Concentrate on You," Powell played prima ballerina, partnered with Astaire, in a dazzling display of technique.

The film's high point is "Begin the Beguine" from Porter's *Jubilee*. The setting is a Caribbean island designed to evoke "a night of tropical splendor" with dancers in diaphanous costumes and the lush-voiced Lois Hodnott (unbilled) providing the vocal. Powell appears in a full-length white dress that flows down her slender frame. She does not so much interpret the lyrics as enact them, gracefully tracing an arc by extending her leg clockwise, leaving a momentary swirl of white.

Astaire enters, for some reason dressed as a matador. They alternate between ballroom and flamenco, absorbing each other's rhythms as if each were the other's alter ego. When Powell and Astaire danced together in their only on-screen appearance, the chemistry was artistic, not erotic; it was an occasion for two artists to demonstrate their art without posturing or feigning physical attraction.

THE PIRATE (1948)

Porter returned to MGM seven years later but to a different studio. Although Louis Mayer was still the studio head, he would be replaced by Dore Shary within five years. It was not the same MGM that doted on him in 1936. He had been hired to write the score for *The Pirate*, freely adapted from S. N. Behrman's play of the same name that starred Alfred Lunt and Lynn Fontanne and which ran for 177 performances during the 1942–43 season. The, Judy Garland and Gene Kelly, superb artists in their own right, did not form a legendary stage couple like the Lunts. As a musical, *The Pirate* had to conform to the public's screen image of the stars: Garland as a singer, Kelly as a dancer. Kelly had the more daunting role, although one would never have thought it from the extraordinary vitality he displayed both as costar and co-choreographer, sharing credit for latter with Robert Alton.

Kelly would be playing a role that required him to walk a tightrope as Lunt had done in the original, and that Kelly did effortlessly on the screen. He also climbed up balconies, danced on ledges, slid down poles, and performed a Cossacks dance with the astonishing Nicholas Brothers. For Kelly, Porter's score was an interval between displays of physical prowess.

Porter would also be working with Garland's second husband, director Vincente Minnelli, who had his own ideas about way the Garland should play Manuela, who has erotic fantasies about a pirate. Kelly also had his ideas about the choreography, particularly "The Pirate Ballet," a hybrid score that incorporated themes from "Mack the Black," which Porter composed for Garland but which was re-orchestrated with the jagged rhythms and the feverish intensity of the "Sabre Dance."

Porter's score was winnowed down to six numbers: "Mack the Black," "Love My of Life," and "You Can Do No Wrong" for Garland—the latter two totally forgettable; "Nina" and "The Pirate Ballet" (less of a musical number than a feat of choreography for Kelly); and "Be a Clown" for both of them.

Some numbers had to be cut because Garland, unhappy with her role as the convent-educated Manuela forced by her financially strapped relatives to marry the wealthy Don Pedro (Walter Slezak), fought openly with Minnelli and ended up missing 99 of 135 shooting days, making Kelly the star by default.

The plot had been totally altered to focus on an arranged marriage between a corpulent plutocrat (Slezak) and a storybook romantic (Garland) yearning for much more than what Don Pedro can offer. Unable to sleep, Manuela hears the sound of a performance taking place under her window given by Serafin (Kelly), head of a troupe of itinerant players. Drawn to their world which offers a respite from her own, she throws on a red skirt, dons a cloak, and mingles with the spectators. Spotting her in the crowd, Serafin makes her part of the act. He hypnotizes her, ridding her of her inhibitions as she launches into "Mack the Black" as if possessed, bringing the song to a climax that leaves her totally spent. Convinced that Serafin is Mack the Black, she soon learns otherwise when the real Mack is unmasked who is none other than (spoiler alert) Don Pedro, who must be the most overweight pirate on the Spanish Main.

The ending is another test of credibility. Garland joins the Serafin's troupe; dressed as circus clowns with matching makeup, she and Kelly leave the audience with a simple message: "Be a clown, be a clown, / All the world loves a clown." It was one of the few times in the film that Garland looked happy. It was as if she were one of the Gumm sisters again working in vaudeville, not the troubled star whose days at MGM were rapidly coming to an end.

HIGH SOCIETY (1956)

Porter returned to MGM on two more occasions, the first of which was to compose the score for a remake of *The Philadelphia Story* (1940), retitled

High Society; the second, to do the same for *Les Girls*, an original musical by John Patrick, who had also done the adaptation of *High Society*. *The Philadelphia Story* (1938) was directed by George Cukor, who distilled the wit and urbanity of Philip Barry's 1938 Broadway play in a wine that never lost its sparkle; it was faithfully adapted by Donald Ogden Stewart, who was a first rate sommelier. *The Philadelphia Story* was the kind of stage play that achieved perfection in its original form, leaving its adapter little choice but to adhere to the text, alter it for mass entertainment, but honoring its underlying humanity that made it a classic.

High Society is to *The Philadelphia Story* what a copy is to the original. The setting has been changed from Main Line Philadelphia to Newport, Rhode Island, making the scent of money more pervasive, the drawing rooms airier, and the aura of privilege less odious. Otherwise, the plot threads remained the same. Tracy Lord (Grace Kelly) is about to marry the proper John Lund, but in a few hours will be reunited with her former husband (Bing Crosby) after an innocent fling with Frank Sinatra, who realizes that he is meant for his associate, Celeste Holm. It was the same four-quadrant plot, with characters at either end moving out of their own space into another's in ways that neither expected. In *The Philadelphia Story*, Katharine Hepburn moves out of her space into the one occupied by James Stewart, a frustrated novelist reduced to writing for a tabloid (and enamored of her), only to be drawn back into her ex-husband's (Cary Grant) space, leaving Stewart free to fill the void left in Ruth Hussey's heart. While *The Philadelphia Story* had sparkle, *High Society* had sheen, radiated in great part by Kelly's porcelain beauty and Porter's score, the best of which derived from his earlier musical, *Du Barry Was a Lady*, and became a tour de force for Crosby and Sinatra.

Interestingly, Porter's final Broadway musical was *Silk Stockings*, an adaptation of Ernst Lubitsch's peerless *Ninotchka*, which, if Hildegarde Neff is correct, turned out more like hash than a soufflé. *High Society* was neither hash nor a soufflé. Rather, it was like Johnny Walker Black Label with a splash of soda, which seemed appropriate for Crosby and Sinatra.

The Philadelphia Story belonged to a different world. Barry had written the play for Katharine Hepburn, who starred in it on Broadway for 415 performances, then on tour, and finally on the screen. There was no trace of belabored line readings that often creep into a stage-to-screen transfer. There was a freshness about Hepburn's Tracy, yet at the same time a feeling of anxiety that a strongly independent woman might experience by becoming so far removed from the norm that she would be inaccessible to mere mortals. Hepburn resolved all these warring aspects within Tracy's character, leaving her palpably human and vulnerable, unable to decide between a stuffy suitor (John Howard) and her ex-husband (Cary Grant) until the latter makes her mind up for her. That same year, Grant performed a similar service for Rosalind Russell in *His Girl Friday*, saving her from marriage to Ralph Bellamy.

There are few surprises in *High Society*, especially after the first scene in which Louis Armstrong and his band arrive at Newport for the Jazz Festival—and to which the film returns at the end as Crosby joins Armstrong for the finale. The film becomes a frame narrative with Armstrong appearing intermittently as commentator and closing the frame at the end.

There was one standout number, and another that became far more popular for other reasons.

In *High Society*, Crosby and Sinatra find themselves at a party at which each feels out of place. They retire to the study and parody the guests' vapid conversations in "Well, Did You Evah!," which Betty Grable and Charles Walters introduced in *Du Barry Was a Lady*. Sinatra and Crosby trade anecdotes about "dear Blanche [who] got run down by an avalanche" and "Mimsy Starr [who] got pinched in the Astor Bar." With the concluding verse, "What a swellegant, elegant party this is," they exit arm in arm to join the other guests. When they realize the boredom in store for them, they rush back to the study for another drink—and an encore. Each then goes his own way—one exiting left, the other right as if on stage and leaving the audience in such a euphoric state that applause would not have been out of place. This was the most sublime moment in the film.

Less so was "True Love," in which Crosby and Kelly recall their honeymoon on the yacht if that name. It is a simple melody in ¾ time sung mostly by Crosby except for the final chorus, when Kelly joins him. The mellowness of Crosby's voice gave it the air of a lullaby, a remembrance of things past. It is hard enough to believe that Crosby and Kelly have been divorced for only two years, and that Crosby is a successful jazz musician, descended from Newport robber barons, which gave him access to Kelly's circle.

In the 1940 original, the four principals were approximately the same age: Katharine Hepburn and James Stewart, both born the same year, were thirty-three; Cary Grant, thirty-six; and Ruth Hussey, twenty-eight. In the 1956 remake, Bing Crosby was fifty-four; Frank Sinatra, forty-five; Grace Kelly, twenty-four; and Celeste Holm, five years older than Ruth Hussey (and the right age for her character). If "True Love" sounds more like a cradle song that pledge of fidelity, it may be the disparity in the characters' ages. *The Philadelphia Story* was a perfect fit; *High Society* was a few sizes too large.

LES GIRLS (1957)

Although *Les Girls* was a financial disappointment for MGM, it was vastly superior to *High Society*. In fact, it seems less of a musical than a melodrama, which explains why director George Cukor, who generally avoided musicals, was drawn to it. A former member of Gene Kelly's company known as Les Girls has now become Lady Sybil Wren (Kay Kendall), who has published a memoir that has triggered a libel suit. Lady Wren has alleged that another member of the troupe (Tania Elg) attempted suicide out of unrequited love for Kelly. Elg takes the stand, claiming it was the other way around. Finally, Kelly sets matters straight (somewhat) by admitting that if he had not broken into their flat, they would both have died from carbon monoxide poisoning caused by a defective heater. Whether Kelly is telling the truth or not is debatable. In the final scene, a man wearing a "What Is Truth?" sign walks the frame, signaling The End. But The End of what? Like Akira Kurosawa's *Rashomon* (1950), which clearly inspired John Patrick's screenplay, truth is often weirder than fiction. In *Rashomon*, what seems to have been a rape and a murder is neither and, in fact, is downright ludicrous.

As Lady Wren, the irresistible Kay Kendall upstaged everyone as an alcoholic who hides liquor in perfume bottles and delivers a drunken "Habanera" from Bizet's *Carmen*. In one sketch, Kendall and the others, dressed in Marie Antoinette costumes with an exposed backside decorated with a bow, list the various ways they serve the King, each time returning from his chamber with the bow resting in their wig. It was the best number in a less-that-lustrous score.

The low point was "Why Am I So Gone About That Gal?" with Kelly in a black leather jacket looking like Marlon Brando in *The Wild One* (1954), who drops into a diner with his fellow bikers where Mitzi Gaynor works as a server. He is interested, she is available, moving from stool to stool and signaling with an outstretched leg. It is the low erotic, a sad attempt to evoke the glory days at MGM when Kelly danced *Slaughter on Tenth Avenue* with Vera-Ellen in *Words and Music* (1948) and partnered with Cyd Charisse in *Singin' in the Rain* (1952). But bikers are not meant for diners, and Kelly and his gang depart, leaving Gaynor with a white handkerchief as a souvenir—and Porter with a five-song score that ranks among his lesser efforts.

CHAPTER 15

COLUMBIA: *YOU'LL NEVER GET RICH* (1941) AND *SOMETHING TO SHOUT ABOUT* (1943)

The first of Porter's two films for Columbia Pictures, *You'll Never Get Rich*, was more adventuresome than the latter, *Something to Shout About*. What it lacked was a hit song which the latter had—a song that was one of the most memorable of the World War II years, "You'd be So Nice to Come Home To," which expressed the sentiments of a nation engaged in a war whose outcome was still uncertain. The song was deceptively simple, with a minimum of imagery and an abundance of warmth—the same combination that attracted such as vocalists as Dinah Shore, Frank Sinatra, Jo Stafford, Julie London, Nina Simone, and Harry Connick Jr. *You'll Never Get Rich*, on the other hand, is memorable for the first pairing of Fred Astaire and Rita Hayworth, who returned to the studio for their second and last musical together, *You Were Never Lovelier* (Columbia, 1942), this time with a score by Jerome Kern that included "Dearly Beloved" and the title song.

You'll Never Get Rich is a strangely disjointed film. The title would only have made sense to moviegoers of the time since the main characters—Fred Astaire as a Broadway choreographer, Rita Hayworth as his most talented dancer, and Robert Benchley as a theater owner—are reasonably well-off. Released in late September 1941, two months before Pearl Harbor, audiences would have had no difficulty identifying the source: "We're In the Army Now (sometimes "You're in the Army Now)," a popular World War I song by Isham Jones, which contained the lines, "You'll never get rich by digging a ditch / You're (we're) in the army now." The alternate version is more colorful but less common: "You'll never get rich, you son of a bitch."

The passage of the selective service act in 1940 gave the song a special relevance. The working title of *You'll Never Get Rich* was "He's My Uncle," a reference to every American's uncle, Uncle Sam. It was impossible to enter a post office without seeing our "uncle's" message to draft-age men, "Uncle Sam Wants You." Another film released a few months after Pearl Harbor, *You're in the Army Now* (1941) took a similar approach to the military draft, which still depicted an America ensconced in the cocoon of isolationism. Although America was by then at war, the sentiments expressed in the film were genuine, at least by Hollywood's standards by which truth is measured by public opinion. If Uncle Sam wants you, only the lily-livered would decline the invitation. When the men in *You're in the Army Now* celebrate their draft status in the rousing "I'm Glad My Number Was Called," you would think they had won the lottery.

The working title made it clear that *You'll Never Get Rich* would center around the (then) peacetime draft with Fred Astaire as such a loyal son of Uncle Sam, and so glad his number was called, that he fakes his weight so he can be eligible. The writers, Michael Fessier and Ernst Pagano, had their setup; now they needed a storyline that would explain why the choreographer of a show in rehearsal would rush off to join the army. The explanation is as questionable as that in any musical. What matters is its credibility. If the actors believe it, chances are the audience will, too.

Theater owner Robert Benchley has become so infatuated with a dancer (Rita Hayworth) that he presented her with a personally inscribed diamond bracelet, which Hayworth, wise to his ways, leaves behind. When Benchley's wife discovers it, she thinks it is an anniversary present until she sees the inscription. Benchley prevails upon Astaire to pretend to be romantically involved with Hayworth so that his wife will assume Astaire had the bracelet inscribed for Hayworth. Their "romance" makes the gossip columns, infuriating Hayworth who blames Astaire. In an attempt to extricate himself from a situation that has spiraled out of control after Hayworth's unofficial fiancé, an army captain, threatens him, Astaire uses his draft notice as an excuse to avoid further complications.

The second half of the film is a continuation of the first. Benchley volunteers to produce a show for the men on the base with Astaire as choreographer, but with a new star, his latest fancy. Astaire wants Hayworth and eventually gets her. Since the production was supposed to end with a wedding, Astaire arranged for a real minister to officiate and legalize their union. Hayworth does not mind, and with her unofficial fiancé transferred to Panama, Astaire has a dancing partner who was every bit his equal, if only for two films.

The writers were obviously familiar with *George White's Scandals* (Fox Film Corporation, 1934), which ended the same way. A producer played by George White himself, knowing that Alice Faye and Rudy Vallee are in love, trick them into signing new contracts, which are really marriage licenses. In the show in which they are starring, they are supposed to exchange vows, which they do—but it is before a real justice of the peace, not an actor.

Hayworth brought out a side of Astaire that was previously concealed behind a façade of stylized movement. With Ginger Rogers, it was the low erotic dance so delicately purged of passion that one was satisfied with merely the sight of two celestial beings dancing to the music of the spheres. You were tempted to say, as Astaire did in Irving Berlin's *Top Hat* (1935), "Heaven, I'm in Heaven."

With Hayworth, Astaire found liberation. When she played the goddess Terpsichore in the musical, *Down to Earth* (Columbia, 1947), she was the embodiment of her character, all fluidity and grace. She was the same in *You'll Never Get Rich*. Astaire responded to her welcoming presence, seeming more relaxed than he had been before, particularly with Rogers, with whom every dance was a competition with no winners. As previously noted, Katharine Hepburn claimed that Astaire gave Rogers class while she gave him sex. If anyone gave Astaire sex, it was Hayworth, who did it so subtly that he seems to have been born with it. In "So Near and Yet So Far," which, sadly, summed up their brief hour together, Porter created a blend of ballroom and rumba, with Astaire responding to Hayworth's sense of the Latin style as if it was as natural to him as it was to her. In "The Wedding Cake Walk," sung by the great Martha Tilton, Astaire and Hayworth celebrated their union atop a tank in the shape of a wedding cake with the dancers, strutting cakewalk style in 2/4 time.

Porter's most original contribution to the score of *You'll Never Get Rich*, "Since I Kissed My Baby Good By," is sung by all-Black quartet, the Four Tones, who had appeared in a number of Black westerns, including *Two-Gun Man from Harlem* (1936) and *Harlem on the Prairie* (1937). The setting is the guard house frequently occupied by Astaire, who thinks of the army as the equivalent of summer camp. What is unusual about this guard house is the presence of Black servicemen on a (then) segregated army base. The Four Tones, unidentified both in the credits and as characters, are Lucius Brooks, Leon Buck, Rudolph Hunter, and John Porter. Why they are there is never made known, but their plight is made wrenchingly clear in Brooks's soulful lament. The singer finds no solace in a tranquil evening or a starry sky and sees no difference between living and dying "since I kissed my baby goodbye." Astaire's tapping does not alleviate the sense of loss; in fact, it intensifies it. Did a 1940s audience wonder what four Black men did to be confined to an all-white guardhouse? We know that Astaire deserved to be punished for impersonating a captain in order to impress Hayworth. Perhaps in 1941 it did not matter. After all, no one knew who the men were.

Something to Shout About, Porter's second and last film for Columba, was also a showbiz musical, less inventive than *You'll Never Get Rich*. Although it may have lacked the star power of Astaire and Hayworth, it had a talented and energetic cast (Don Ameche, Janet Blair, and Jack Oakie, who runs a boarding house where the supremely talented pianist, Hazel Scott, is one of the boarders). The plot is built around a set of showbiz tropes that have been reworked for a plot about an aspiring composer (Janet Blair), who has come to New York from Altoona, Pennsylvania, to interest music publishers in her songs. She is befriended by Don Ameche, a publicist who has just lost his job, and Jack Oakie, who not only offers her a place to stay but also an appreciative audience for her music. Just when you think how refreshing it is to watch a film about a composer instead of one about a dewy-eyed ingénue, the plot takes a sharp detour into the show business netherworld where anything is possible, including a composer with a pleasant voice but with no stage experience who finds herself as the star of a musical revue when the monumentally untalented star (Cobina Wright) leaves in a huff. The composer-music teacher is a sensation, dancing "Hasta Luego" with David Lichine as if she had been coached by Carmen Miranda.

When the star (and principal backer) closes the show, all is not lost. She had taken a two-month lease on the theater, just enough time for Ameche and Oakie to mount a vaudeville show whose main attraction is an animal act with dogs on scooters and leaping out of windows into baskets. It requires a giant leap of faith to believe that audiences prepared for a musical revue would settle for a journey to the past. But if it was good enough for Mickey Rooney and Judy Garland in *Babes in Arms* (MGM, 1938), it's good enough for Broadway. What matters is that boy gets girl (what happens to her songwriting career is unresolved). The show is a success, and a producer with a succession of flops (William Gaxton) finally has a hit even if it is not in the legitimate theatre.

Something to Shout About does not make overt references to World War II, except for Hazel Scott's song, "I Can Do without Tea in My Teapot," a typical Porter list song about rationing, in which she enumerates everything she can do without (gas, gin, silk underwear, French perfume), striking each key as if it were an item to be discarded, but admitting that while she can do without a girdle, "But baby, never / Without you."

"Lotus Bloom" is subtler. It is a lullaby sung by Janet Blair and danced by a very young Cyd Charisse and David Lichine, in which Blair encourages a young Chinese girl to dream of a prince who will take her away "from this world of gloom"—a world that was described in an unused version that reflected Porter's mood at the time. The prince will take her away from a world "of bombs that kill." Meanwhile, "trust in heaven and your Uncle Sam." "Lotus Bloom" was to have been in the original production, suggesting a musical revue that did not shy away from the topical, even amid wartime. Instead, it was replaced by a vaudeville show whose main attraction was an animal act.

If *Something to Shout About* is remembered at all, it is for the World War II favorite, "You'd Be So Nice to Come Home To." It is sung twice by Janet

Blair, first at the boarding house and later when she returns to Altoona after her disillusioning experience in the theater; and in the finale by Blair and Don Ameche. In each instance only the refrain is sung. If the verses were included, it would never have become the classic it did.

In verse 1, a brash young man makes his intentions known to the object of his affection, comparing her to "asparagus out of season" and assuming she is impressed by the metaphor. In verse 2, the woman, wise to his brand of flattery, informs him that she might be interested if he "behaved like a grown up." Sandwiched between the verses is the refrain. With the verses, you have the age-old story of a man on the make and the woman who puts him in his place. With only the refrain, you have a ballad that spoke to a generation going through a war that was far from over.

In his analysis of the song, Don Randel notes that the refrain is built around a set of conditions. The song is not entitled "You'll Be So Nice" but "You'd Be So Nice"—not the future indicative but the conditional. "You'd" is repeated five times in the eleven-line refrain. "You'd" implies an "if," but if *what*? Porter does not specify the conditions, but they are easily inferable: an Allied victory, a return to normalcy, a period of peace before the next conflict.

Meanwhile, "trust in Heaven and your Uncle Sam."

Porter's original scores for movie musicals included some standards ("Begin the Beguine," "Easy to Love," "I've Got You Under My Skin," "True Love"), but the musicals themselves were, except for *High Society*, not especially memorable. They were certainly not on the order of Rodgers and Hammerstein's only original screen musical, *State Fair* (Twentieth Century-Fox, 1945); Irving Berlin's *Holiday Inn* (Paramount, 1942); Jerome Kern's *Swing Time* (RKO, 1936), *High, Wide and Handsome* (Paramount, 1937), *You Were Never Lovelier* (Columbia, 1942), *Cover Girl* (Columbia, 1944), *Can't Help Singing* (Universal, 1944); or Harold Arlen's *The Wizard of Oz* (MGM, 1939) and *A Star Is Born* (Warner Bros., 1954). Cole Porter was meant for Broadway; Hollywood was a side trip.

CHAPTER 16

A Less-Than-Grand Finale

Aladdin

Porter's sole musical for television, *Aladdin*, was a DuPont Show of the Month presentation, telecast live on CBS-TV on February 21, 1958. It was also his last musical venture. The previous year, Rodgers and Hammerstein scored a triumph with their television musical *Cinderella* on CBS-TV, March 31, 1957, directed by Ralph Nelson and starring in the title role Julie Andrews, then appearing opposite Rex Harrison on Broadway in *My Fair Lady*. The score was rich in melody, and although the songs never became part of the American Songbook, "Do I Love You Because You're Beautiful?" became popular through recordings by Vic Damone and John Coltrane.

It seemed that audiences could not get enough of *Cinderella*. It was telecast two more times with different heroines, Lesley Ann Warren in 1965 and Brandy Norwood in 1997; it was converted into a stage musical that premiered at the London Coliseum in 1958, followed by international tours, performances at New York City Opera, and finally a Broadway production in 2013 with a considerably revised book by Douglas Carter Beane. The producer of the 1957 telecast, Richard Lewine, believed that if Rodgers and Hammerstein could lend their musical talents to television, so could Cole Porter. And if Rodgers and Hammerstein could make a musical out of a fairy tale seen by more viewers than any television show up to that time, Porter might be able to do the same with a tale from the *Arabian Nights*.

Richard Lewine and Ralph Nelson returned as producer and director of *Aladdin*. Since it would be televised live, a cast was recruited consisting mainly of actors with stage experience, who could bring the immediacy of theater to a multi-set television production. The cast that was assembled included actors who had appeared a year or two earlier on Broadway or were slated to appear the following season: Cyril Ritchard (Sui-Janel, the Sorcerer) had just completed a run of Gore Vidal's *Visit to a Small*

Planet, which closed on January 11, 1958. Dennis King (the Astrologer) had costarred with Robert Preston and Lili Darvas in *The Hidden River* (1957). Una Merkel (Aladdin's mother) won a Tony for best featured actress in *The Ponder Heart* (1956). Akim Tamiroff (unbilled as the Governor) would play the Woodcutter in the stage adaptation of *Rashomon* (1959). The great dancer Geoffrey Holder (the Genie) had been principal dancer with the Metropolitan Opera Ballet, created the role of the Champion in the Harold Arlen-Truman Capote musical *House of Flowers* (1954), for which he also choreographed the Banda dance, and played Lucky in the all-Black revival of Samuel Beckett's *Waiting for Godot* (1957). Basil Rathbone (the Emperor) replaced Raymond Massey as Mr. Zuss in Archibald MacLeish's *J.B.* during the 1958–69 run. Howard Morris (Wu Fang, the pickpocket) was a veteran of live television, well remembered from Sid Caesar's *Your Show of Shows*. Sal Mineo (Aladdin) had worked in live television (*Omnibus*, *Climax!*, *Philco Television Playhouse*). Anna Maria Alberghetti (the Princess), who had performed on the concert stage and *The Ed Sullivan Show*, would make her Broadway debut two years later in *Carnival!* (1960).

The book was by humorist-screenwriter-playwright S. J. Perleman (*Monkey Business*, *Horse Feathers*, the book for Kurt Weill's *One Touch of Venus*). Rod Alexander, who staged the dance sequences in the film version of *Carousel*, choreographed the production, and Irene Sharaff (*An American in Paris*, *Call Me Madam*, *Brigadoon*, and numerous others) designed the costumes. And with a score by Cole Porter, how could such a stellar production fail?

It did.

The problem was Perleman's book. It was obvious Perleman had little interest in *Aladdin* and more in the sorcerer Sui-Jamal, which is understandable, since it was the starring role played with foppish flamboyance by Cyril Ritchard. Sui-Jamal pretends to be the brother of Aladdin's dead father in order to trick the lad into retrieving a magic lamp from a far-off mountain cave. Desperate to return to his widowed mother, Aladdin clutches the lamp, unaware of its magical properties, and is whisked back home. Determined to regain the lamp, Sui-Jamal dons an eye patch and poses as a peddler trading old lamps for new. Wu Fang persuades Aladdin's mother to make the exchange, which she reluctantly does. Meanwhile, in the "princess and the commoner" subplot, Aladdin fall in love with the Emperor's daughter. Sui Jamal stages a coup against the Emperor, who is imprisoned along with his daughter, Aladdin, and Wu Fang, who has the new lamp. Just when they are about to be beheaded, the lamps get mixed up, the right one is rubbed, the captives are free, Aladdin marries the princess (if a prince can marry Cinderella, a princess can marry Aladdin), and the genie subjects Sui-Jamal is to torture by tickling.

Although Mineo and Alberghetti make an attractive couple, they remain storybook characters. Mineo, who has a pleasantly generic voice and does what little dancing is required of him, can only express the emotional range Perleman has given his character, which never moves beyond zero. Alberghtti's bell-like soprano was familiar to moviegoers from *Here Comes the Groom* and *The Stars Are Singing*, in which she performed "Caro nome" in the former and selections from *Lucia di Lammermoor*, *La Traviata*, and *The Barber of Seville* in the latter. Anyone expecting operatic vocalism in *Aladdin* was disappointed. Alberghetti had little to do except look virginal and sing the dreamy title song in which "Aladdin" is repeated five times, rhyming with "gladden" and "sadden." She joins Mineo in a duet, "I Adore You," with "adore" rhyming twice with "implore" as if Porter could not come up with another verb. Both were boilerplate numbers: a solo (literally, since it was Alberghetti's only one) and a love duet. The feelings expressed in "I Adore You" were more poetically rendered in "I Worship You," which, for some reason, was dropped from *Fifty Million Frenchmen*. "I Worship You" goes far beyond the gooey sentiments of "I Adore You" in its elevation of love to a form of worship, as if love were a religion and the beloved an object of veneration.

The musical should have been entitled "The Sorcerer," since Ritchard not only steals every scene he's in but also has the best numbers. Porter's rhymes come trippingly off Ritchard's tongue in the list song, "Come to the Supermarket in Old Peking," which he tosses off with impeccable enunciation as if it were a Gilbert and Sullivan patter song. "Come to the Supermarket in Old Peking" lacks the sophistication and inside references of "Anything Goes," but the idea is the same: anything you want you can get—from lizard cakes and pickled snakes to calico and buffalo to seaweed soup and poodle soup. Ritchard's verbal dexterity is also on display in "No Wonder Taxes Are High," which catalogues the Emperor's passion for such extravagances as marble dragons, emeralds and rubies, satin and perfume, while the masses work with faces covered in grime and no hope of getting overtime. Porter avoids contemporary parallels; the title speaks for itself.

Ritchard's Sui-Jamal is a light-footed Chinese Captain Hook who behaves like the charmingly affected dandy Sir Fopling Flutter in George Etheridge's Restoration comedy *The Man of Mode*. (In 1950, Ritchard starred on Broadway as Lord Foppington in Sir John Vanbrugh's Restoration comedy *The Relapse*, which he also directed.) Ritchard brought the high style of classic English comedy to the role; as the Emperor, Basil

Rathbone was properly autocratic when he was in power and resigned to powerlessness when he was in prison. While Ritchard and Rathbone played versions of their stage and screen personas, the extraordinarily versatile Dennis King, who was equally at home in operetta and serious drama, understood that *Aladdin* was essentially operetta and played the astrologer as he did the leads in Sigmund Romberg's *Rose-Marie* and Rudolph Friml's *The Vagabond King*. At sixty-one, his baritone was still serviceable, as he showed in the musical's only serious song, "Trust Your Destiny to Your Star," which he delivered with the measured tones of one who knew his way around the Zodiac.

Unlike *Cinderella*, *Aladdin* never made it to Broadway, but in December 1959, a stage version arrived at London's Coliseum with a considerably reworked book by actor-playwright Peter Coke, best known for his comedy *Breath of Spring* (1958), filmed as *Make Mine Mink* (1960) as a vehicle for Terry Thomas. *Aladdin* starred the hugely popular Bob Monkhouse, who was thirty as opposed to Sal Mineo, who was nineteen when he played the part on television; it did not matter to British audiences, to whom Monkhouse had endeared himself from his many appearances on radio and especially television as both a game show host and the star of *The Bob Monkhouse Show* and *The Bob Monkhouse Hour*. He had, in fact, become such an institution that in 1993 he was made an Officer in the Order of the British Empire for his contribution to British media.

The casting of Doretta Morrow—Tuptim in *The King and I* (1951) and Marsinah in *Kismet* (1954) on Broadway, and Mario Lanza's costar in *Because You're Mine* (MGM, 1952)—as the Princess meant additional musical numbers. Her solo "Aladdin" and the "I Adore You" duet were retained. Two songs were interpolated from *Out of This World*: "I Am Loved," which was far more suited to her full-bodied soprano than it was to Priscilla Gilette's lighter voice in the original; and the bouncy "Cherry Pies Ought to be You" as a second duet for Aladdin and the Princess.

Coke added a new character, the magician Abanazar from the popular British pantomime also called *Aladdin*. Abanazar is a comic villain, which is how Alan Wheatley played him. Wheatley was another familiar face, having appeared on stage, screen, and especially television, notably as the Sheriff of Nottingham in *The Adventures of Robin Hood* series (1958–59), which starred Richard Greene as Robin. Coke replaced the Astrologer with the Widow Twankey, another character from the *Aladdin* pantomime, always played by a male in drag—in this case by another British favorite, the comedian Ronald Shiner. The Astrologer's solo, "Trust Your Destiny to Your Star," became a duet between the Emperor and Twankey.

To make Aladdin the central character, Sui-Jamal was also eliminated, but not his list song, "Come to the Supermarket in Old Peking," which Monkhouse inherited. Monkhouse needed an opening number, which *Aladdin* did not have in the television version. He was given "There Must Be Someone for Me" from *Mexican Hayride*, which required some changes in gender, having been introduced by June Havoc as a female bullfighter. It was another list song, goofier than most, which, depending on one's taste, would either come off as tedious or hilarious; either way, it is an overlong enumeration of various species that easily find their mates (cats, bats, rats, snails, quails, whales, even loons and prunes). Ergo, there must be someone for Aladdin—and that person is, of course, the Princess.

In the television original, Basil Rathbone was to have performed the very last song that Porter wrote, "Wouldn't It be Fun?," in which the Emperor wishes he could have been an ordinary person, not a monarch who must attend executions, entertain Huns, and inspect slave labor camps. "Wouldn't it be fun to be nearly anyone / Except me, mixed up me!" The song begins on a reflective note, then veers off into dark humor, and concludes with a wish for anonymity. Six weeks after the *Aladdin* telecast, Porter's right leg was amputated. He would never be anonymous, but his composing days were over.

Basil Rathbone had recorded "Wouldn't It Be Fun?" for the soundtrack. Although it is on the remastered *Aladdin* CD, it was not part of the telecast either because Rathbone's singing voice was considered inadequate or, more likely, because the references to slave labor and executions made the Emperor sound like a tyrant and was at odds with his change of character, which Rathbone conveyed by his newly acquired gravitas after being overthrown. The song was restored for the London production and performed like an operatic monologue by bass-baritone, Ian Wallace, whose repertoire included in Schaunard in Puccini's *La Bohème*, Leporello in Mozart's *Don Giovanni*, Pistol in Verdi's *Falstaff*, and Doctor Bartolo in Mozart's *The Marriage of Figaro*. Wallace was also no stranger to musical theater, having starred opposite Robert Morley in a West End production of *Fanny*.

As a stage musical, the London *Aladdin* was vastly superior to the television original, not merely because it had a stellar cast but also because it was directed and choreographed by the astonishingly versatile Robert Helpmann, who excelled in whatever he attempted: ballet, acting (theater and film), and directing (stage and opera). He performed on stage with such artists as Sir Laurence Olivier, Vivien Leigh, Katharine Hepburn, Richard Burton, and Claire Bloom. Moviegoers with a fondness for ballet would remember him as Ivan in *The Red Shoes* (1948) and as each of the four villains in *The Tales of Hoffman* (1951).

Aladdin should never have been a television musical. Coke's much improved book with elements of British pantomime and Helpmann's lavish staging brought *Aladdin* out from the narrow confines of operetta and into the broader world of musical theater. Coke, Helpmann, and a first-rate cast did Porter justice. It is a pity that he never saw the production.

Cole Porter died on October 16, 1964.

Epilogue

Classic films are screened regularly at New York's Museum of Modern Art. They are shown on a channel devoted to classic American and European films, Turner Classic Movies (TCM). Concert halls program music by the famous, the less famous, and the potentially famous. Opera houses stage rarely heard Verdi operas. New York City is home to the New York City Ballet, the Alvin Ailey Dance Company, and the American Ballet Theatre.

All the arts have a home. Broadway has revivals.

There is no organization committed to preserving the legacy of the Broadway musical, nothing to remind theatergoers that before there was Stephen Sondheim, there were George Gershwin (1898–1937), Irving Berlin (1888–1989), and Jerome Kern (1885–1945). And Cole Porter.

On Broadway, the past is either revived or languishes in an archive until some visionary gets enough backing to restore a work to a semblance of its former self, even if the text has to be made to conform to present cultural norms. In the 2019 revival of Cole Porter's *Kiss Me, Kate*, Kelli O'Hara as Lilli Vanessi, who is playing Katherine in a musical version of Shakespeare's *The Taming of the Shrew*, no longer sings Katherine's advice to wives, "I am ashamed that women are so simple"—Shakespeare's words that Porter had set to music; instead, she sings, "I am ashamed that people are so simple."

Rather than have an old roué sing "Thank Heaven for Little Girls," as Maurice Chevalier did in Vincente Minnelli's *Gigi* (MGM, 1959) before it was converted into a stage musical, the number was entrusted to Gigi's grandmother (Victoria Clark) and aunt (Dee Hoty) in the 2015 Broadway revival. As Chevalier sang it in the film, it was evident that he could not wait for little girls to blossom into womanhood. In an age that has seen its share of pedophiles, it seemed prudent to switch genders.

Cole Porter has suffered the same fate as Jerome Kern, George Gershwin, and Irving Berlin. Only Porter's *Anything Goes* and *Kiss Me, Kate* have had major revivals. Neither requires much updating to be successful. The title song in *Anything Goes* can be sung alone without the references to contemporaries who would be unfamiliar to present day audiences. As we have seen, *Kiss Me, Kate* requires a climactic number that does not come off as sexist, accomplished by a simple change of "women" to "people."

Of all Jerome Kern's musicals, only *Show Boat* has proved a favorite. It has been revived five times on Broadway: in 1932, 1946, 1966, 1983, and 1994. George Gershwin won a Pulitzer Prize for *Of Thee I Sing* (1931), the first musical to ever win that award. It was revived unsuccessfully in 1952 and most likely will never be again. The humor, once topical, has become dated. If the name of George Gershwin is associated with any stage work, it is with *Porgy and Bess*, once considered a mere folk opera, and now a staple in major opera houses, including the Metropolitan Opera. *Porgy and Bess* premiered at a Broadway theatre, the Alvin (now the Neil Simon) on October 10, 1935. Since then, it has been revived in 1942, 1954, 1977, 1983, and most recently as *The Gershwins' Porgy and Bess* in 2012, proving that orchestrated differently, the same work can straddle two different worlds.

Irving Berlin may be America's greatest songwriter, but not of stage musicals. Only *Annie Get Your Gun* (1946) gets revived, the last time in 1999 with Bernadette Peters in the role created by Ethel Merman. Since Berlin's lyrics were deemed offensive to Native Americans, "I'm an Indian, Too" was cut.

Film has afforded a greater form of longevity to composers like Irving Berlin, George Gershwin, and Jerome Kern than has Broadway. Think of such films as Irving Berlin's *Top Hat* (RKO, 1935), *Alexander's Ragtime Band* (Twentieth Century-Fox, 1938), *Holiday Inn* (Paramount, 1942), *Blue Skies* (Paramount, 1946), *Easter Parade* (MGM, 1948), *Call Me Madam* (Twentieth Century-Fox, 1953, *White Christmas* (Paramount, 1954), *There's No Business Like Show Business* (Twentieth Century-Fox, 1954); George Gershwin's *Shall We Dance?* (RKO, 1937), *Lady Be Good* (MGM, 1941), *Girl Crazy* (MGM, 1943); the biopic *Rhapsody in Blue* (Warner Bros.,1945); *An American in Paris* (MGM, 1951), *Porgy and Bess* (Goldwyn-Columbia, 1959); Jerome Kern's *Music in the Air* (Twentieth Century-Fox, 1934), *Roberta* (RKO, 1935), *Swing Time* (RKO, 1936), *Sunny* (RKO, 1941), *You Were Never Lovelier* (Columbia, (1942), *Cover Girl* (Columbia, 1944), *Can't Help Singing* (Universal, 1944), *Centennial Summer* (Twentieth Century-Fox, 1946), *Lovely to Look At* (remake of *Roberta*, MGM, 1952); and the biopic *Til the Clouds Roll By* (MGM, 1946).

Film has also ensured Cole Porter's legacy. Porter has been the subject of two biopics, neither of which did him justice, although the latter at least portrayed him as a gay man—or as gay as a PG-13 rating would allow.

According to the credits, *Night and Day* (Warner Bros., 1946), directed by Michael Curtiz and starring Cary Grant as the composer and Alexis Smith as Linda Lee Thomas, was "based on the career of Cole Porter," which absolved the screenwriters of factual accuracy. At the opening of Porter's first New York musical, *See America First,* Jane Wyman is in the middle of singing "You Do Something to Me" when news of the sinking of the *Lusitania* causes a mass exodos from the theatre. "You Do Something to Me" is from the score of *Fifty Million Frenchmen,* and the *Lusitania* was torpedoed by a German U-boat on May 7, 1915. It is true that *See America First* was a failure, but it was not because of the *Lusitania.*

Night and Day is worth watching to hear Mary Martin sing "My Heart Belongs to Daddy" as suggestively as an abridged version would allow. Unless you know the context, you might wonder why Martin is wearing a fur jacket over her tights and singing to a group of Eskimos. The number is from *Leave It to Me,* in which Martin's character ends up at a Siberian train station where she entertains the natives with her impish vow of flexible fidelity to her "daddy."

De-Lovely (MGM, 2004), directed by Irwin Winkler from a screenplay by Jay Cocks, starred Kevin Kline as Porter and Ashley Judd as Linda, neither of whom had the stature of Grant and Smith, yet succeeded in being far more believable. They were not movie stars in a biopic but a brilliant composer with male lovers and a wife who understood his needs as best she could.

Cocks used a framing device beginning with Porter at the close of his life visited by the angel Gabriel (Jonathan Pryce), the same Gabriel that Reno Sweeney invoked in "Blow, Gabriel, Blow" in *Anything Goes.* Gabriel is entrusted with the task of having Porter review his past, which unfolds like chapters in a book interleaved with musical segments. Samson Raphaelson used a similar technique in Ernst Lubitsch's *Heaven Can Wait* (Twentieth Century-Fox, 1943), in which a recently deceased lothario (Don Ameche) awaits judgement as he reviews his past indiscretions which will determine whether he will be taking the elevator up or down. Porter is spared the elevator ride; since Gabriel is an archangel, he seems to be only headed in one direction.

Details from Porter's life alternate with the musical numbers, most of which are out of context and designed as interludes between the plot threads. "Be a Clown," the climactic song in *The Pirate* (MGM 1948), becomes a full-scale production number on the MGM lot. "Love for Sale" (*The New Yorkers,* 1930) is sung at a club with a decidedly gay clientele. When Monty Woolley bets Porter that he cannot write a love song that begins with the words "I love you," Porter does, and it becomes the only hit song in *Mexican Hayride*. In the film, it is written for an MGM musical that looks like *Rose-Marie* (MGM, 1936), but not with the original stars Jeanette MacDonald and Nelson Eddy. When Porter is watching a run-through of the opening number in *Kiss Me, Kate*, he is critical of a "Miss Morison," one of the dancers. In the musical, Patricia Morison is not a lady of the chorus but Alfred Drake's costar. Perhaps this was a nod to those who knew that in the original Drake criticized the way Morison was taking her curtain call. But it did not really matter. In a musical biopic, what matters are the songs, not as they were sung in the original stage production, but as they exist within a newly created musical context.

Winkler was unusually discreet about Porter's gay lovers. Porter gives a quick kiss to dancer Boris Kochno before leaving the bedroom. Linda is about to join her husband at their swimming pool where he is surrounded by men, but then decides otherwise and leaves. Monty Woolley decides to check out the action in the Ramble in Central Park. Some may have gotten the reference, but one wonders how many native New Yorkers even knew that the Ramble was notorious for gay sex. In the film's most touching scene, Linda, after seeing how natural Porter behaved around Gerald and Sara Murphy's children, suggests that they too might start a family. You would think that the Production Code was still in effect from the way Linda broached the subject. In the film, Porter admits that he is open to any kind of love, so the idea of his impregnating Linda seems plausible. But Linda miscarries, and there is no further talk of a family.

At near the close of *De-Lovely*, there is a superb example of intercutting between Porter at the piano singing "So in Love" to Linda to Porter at the opening night of *Kiss Me, Kate* as the song is sung on stage by the stars, Alfred Drake and Patricia Morison. At this point, we forget that "So in Love" is first sung by Morison on Act 1 and reprised by Drake in Act 2. It was never a duet, and yet it could easily have been one.

Night and Day and *De-Lovely* have their faults as biopics, but Porter's music redeems them. Porter did not think much of *Night and Day*. In *De-Lovely*, after a screening, he tells Linda, "If I can survive this, I can survive anything." Ironically, film has become the preserver of the Broadway musical, allowing it to continue in another medium.

The Musicals of Cole Porter (1891–1964)

BROADWAY

See America First (1916)
Hitchy-Koo of 1919
Hitchy-Koo of 1922
Greenwich Village Follies (1924)
Paris (1928)
Wake Up and Dream (1929)
Fifty Million Frenchmen (1929)
The New Yorkers (1930)
Gay Divorce (1932)
Anything Goes (1934)
Jubilee (1935)
Red, Hot and Blue (1936)
You Never Know (1938)
Leave It to Me (1938)
Du Barry Was a Lady (1939)
Panama Hattie (1940)
Let's Face It! (1941)
Something for the Boys (1943)
Mexican Hayride (1944)
Seven Lively Arts (1944)
Around the World (1946)
Kiss Me, Kate (1948)
Out of this World (1950)
Can-Can (1953)
Silk Stockings (1955)

LONDON

Nymph Errant (1933)
Aladdin (1959)

HOLLYWOOD STAGE-TO-SCREEN TRANSFERS

Anything Goes (Paramount, 1936)
Panama Hattie (MGM, 1942)
Du Barry Was a Lady (MGM, 1943)
Let's Face It (Paramount, 1943)
Something For the Boys (Twentieth Century-Fox, 1944)
Mexican Hayride (Universal-International, 1948)
Kiss Me Kate (MGM, 1953)
Silk Stockings (MGM, 1957)
Can-Can (Twentieth Century-Fox, 1960)

HOLLYWOOD STUDIO MUSICALS

Born to Dance (MGM, 1936)
Rosalie (MGM, 1937)
Broadway Melody of 1940 (MGM, 1939)
You'll Never Get Rich (Columbia, 1941)
Something to Shout About (Columbia, 1943)
The Pirate (MGM, 1948)
High Society (MGM, 1956)
Les Girls (MGM, 1957)

RADIO

Around the World, Mercury Summer Theater of the Air, June 1946 (archive.org/details/1946MercurySummerTheatre)

TELEVISION ADAPTATIONS

Anything Goes, live telecast with Ethel Merman, Frank Sinatra, and Bert Lahr, NBC-TV. February 28, 1954
Panama Hattie, live telecast with Ethel Merman and Ray Middleton, CBS-TV, November 10, 1954

Kiss Me, Kate, live telecast with Alfred Drake and Patricia Morison, NBC-TV, November 28, 1958

ORIGINAL TELEVISION PRODUCTION

Aladdin CBS-TV's *DuPont Show of the Month,* February 21, 1958

Notes

CHAPTER 1. FOLLOWING HIS FANCY: *SEE AMERICA FIRST, HITCHY-KOO OF 1919, GREENWICH VILLAGE FOLLIES*, AND *PARIS*

3 **mere fifteen**: *See America First, The Complete Lyrics of Cole Porter*, ed. Robert Kimball (New York: Vintage, 1984), 41–63; hereafter cited as *CLCP*.
3 **anything in the Old World**: Margaret S. Shaffer, "See America First: Re-Envisioning Nature and Region through Western Tourism," *Pacific Historical Review* 65, no. 4 (1966): 559–581.
5 **"SHOW MOST ENTHUSIASTICALLY RECEIVED"**: *The Letters of Cole Porter*, eds. Cliff Eisen and Dominic McHugh (New Haven: Yale University Press, 2019); hereafter cited as *LCP*.
5 **costumed as Pavlova**: *CLCP*, 19.
6 **"Cute Clifton"**: *LCP*, 105–6.
7 **composed the complete scores**: Thomas S. Hischak, *The Jerome Kern Encyclopedia* (Lanham, MD: 2003), 257–58.
7 **Linda had custom made**: William McBrien, *Cole Porter: A Biography* (New York: Vintage, 1998), 77–78.
8 **Porter composed seven songs**: *CLCP*, 85–89.
11 **Oo-la-la!**: Ad for *Paris*, Loews Warfield West Coast Theatres.

CHAPTER 2. THE LIST SONG: *WAKE UP AND DREAM, FIFTY MILLION FRENCHMEN*, AND *THE NEW YORKERS*

12 **"I've a Shooting Box in Scotland"**: *CLPC*, 36–37.
14 **"Operatic Pills"**: *CLPC*, 113–14.
15 **According to one source**: sondheimguide.cole.porter/you-never-know.
15 **Another lists**: Wikipedia/You Never Know.
16 **An undated program**: Charlesmortimerweekly.com/wake-up-and-dream
16 **Porter's claim**: Charlesmortimerweekly.com/wake-up-and-dream, 56.
19 **the setting was changed**: McBrien, *Cole Porter*, 131.

CHAPTER 3. CA, C'EST L'AMOUR: THE COLE PORTER LOVE SONG

- 20 **"What Love Is"**: *CLPC*, 31.
- 24 **also had procurers**: Charles Schwartz, *Cole Porter, A Biography* (New York: DaCapo, 1992), 114.
- 25 **Porter refused**: *LCP*, 359–60.
- 25 **Sylvain took care**: *LCP*, 398–99.
- 25 **When Porter learned**: *LCP*, 957.
- 25 **"the most perfect"**: *LCP*, 35–36.
- 26 **"Je t'adore,"**: *LCP*, 53–70.
- 26 **"Write me"**: *LCP*, 53–70.
- 27 **"I actually miss you"**: *LCP*, 62.
- 28 **"because I love you"**: *LCP*, 201.

CHAPTER 4. LA VIE EST GAI: GAY DIVORCE

- 31 **unproduced play**: imdb.com/J.Hartley Manners/biography.
- 31 **Gertrude Stein seems**: Martha Stone, "Who were Miss Furrer and Miss Skene?," Gay-lesbian-review-worldwide, September 1, 2002.
- 39 **"almost in tears"**: *Gay Divorce*, music and lyrics by Cole Porter, book by Dwight Taylor, 31, Nyk Public Library for the Performing Arts, Special Collections, RM 5732, hereafter cited as NYPLPA-SC.
- 39 **Astaire admitted**: Fred Astaire, *Steps in Time*, foreword by Ginger Rogers (New York: Harper & Row, 1959), 176.
- 40 **"an elegant"**: Richard Barrios, *Dangerous Music: Why Movie Musicals Matter* (New York: Oxford University Press, 2014), 64.
- 40 **Edward Tauch**: McBrien, *Cole Porter*, 155.

CHAPTER 5. AN ERRANT NYMPH AND AN EX-EVANGELIST: NYMPH ERRANT AND ANYTHING GOES

- 42 **a recording was made**: *Cole Porter's Nymph Errant*, Recorded live in concert at Theatre Royal Drury Lane, May 21, 1989, EMI Records.
- 46 **"I held"**: Ethel Merman, *An Autobiography*, with George Ells (New York: Simon and Schuster, 1978), 49.
- 46 **"Reportedly, she did"**: Caryl Flinn, *Brass Diva: The Life and Legends of Ethel Merman* (Berkeley: University of California Press, 2007), 12.
- 46 **early draft**: Lindsay and Crouse, *Anything Goes* Typescript, NYPLPA-SC, #7446.
- 53 **raised an important question**: Geoffrey Block, *Enchanted Evenings; The Broadway Musical from Show Boat to Sondheim* (New York: Oxford University Press, 1987), 56–59.
- 55 **Paramount did not pay**: Gary Giddins, *Bing Crosby, A Pocket Full of Dreams: The Early Years, 1903–1930* (New York, Little Brown, 2021), 191.

CHAPTER 6. A COLE PORTER PRIMER: PROSODY AND FIGURATIVE LANGUAGE

56 **The Tudor rhetoricians:** Sister Miriam Joseph, *Rhetoric in Shakespeare's Time* (New York, Harcourt, 1947), 36–40.
56 **"When Shakespeare began writing plays":** S. Schoenbaum, *Shakespeare's Lives* (New York: Oxford University Press, 1970), 781.
57 **In Porter's day:** See "Glossary of Poetic Terms," *The Golden Treasury, Selected and Arranged by Frances Turner Palgrave* (London: Collins, 1861, Rpt. 1959), 571–76.
57 **"At the Dawn Tea":** *CLCP*, 26.
59 **For example:** Edward P. J. Corbett, *Classical Rhetoric for the Modern Student* (New York: Oxford University Press, 1990), 427–60.

CHAPTER 7. STRANGE BEDFELLOWS: COLE PORTER AND MOSS HART'S *JUBILEE*

67 **during a four-and-a-half-month cruise:** Schwartz, *Cole Porter*, 138.
68 **slow start:** *Jubilee*, music and lyrics by Cole Porter, book by Moss Hart, NYPLPA-SC, #4340.
69 **Whether Porter heard:** McBrien, *Cole Porter*, 88.
70 **"Aphrodite's Dance":** *CLCP*, 191.

CHAPTER 8. TRIPLE THREAT: ETHEL MERMAN, JIMMY DURANTE, AND BOB HOPE IN *RED, HOT AND BLUE*

72 **one of the weakest books:** *Red, Hot and Blue* typescript, collections.yale.edu/catalog/32212554.

CHAPTER 9. 1938, A YEAR TO REMEMBER: *YOU NEVER KNOW* AND *LEAVE IT TO ME*

76 **"that means":** *LCP*, 150.
77 **full-scale musical comedy:** *LCP*, 154.
77 **the longest of any Porter show:** *CLCP*, 215.
78 **closed after two months:** McBrien, *Cole Porter*, 215.
78 **Lazarus's revision:** *Cole Porter's You Never Know*, additional adaptation by Paul Lazarus (New York: Samuel French, 2001).
81 **which is precisely what happened:** *Leave It to Me*, a musical play by Bella and Sam Spewack, songs by Cole Porter, NYPLPA-SC, #8703.

CHAPTER 10. PORTER'S BAWDY: *DU BARRY WAS A LADY*

86 **Lahr joined the cast:** Hugh Fordin, *MGM's Greatest Musicals: The Arthur Freed Unit* (New York: DaCapo, rpt., 1975), 20.
86 **Lahr worked on the film:** Aljean Harmetz. *The Making of the Wizard of Oz* (New York: Hyperion, rpt., 1988), 131.

CHAPTER 11. THE WAR YEARS: *PANAMA HATTIE, LET'S FACE IT!, SOMETHING FOR THE BOYS,* AND *MEXICAN HAYRIDE*

91 **Merman was not Jewish**: Flinn. *Brass Diva*, 4.
92 **available on**: *Ethel Merman, 12 Songs from Call Me Madam (with selections from Panama Hattie)*, MCA Classics, Broadway Gold.
94 **"The attack on Pearl Harbor"**: imdb.com/panamahattie/filming&production.
95 **It all began**: Theodore Strauss, "The Career of 'Let's Face It': From the Idea to the Subsequent Hit" *New York Times*, November 18, 1941, D, 1–2.
102 **authorized a transmission**: *Something for the Boys*, AEI Records, CD-804.
102 **incurred Merman's wrath**: Flynn, *Brass Diva*, 114.
103 **which cost $2 million**: Aubrey Solomon, *Twentieth Century-Fox: A Corporate and Financial History* (Lanham, MD: Scarecrow Press, 2022), 229, 241.
103 **signed a contract**: *CLCP*, 343.
104 **Clark romped**: Abe Laufe, *Broadway's Greatest Musicals* (New York: Funk & Wagnalls, 1969), 365.
105 **"The idea"**: Booklet Notes, *Mexican Hayride* CD, Decca Broadway.
105 **The State Department**: Neal Gabler, *Walt Disney: The Triumph of the American Imagination* (New York: Knopf, 2006), 394–95.
108 **had been opposed**: Bob Furmanek and Ron Palumbo, *Abbott and Costello in Hollywood* (New York: Penguin), 181.

CHAPTER 12. STRANGE INTERLUDES: *SEVEN LIVELY ARTS* AND *AROUND THE WORLD*

110 **At one point**: James O'Leary, "Keeping Faith with John Q. Public: Cole Porter, Billy Rose, and *Seven Lively Arts*," *A Cole Porter Companion*, eds. Don M. Randel, Matthew Shaftel, and Susan Forscher Weiss (Urbana: University of Illinois Press, 2016), 166.
112 **a playbill**: Playbill for the Ziegfeld Theatre, *Seven Lively Arts*, week of December 26 1944. Private Collection.
118 **"learned in part"**: Charles Higham, *The Films of Orson Welles* (Los Angeles: University of California Press, 1971), 5.
118 **"a magician whose"**: James Naremore, *The Magical World of Orson Welles*, rev. ed. (Dallas TX: Southern Methodist University Press, 1989), 30.
119 **"half-hour version"**: "Around the World, The Mercury Summer Theatre of the Air," http//archive.org/details/1946MercurySummerTheatre.

CHAPTER 13. JOURNEY'S END: *KISS ME, KATE*

121 **The genesis of**: Miles Krueger, "The Genesis of *Kiss Me, Kate*: The Making of a Masterpiece," CD booklet, *Kiss Me, Kate*, Columbia Broadway Masterworks, 1949, Sony Music Entertainment, 1959.
121 **tying her hands**: William Shakespeare, *The Taming of the Shrew*, Arden Edition, ed. Brian Morris (London: Methuen, 1981), 197.
121 **according to the stage directions**: Shakespeare, *The Taming of the Shrew*, 185.

122	**tame his shrewish wife**: Shakespeare, *The Taming of the Shrew*, 305–6.
127	**three-act redaction**: Shakespeare, *The Taming of the Shrew*, 195.
128	**As late as**: *Kiss Me, Kate* by Cole Porter and Bella Spewack, final, October 30, 1948, NYPLPA-SC, #183.
130	**One writer**: Block, *Enchanted Evenings*, 150.
136	**Porter obliged**: McBrien, *Cole Porter*, 310.

CHAPTER 14. REGARDS TO BROADWAY: *OUT OF THIS WORLD*, *CAN-CAN*, AND *SILK STOCKINGS*

144	**In the booklet**: Didier C, Deutsch, *Out of This World*, CD booklet, 8, Sony Broadway, 1950.
144	**Porter's biographer**: McBrien, *Cole Porter*, 322.
146	**"Don't speak to me"**: Jean Giraudoux, *Amphitryon 38*, *Three Plays*, vol. 2, trans. Phyllis LaForge, with Peter H. Judd (New York: Hill and Wang, 1964), 111.
146	*Amphitryon 38*: *Amphitryon 38*, 104.
152	**"Mr. Jekyll and Mr. Hyde"**: Bill Rosenfeld, *Silk Stockings*, CD booklet, 2, original cast recording, RCA Victor.
152	**graduated from Julliard**: Bernard F. Dick, *Engulfed: The Death of Paramount Pictures and the Birth of Corporate Hollywood* (Lexington: University Press of Kentucky, 2001), 91–92.
152	**"Ernie was the sparkplug"**: Mel Gussow, "Ernest H. Martin Dies at 75," *New York Times*, May 9, 1995, D, 4.
155	**Abe Laufe could**: Laufe, *Broadway's Greatest Musicals*, 175–76.
161	**"not a good script"**: Darryl F. Zanuck to Henry Ephron, November 29, 1955, Darryl F. Zanuck Papers, Margaret Herrick Library.
161	**"vague and thinner storyline"**: Zanuck to Ephron, December 8, 1955.
161	**international cast**: Zanuck to Ephron, January 27, 1956.
162	**"out of this world"**: Zanuck to Ephron, January 31, 1956.
162	**only brought in**: Solomon, *Twentieth Century-Fox*, 228.
164	**abounds in such characters**: Howard Teichmann, *The Wit, World and Life of Alexander Woolcott* (New York: Morrow, 1976), 257.
166	**"Kaufman's soufflé"**: Hildegard Knef, *The Gift Horse: Report on a Life*, trans. David Anthony Palastagna (New York: McGraw Hill, 1971), 312.
166	**"play with music"**: LCP, 300.
167	**"a fascinating actress"**: Bill Rosenfeld, *Silk Stockings*, CD booklet, 9, original cast recording, RCA CD.

CHAPTER 15. PORTER IN HOLLYWOOD

172	**wooed by MGM**: George Eels, *Cole Porter: The Life That Late He Led* (New York: Putnam's, 1967), 147.
172	**"This is not personal"**: Eels, *Cole Porter*, 165–66.
174	**Eddy had difficulty**: Eels, *Cole Porter*, 179.

184   **Porter, knowing**: Don Randal, "About Cole Porter's Songs," *A Cole Porter Companion*, 232–36.

CHAPTER 16. A LESS-THAN-GRAND FINALE: *ALADDIN*

188   **a second duet**: Cole Porter, *Aladdin*, original cast recording, 1960, EMI UK; Stet Records, 1983.

Index

Abbott (Bud) and Costello (Lou), 108–9
Abercrombie, Dean Daniel Webster, 57
"After You, Who?," 25
Aladdin (television), 183–88; stage musical, 188–90
Alberghetti, Anna Maria, 186, 187
"Always True to You in My Fashion," 136, 137
Ameche, Don, 166, 167, 183
Amphitryon (Plautus), 144–45, 147
Amphitryon 38 (Giraudoux), 145–46, 147, 149–50
Anderson, John Murray, 8, 9
"Another Op'nin', Another Show," 129–30
"Anything Goes," 51–52
Anything Goes (stage), 45–54; film, 54–55
Arden, Eve, 96, 97
Arno, Peter, 18–19
Around the World (stage), 117–18, 119; radio, 119–20
Ashley, Barbara, 147, 149
Astaire, Fred, 34, 35, 40, 169, 170, 171, 180–82
"At Long Last Love," 22
"At the Dawn Tea," 57–58

Ball, Lucille, 87–88
Barber of Seville, The, 12
Barcliff, Nelson, 26–27, 28
"Begin the Beguine," 69–70, 175
"Bianca," 136–37
Birkmayer, Toni, 14, 15, 16, 17
Blaine, Vivian, 102
Blair, Janet, 183, 184
Bordoni, Irene, 9, 10
Born to Dance, 173–74

Broadway Melody of 1940, 174–75
Bruce, Virginia, 173–74
"Brush Up Your Shakespeare," 137–38
Burrows, Abe, 153, 154, 157, 168
"But in the Morning, No," 87

Can-Can (musical), 154–57; film, 157–62
Ceballos, Larry, 17
Charisse, Cyd, 169, 170, 185
Chevalier, Maurice, 159, 160
Cinderella (television), 188
Clark, Bobby, 104, 105, 106, 107
Clear All Wires!, 79–80
Clift, Montgomery, 67
Columbia Pictures, 180–84
"Come Away with Me," 160
Como, Perry, 103
Conreid, Hans, 153
Cookson, Peter, 153, 154
Cradle Snatchers, 95
Crosby, Bing, 54, 55, 178
Crouse, Russel, 46, 47, 48, 53–54, 172
Crouse, Timothy, 47, 49

DaSylva, B. G., 84
De-Lovely (film), 193–94
DelRuth, Roy, 172
Don Giovanni, 12
Drake, Alfred, 137, 142, 194
Driscoll, James, ix
Du Barry Was a Lady (musical), 84–87; film, 84–88
Durante, Jimmy, 18, 72, 73
Durbin, Deanna, 38–39

INDEX

"Easy to Love," 22
Eddy, Nelson, 74
Errol, Leon, 105
Evans, Wilbur, 106, 107
"Ev'ry Time We Say Goodbye," 117

"Farming," 34
Feuer, Cy, 152–53, 165
Fields, Dorothy, 96, 100, 103
Fields, Herbert, 18, 84, 96, 100, 103
Fifty Million Frenchmen (musical), 17–18
Fine, Sylvia, 98
Fosse, Bob, 141
Foster, Sutton, 47
Freedley, Vinton, 95
"From This Moment On," 140–41

Garland, Judy, 175–76
Garrett, Betty, 102
Garrick, David, 127
Gaxton, William, 7, 8, 53, 83
Gay Divorce (musical), 33–41
Gay Divorceé, The (film), 39–40
Gaynes, George, 148
Gaynor, Mitzi, 179
Gershwin, George, 45
Gillette, Priscilla, 147, 148
Girl Crazy (musical), 45–46
Goetz, E. Ray, 10
Grable, Betty, 85, 86
Grayson, Kathryn, 140, 141
Green, Charles, 25
Greenwich Village Follies of 1924, 7, 8–9
Greenwood, Charlotte, 148, 149, 150, 151
Grey, Joel, 47
Grey, Virginia, 109
Guys and Dolls (musical), 160

Haney, Carol, 141
Hart, Moss, 68, 110, 116
Hartley, J. Manners, 33, 34
Havoc, June, 104–5, 106, 107
Hayworth, Rita, 180–82
Healy, Mary, 119
Helpmann, Robert, 189–90

Hepburn, Katharine, 177–78
High Society (film), 176–78
Hitchy-Koo of 1919, 6
Holder, Geoffrey, 86
Holm, Celeste, 178
Hope, Bob, 72, 73, 75, 99–100
Hutton, Betty, 109

"I Am Ahamed That Women Are So Simple," 139–40
"I Am Loved," 21
"I Get a Kick Out of You," 50–51
"I Happen to Like New York," 79
"I Hate Men," 133
"I Love Paris," 155–56
"I Love You," 106, 109
"I'm In Love Again," 8, 21, 28
"In the Still of the Night," 174
"It's All Right with Me," 156–57, 159
"It's De-Lovely," 74–75
"I've Come to Wive It Wealthily in Padua," 134
"I've Got You Under My Skin," 173

Jourdan, Louis, 160
Jubilee (musical), 67–71
"Just One of Those Things," 21–22

Kaufman, George S., 110, 163, 164
Keel, Howard, 140, 141–42
Kelly, Gene, 88, 175–76, 179
Kelly, Grace, 177, 178
Kelly, William, xi
Kendall, Kay, 179
Kern, Jerome, 7
Kidd, Michael, 153
Kimball, Robert, ix
King, Dennis, 186, 188
Kingsley, Dorothy, 140
Kirk, Lisa, 44
Kiss Me, Kate (musical), 121–40; film, 140–42
Kochno, Boris, 26–27

Lahr, Bert, 84, 86, 111, 113, 114, 115
Lawrence, Gertrude, 42, 44, 76

Lawrence, Paula, 100, 101, 102
Lazarus, Paul, 78
Leave It to Me (musical), 80–83
Les Girls (film), 179–80
"Let's Do It," 10, 12
Let's Face It! (musical), 6, 34, 105–8; film, 108–10
"Let's Misbehave," 10
"Let's Not Talk about Love," 99
Library of America Poets Project, The, ix, 32
Lillie, Beatrice, 111, 113, 114, 115, 116
Lilo, 155, 156
Lindsay, Howard, 46, 47, 48, 53–54, 72
list song, 12–14, 18
Losch, Tilly, 14, 15, 16, 17
"Lotus Bloom," 84
"Love for Sale," 19, 24, 29–30
love songs, 20–32
Luce, Claire, 34, 39
LuPone, Patti, 48

MacGrath, Leween, 167
MacLaine, Shirley, 157, 159, 160–61
"Make It Another Old-Fashioned, Please," 93
Margetson, Arthur, 119–20
Martin, Ernest, 152–53, 166, 167
Martin, Mary, 80, 193
"Melody in 4-F," 98–99
Merkel, Una, 16
Merman, Ethel, 45–46, 54–55, 72–76, 84–94, 100–102
Mexican Hayride (musical), 103–7; film, 107–8
MGM, 170–80
Miller, Ann, 140, 141
Mineo, Sal, 186, 187
Miranda, Carmen, 102, 103, 105
Monkhouse, Bob, 188, 189
Moore, Victor, 60
Morison, Patricia, 191, 194
Mura, Corinna, 106, 107
Musicals Tonight, 66, 67
"My Heart Belongs to Daddy," 83

Neff, Hildegarde, 168, 169
Nicholas Brothers, 175
"Night and Day," 29, 30–31, 36–37, 38–39
Night and Day (film), 193
Ninotchka, 162–63, 165
"Nobody's Chasing Me," 150
Nymph Errant (musical), 42–45

Oakie, Jack, 182
"Old Fashioned Garden," 6
Out of This World (musical), 147–51

Paige, Janis, 169–70
Panama Hattie (musical), 91–94; film, 94–95
Paranoia, 6, 12
Paris (musical), 9–10; film, 10–11
Perleman, S. J., 186, 188
Philadelphia Story, The, 177–78
"Physician, The," 44
Pirate, The, 175–76
Pirates of Penzance, The, 3
Porgy and Bess, 16
Porter, Cole: classical education, x, 57–58, 171; list songs, 12–14, 18; love songs, 20–32; lovers, 25, 26, 27, 28, 40, 41; movie musicals, 172–84; use of figurative language, 59–63; use of rhyme, 63–65; Yale fraternity shows, 6, 7, 57–58
Porter, Linda Lee, 7, 24, 28, 172, 194
Pot of Gold, The, 5, 7
Powell, Eleanor, 172–75
Prouse, Juliet, 157, 158, 159

Rall, Tommy, 141
Rathbone, Basil, 186, 189
Red, Hot and Blue, 75–79
Rhetoric in Shakespeare's Time, ix
Ritchard, Cyril, 187–88
Rosalie, 174
Rose, Billy 109–10, 111

Saint Subber, Arnold, 121
Scott, Hazel, 184
See America First, 3–6
Seldes, Gilbert, 109

Seven Lively Arts, The, 109–17
Shakespeare, William: *Julius Caesar*, 56; *Measure for Measure*, 146; *Much Ado About Nothing*, 48; *The Taming of the Shrew*, 121–27, 134, 135, 137, 149; *Twelfth Night*, 4, 22, 119
Short, Bobby, 10
Short, Hassard, 103
Sidney, George, 141
Silk Stockings (musical), 162–69; film, 170–71
Sinatra, Frank, 36–37, 157, 159, 177, 178
Skelton, Red, 87–89, 194–95
"So in Love," 31–32, 131, 132, 133, 137
"Solomon," 45
Something for the Boys, 100–101; film, 101–3
Something to Shout About, 183–84
Sothern, Ann, 94–95
Spewack, Bella, 79–80, 121, 131, 133
Spewack, Sam, 79–80
Stein, Gertrude, 24
"Stereophonic Sound," 168
Stewart, James, 173, 178
Sylvain, Paul, 24–25

"Tale of the Oyster," 18
Taming of the Shrew, The. See Shakespeare, William
Tauch, Edward, 40–41
Taylor, Dwight, 33, 147
"They Couldn't Compare to You," 149
This Is the Army (musical), 26, 27
Todd, Michael, 103
"Too Darn Hot," 130, 135
"True Love," 178
"Two Babes in the Woods," 8, 9

"Use Your Imagination," 148

Valez, Lupe, 105
Van, Bobby, 141
Verdon, Gwen, 155–56, 158–59

Wake Up and Dream, 14–17
Walters, Charles, 69, 70, 85, 86
Warner Bros., 18
Webb, Clifton, 6, 78
Welch, Elizabeth, 19, 41, 45
"Well, Did You Evah!?," 85
"What Love Is," 20
"When I Used to Lead the Ballet," 6
"Where, Oh Where?," 149
"Where Is the Life That Late I Led?," 135–36
"Why Can't You Behave?," 131, 132
Wizard of Oz, The, 68
Worchester Academy, x, 57–58, 71
"Wunderbar," 132
Wyler, Gretchen, 168

"You Don't Know Paree," 7, 17
You Never Know (musical), 76–78; sources, 76–77
"You'd Be So Nice to Come Home To," 28, 29, 183–84
You'll Never Get Rich (film), 180–82
"You've Got That Thing," 20

Zanuck, Darryl F., 161–62

About the Author

Credit: Autumn Years

Bernard F. Dick is retired professor of communication and English at Fairleigh Dickinson University. He is author of many books, including *The Golden Age Musicals of Darryl F. Zanuck: The Gentleman Preferred Blondes*; *That Was Entertainment: The Golden Age of the MGM Musical*; *The Screen Is Red: Hollywood, Communism, and the Cold War*; *The President's Ladies: Jane Wyman and Nancy Davis*; *Hollywood Madonna: Loretta Young*; *Forever Mame: The Life of Rosalind Russell*; and *Claudette Colbert: She Walked in Beauty*, all published by University Press of Mississippi.